LEAVING
CRAZY
TOWN

My true journey through severe mental
illness into complete mental health.

GRACE ANN CARLSON

BALBOA.
PRESS

A DIVISION OF HAY HOUSE

Balboa Press books may be ordered through booksellers or by contacting:

Balboa Press
A Division of Hay House
1663 Liberty Drive
Bloomington, IN 47403
www.balboapress.com
1-(877) 407-4847

Because of the dynamic nature of the Internet, any web addresses or links contained in this book may have changed since publication and may no longer be valid. The views expressed in this work are solely those of the author and do not necessarily reflect the views of the publisher, and the publisher hereby disclaims any responsibility for them.

The author of this book does not dispense medical advice or prescribe the use of any technique as a form of treatment for physical, emotional, or medical problems without the advice of a physician, either directly or indirectly. The intent of the author is only to offer information of a general nature to help you in your quest for emotional and spiritual well-being. In the event you use any of the information in this book for yourself, which is your constitutional right, the author and the publisher assume no responsibility for your actions.

Any people depicted in stock imagery provided by Thinkstock are models, and such images are being used for illustrative purposes only.

Certain stock imagery © Thinkstock.

Printed in the United States of America

ISBN: 978-1-4525-6989-5 (sc)
ISBN: 978-1-4525-6990-1 (hc)
ISBN: 978-1-4525-6991-8 (e)

Library of Congress Control Number: 2013904018

Balboa Press rev. date: 3/6/2013

In memory of my Dad, Stan Clarke &
My Grandmother, Myrtle Turner

In dedication to the three people
who never left my side; I love you
forever and beyond words.

My long time friend and
husband, Ron Carlson

My Son Derrick Carlson

My Daughter Sherrie Carlson

– PATIENCE –

waiting for what you want
is separate from the virtue
patience.
Tolerance – Forgiving – Caring
not only words to aspire to.
Tolerant when pushed to
your limit,
Forgiving when pain flows
from head to toe,
Caring when those around
you need your help.
Waiting for nothing,
accepting what you have
and creating your life
with it.
The virtue
– Patience –

written by Derrick Carlson

CONTENTS

ACKNOWLEDGEMENTS

Amanda Jackson, Artist & friend; humble appreciation to you
for designing & painting the cover art for *Leaving Crazy Town*.

amanda.jackson.50746444@facebook

or

tinker__bell17@hotmail.com

Garry Carlson, friend, inspirer and brother-
in-law; grateful for your help!

Bonnie Williamson, mentor; thank you for seeing my potential.

Patricia Gunn, friend & minister; thank you for believing in me.

Lana Ryan, your friendship is deeply appreciated
and thank you for taking me up the mountain to
physically touch the giant white cross.

All the Medical Professionals; sincere
appreciation for helping me to heal.

All Spiritual Healers, your loving prayers
helped me become well; thank you.

To those who helped in ways you might never know; Heartfelt
Gratitude:

Sharon Bell, Dianne & Peter Burroughs, Lee Chance, Libby Clark,
Jackie Cole, Sister Eileen Curteis, Eileen Davies, Kirsten Dueck,

Frank Enns, Kathy & Wayne Enslow, Bev Forshner, Chris Friesen, Christine Geith, Doug Gibbs, Melinda & Rick Haslem, Marilyn Hill, Sensei Hyakuten Inamoto, Jan Jameson, Anji Jones, Jan Laidlaw, David Large, Lise Lelievre, Kathy Love, Pam Malt, Bruce Mason, Nancy & Brian McLennon, Sue McQuay, Phyllis Memphis, Sister Mary Michael, Beverly Stretch, Nancy & Ron Tate, Myrna & Ted Valleau, Amy van Reeuwyk, Christine van Reeuwyk, Sandi Weagant, Lynn Weir, Connie Wilson, Leanne White, Pam & Innes Wight…

Although I have not been able to write the name of every person who has made a positive difference in my life, YOU know who you are and please remember my heart will always hold you with love and thankfulness.

All interior art drawn by Grace Ann Carlson

INTRODUCTION

Born in 1958, Duncan, BC, my name is Grace Ann Carlson (nee Clarke). My older brother and I were raised by our parents Stanley and Marjorie Clarke in the small, lake side town of Honeymoon Bay, on Vancouver Island, BC, Canada.

In 1976, I graduated high school, moved out of my parents' house and into my own apartment in Victoria, BC; to attend a business college. While in the big city I eventually met and married my soul mate, Ron Carlson. Later came a son, Derrick, born in 1980; and in 1982, a daughter, Sherrie.

Although there have been several moves to different locations on Vancouver Island, Ron and I made this *island paradise* our permanent home.

As a psychiatric patient who suffered with severe mental illness, life was no picnic. But boy do I have a story to tell and it is a true story. Not to give away the ending, I will only say that my battle with insanity has a happy conclusion.

Enduring episodes of psychosis that ranged from manic euphoria, depression, racing thoughts, delusions, paranoia and hallucinations was challenging. The severity of my mental decline required various stays on the psychiatric ward of Hospitals and anti-psychotic medication became my daily routine.

Doctors diagnosed me with severe, hereditary, bipolar disorder and the prognosis was to remain on psychiatric medication for my lifetime.

Parts in my book have been altered slightly by changing names of locations and people to protect the privacy of certain individuals. Yet, I do have permission from close family members to use their authentic names.

It is my belief that we all face various degrees of personal challenge. I have experienced a place of inner grief and desperation so intensely void of joy, that at one time, death seemed my only relief. Other people have told me they also endured similar anguish. Some of us survive this place of emotional pain and some do not. For me, fortunately, I made the choice to continue my physical existence; only through the Grace of God.

Had I ended my life, I would never have realized the only thing making me feel bad was my own thoughts.

Chapter #1

HEREDITARY ILLNESS

As MY HUSBAND RON AND I prepared to meet with my Mother's Doctor, I browsed through my clothing choices. Jeans were out, too casual. A dress or skirt, nope not the look I'm going for. Around my feet were piles of clean clothes I had yanked off hangers and pulled out of drawers. My stress was building as I kicked through the pile desperate to find something to wear! It was when a string of intensely vulgar words spewed from my mouth that I realized my anxiety wasn't over what clothes to wear, more so, it was my concern over what Mom's Doctor was going to tell us about her recent diagnosis.

Ron knew exactly what would help distract me from my worry, regarding Mom. Before we arrived at her Doctors office, Ron stopped at a bakery and thoughtfully bought us each a cream filled donut with coffee. I devoured my treat and latched onto his, while he was in mid bite. After twelve years of being married to me, he should have expected that was going to happen. *Snooze you lose* was my motto! Yikes, those eyes of Ron's said it all; my antics were not funny from his point of view.

The Doctor's small office had just the right number of seats to accommodate the family members who attended this meeting. He wasted no time with us, as he stated Mom's condition as hereditary bipolar disorder.

He went on to say that it's predominantly a biological disorder that occurs in a specific part of the brain and is due to a malfunction of the chemical messengers in the brain. Bipolar disorder causes the body chemistry to spike, which influences the electrical input of the brain to misfire and leads to incorrect information flooding the mind. It is a hereditary illness and a person who has one parent with bipolar disorder has a 25% chance of having the condition.

For a moment I considered his statement and my fear of getting mental illness, through my DNA link, was unbearable! I quickly refocused my attention back on to the rest of what the Doctor was saying. He gave us a list of concise symptoms commonly associated with bipolar illness.

>> grandiose ideas and unusual optimism

>> unrealistic beliefs about ones abilities or powers

>> sleeping very little, but feeling extremely energetic

>> talking so rapidly that others can't keep up

>> racing thoughts; jumping quickly from one idea to the next

» easily distracted, unable to concentrate

» acting recklessly without thinking about the consequences

» delusions and hallucinations (in severe cases)

» feeling hopeless, sad or empty

» inability to experience pleasure

» fatigue or loss of energy

» extreme irritability

» physical and mental sluggishness

» appetite or weight changes (gain or loss)

» sleep problems

» memory problems

» feelings of worthlessness, guilt or shame

» thoughts of death or suicide

Two additional points were explained by the Doctor. One, since bipolar disorder is a chronic, relapsing illness, it's important to continue medication as treatment, even when you're feeling better. Two, medication alone is usually not enough to fully control this illness. The most effective treatment strategy for bipolar disorder involves a combination of medication, therapy, lifestyle changes and social support.

As the meeting with Mom's Doctor drew to a close, I felt relief knowing her occasional bizarre behavior was not her fault. She had no control over the chemistry of her body. Today's meeting was exceptionally helpful as a means of educating me about what mental illness is. Knowledge is empowering.

I talked with Ron, on the drive home, describing the more difficult parts of my childhood. Witnessing my Mom having mood swings often confused me. Adults close to me said Mom had 'bad nerves' and that I'd better be especially good around her. This led me to believe, with Mom not being well, that it was my fault for not being quiet enough. I could sense the tension in our house at times and wasn't able to put a finger on quite what I was doing wrong to cause it.

"I really get it now", I told Ron *"My childish clowning around had absolutely nothing to do with Mom's behavior"*. A release of tears flowed down my cheeks. Ron took his hand off the steering wheel, reached over and lovingly squeezed my hand.

A few days later, getting back into my daily, uneventful routine, proved troublesome. Geez, I seemed to be obsessed with whether I was going to fall into that 25% category of getting this hereditary illness. Then again, thinking about it, I've got a brother maybe the gene pool will pick him for the lottery. Oh no, I couldn't believe I actually entertained that thought, what did that say about me? Feeling a twinge of guilt, I tossed another load of laundry in. By the time I got around to making the kid's lunches for the next school day, the need to vent my thoughts were tugging at me. With no one to call on, I grabbed my pen and began to journal what I was feeling.

February 1991 – Ann's Journal Entry:

My Mom's mental illness IS hereditary. So what now? Am I going to get it too or am I safe at 32 years of age? I'm so scared, what if I develop this horrid illness? The Doctor assures us that Mom is now on the right medication, I pray she is. I never want to see my Mom suffer another episode. What's bothering me is that I recognize some of the symptoms of bipolar illness in my own behaviour. I haven't had any euphoria, paranoia, delusions or hallucinations, but sometimes, I've been depressed and I escape the hardships of reality through creating day dreams. Fantasizing seems to help me build up my confidence. Is that mentally ill behaviour? I'm sure it's not. I do have uncontrollable crying at times and intense anger, but I know that only leaks out of me when I'm stressed out and frustrated. Isn't that normal? I remember my Dad had an awful temper and he wasn't sick. Doesn't everyone sometimes need to yell and cry it out? I have to stop freaking out about this illness affecting me! I've gotten by all these years quite nicely. I have two beautiful kids to focus on and the best Husband in the world. There is absolutely nothing for me to be upset about.

As I put the pen down and closed my journal, a wave of sadness swept through me. Shaking it off was hard and getting up to finish my household chores was a welcome distraction.

It's surprising how quickly days turn into weeks and weeks turn into months. Spring arrived. Watching nature wake up under the gentle April showers was always an enjoyable sight. Well where I lived, torrential down pour is a more accurate description. I loved the rain though, so refreshing and good memories of outdoor adventures as a kid.

With payday arriving, it was time to fill the house with some necessities and even a few indulgences. Grabbing my grocery list I made the thirty minute drive into town. The kids were in school, my son age eleven and my daughter two years younger. I was looking forward to seeing their faces when they got home and saw the fridge stocked with some of their favorite treats!

Wandering the grocery store isles, I appreciated the quiet early morning with few customers. Simply breezing through the checkout without having to stand in line was such a delight. I practically skipped to my car with the full cart of groceries. Is it normal to be this happy about food, I wondered? Loading the bags into my trunk I considered stopping to visit my parents, but then remembered they had plans for the day. It was a satisfied feeling basking over me while reflecting on my Mom's happier demeanor. She had improved over the past couple months and seemed content with a renewed energy about her.

While enjoying this gorgeous day and loading the last grocery bag into the trunk of my car; I heard a familiar voice call my name. Turning my head to see a woman coming towards me who I recognized, caused a knot in the pit of my stomach. She was well known by all to be quite a busy-body and rather brutal in her efforts to pry into the lives of others. Oh, and quite a gossip.

"Hello Beatrice" I smiled, *"How are you doing today?"* It took a few minutes for her to shoot me with a barrage of sarcastic comments; putting my kids down, as was her habit. Then she scrunched up her face and shook her head as she proceeded to toss out subtle insults directed at my husband. None of her slurs troubled me too much because I supposed it might be coming from a lack of self-esteem. This day she crossed a sacred line though by adding my Mom to her verbal attack. Tolerating bad judgment and poor choice is one thing but some comments are just downright hurtful. Beatrice, speaking in a loud voice, went on to say *"I heard your Mom 'lost it' and was committed to the psyche ward."* I corrected her by saying *"My Mom didn't lose anything. She has a condition where her body's chemistry can spike without warning and cause an imbalance of chemicals to her brain. It's an illness that she has no control over."* Beatrice didn't have any compassion in her voice when she added, *"Whatever, she still went nuts and had to be put on the Psyche Ward."* then she quipped, *"I saw her shopping the other day. She looked so odd, staring off with a blank look on her face. I don't think she's okay, should she even be out of the hospital yet?"* After hearing Beatrice

make her gormless comment, I had to hold myself back from the desire to smack her upside the head. Common sense reigned me in where I politely said, *"That's enough Beatrice, you have no idea what you're talking about, goodbye,"* and I slammed my trunk closed, climbed in the car and convinced myself it would not be helpful to back my car over top of Beatrice.

So much, for my happy Spring feeling. Driving home, in tears, I realized that everyone is going to have their own opinion of my family and it didn't really matter who thought what. The truth is; I was feeling the shame and stigma of having mental illness in my family. No amount of sticking up for my Mom was going to help me over come my own embarrassment.

Chapter #2

THE GREAT PRETENDER

A S A CHILD MY SHYNESS got in the way of being a part of group activities. Now an adult and still suffering from an inferior self-image, I had become proficient with unique excuses that kept me away from socializing. The worst of it was not being able to manage my low self image to attend my children's school events. The rare times I went to my kids activities, Ron was with me, to lean on.

Whenever faced with no way out of a social event, it took me hours to prepare myself. Makeup, hair, clothing all had to be perfect in my eyes. Most people teased me, when they realized it took upwards of three hours to get ready; even for a simple card game at the neighbors. What they didn't know is that three hours was also preparing my mental state to interact with people. This involved pretending to be someone I was not. Fantasizing, believing myself to be a brilliant, successful and well-liked personality. It was easy for me to get lost in my self-deluded imagination to the point that I appeared to others to be confident and fun to be around. It was easy to maintain my pretend world anywhere from one to two hours. After that the image faded from sight and I would again fall into fear based thoughts of being worthless, stupid and less than everyone else. That's when I'd grab Ron and insist we go home, immediately, with the cliché excuse of having a headache.

For most of my existence, I'd flip flop between shyness, depression and bouts of rage. All the time thinking this was normal to experience life like this. My family just thought I was moody.

Regardless of my introverted behaviour, I was befriended by some neighbourhood women, who had children near the same age as mine. Most of them mocked me about my quietness, but generally they were kinder than most ladies I'd met in the past. It wasn't long before I felt a part of their group and much more at ease with myself. They invited me to join them at their aerobic class one day. In my excitement, I bought matching exercise tights, leggings and head-band, which was the fashion of the eighties. Feeling accepted in the neighbourhood allowed me to let go of the need to fantasize I was someone else. It was exhilarating to feel this good, just being me. This was not something I was accustomed to.

As I got to my first aerobic class and walked up the long flight of stairs to the hall, it seemed they could easily suffice as the entire workout!

Seeing my friends at the far end of the hall I walked across the floor, with enthusiasm, to join them. Setting my water bottle on a table and taking off my sweat pants, revealed my aerobic gear. It didn't take me long to realize no one else was in tights and leg warmers, I felt a bit uncomfortable.

The sweaty workout lasted about thirty minutes and felt fabulous. Wiping down with my towel and saying my goodbyes to everyone I felt a smile in my heart, while walking down the stairs. WOOPS. At the bottom of the stairs realizing I'd forgotten my water bottle, back up I trotted. Nearing the top step I overheard several of the women making fun of me. *"She's so stupid, did you hear her say how excited she was to workout with us, what a loser."* Someone else chortled, *"Did you see her ridiculous workout clothes, a headband yet! Who does she think she's impressing?"* At that moment I sobbed and was heard by them. Someone called out, *"Who's there?"* Embarrassed I admitted *"It's just me"* and walked across the floor with my head down as I picked up my water bottle; muttering quietly, *"I forgot this"*. Pretending I hadn't heard their nasty remarks, a fake smile spread across my face, *"have a good day you guys, see you later"*. Fully understanding their dislike of me, showing up at a second aerobic class was out of the question.

My home became a hibernation cave. Curtains pulled tight even on a sunny day. My own feelings of unworthiness had been confirmed through the remarks of others. I began pretending my way through life again, reality was too harsh.

The more severe depression snuck up on me without much notice at first and it was my kids who took the brunt of this emotional decline. Everything in our house had to be perfect and that meant to my unattainable standards. Control had become my middle name. This temporarily gave me a false sense of stability. It was hard on my children because they couldn't feel free to bake cookies, haul out crafts, or even spread games around because I would get upset with the mess. Even walking the family dog was an ordeal for my children as I had so many rules in place. When I yelled in rage towards the kids, it was my Son who endured the worst of it. My Daughter would take cover by hiding somewhere. My apologies always came later and the kids were quick to forgive. Try as I might, it seemed there was no way to be in command of my emotions or my mouth. Yelling, crying and slamming doors were common in our home and I was the only one doing it. Tragically, my mental state turned an otherwise happy household into a house of horrors.

Even though a poor self image plagued me, I did work up the courage once to help as a volunteer in the concession stand for my children's baseball team. That proved disastrous when my mind would often 'freeze' and I couldn't add or subtract to count change. The kids purchasing foods laughed at me and the other adult volunteers scolded me for being slow. Again I was left believing that all the negative insults dumped on me, were indeed true. Now I was not only a loser but a stupid one at that. Never again did I volunteer at the kid's events. The panic that flooded my body every time the school or a team coach phoned, requesting my help, caused me to be prepared with a long list of excuses.

At this point in my life, thoughts of unworthiness caused me to end all contact with friends for a long while. If the phone rang during the day it went unanswered and at night I made excuses so the kids or Ron would pick up the calls. When someone knocked on the door, I hid in the back part of my house. Absolute terror struck me at the mere idea of having to talk with anyone. Not being able to hold up my end of a conversation caused me feelings of disgrace.

Although able to avoid volunteering help with the kid's activities, there were times my excuses didn't get me out of an adult social event. During these stressful moments my awkward shyness often gave way to nervous ramblings of run on sentences. Seeing the discomfort on people's faces and watching them back away from me as I carried on, was humiliating. It seemed I was powerless to stop my thoughts from bursting out of my mouth.

Ron didn't know about my feelings of shame, guilt and embarrassment. He had no clue how panicked I felt when around people. Truly a capable faker, it was easy to convince my family as to why I couldn't participate in an event, using the multitude of excuses I'd developed. Some of my strange behaviour was graciously overlooked by Ron or simply not even noticed.

In my loneliness, self disgust was magnified by the constant memories of ridicule from others. Truly unhappy, it was hard for me to hear of peoples' success and joy.

One early evening was especially hard for me. Ron came home from work smiling, after a long day of house building. He looked satisfied with himself. My envious eyes were boring holes in the back of his head, how could he act that happy when I felt so forlorn.

My complaints of the day began the moment he put his feet up. Ron barely took notice of my hurts and frustrations. Was he ignoring me? I grabbed hold of the kitchen cupboard door and slammed it. BANG. He didn't even glance in my direction. I slammed the fridge door, the kitchen door, the cabinet door – still he didn't look at me. Soon I graduated to throwing small objects against the wall and watched some of them bounce onto the floor and others shatter into pieces. It felt good to lash out and I didn't give a rat's ass if some of my favorite ornaments were broken. This was my routine behavior when upset, Ron had learned not to take much notice of my tantrum. In the meantime, my feelings of anger escalated to rage and I lost all conscious thought of right or wrong. Grabbing a wooden cutting board, in the shape of a pig, I threw it as hard as possible across the room! One of my kids had made that cutting board in a woodwork class at school. THUD, that pig was now firmly lodged, about eye level, into the wall. It jutted out as if it had been placed there to hold perhaps a small plant or maybe a nice ornament. Oh Crap, what had I done! Starring at the new shelf I'd created and feeling immediate regret. The horror and guilt of my actions made my stomach feel clenched by a fist. Now shocked and back to my senses, I couldn't understand how I got so mad that I was throwing and slamming things. Oh God, what's wrong with me? No words came, only deep sobs escaped from me.

Ron quietly got up from his chair and with a pleasant look on his face, walked toward me. Gently, he placed his hand in mine and walked me over to have a look at the cutting board jammed in the wall. He chuckled and said, *"Ann, that's a nice look, but I think maybe a shelf there won't work out. How do you feel about enrolling in a drywall class?"* Ron then hugged me tightly and whispered in my ear how much he loved me and that it was all okay, not to worry. While I appreciated his kindness I felt undeserving of his compassion.

Promising never again to allow my emotions to become rage, was a lovely thought but I found out quickly it's like jumping in front of a speeding 240 ton train. You might think you're going to stop it by standing on the railway tracks but truly the train WILL run you down!

It appeared my temper was bad and out of control, when in truth I was suffering a chemical imbalance complicated by past unresolved issues. Not yet aware that I had won the mental illness lottery, we all just carried on as usual.

There was a long ways to go before I learned how to stop that runaway, speeding train of irrational emotions. Alas, there was going to be some carnage on route.

Chapter #3

THE BROKEN GLASS

NOTHING SEEMED TO HELP KEEP my temper balanced and my frequent tirades of verbal abuse became intolerable for us all. The depth of my emotional pain was now beyond what I could bare. The ongoing sense of despair and mental torment seemed overwhelming to me.

Trying to reach out to family or friends was often frustrating. My words were either misunderstood or I wasn't able to articulate my sorrow. Soon came isolating myself and not even trying to confide in anyone. There was no more hope to be found anywhere, so I gave up.

Waiting until the kids & Ron had left the house so I could end my life required patience. It was with certainty that I believed they could be happier with me gone. Thinking suicide was a kindness to them made my choice easier. I considered they'd be upset for a while, but figured their happiness would soon return. In truth I was the cause of all the anxiety in the household and it was now time to get myself out of the way. Take responsibility, I thought.

The decision to cut my wrists had previously been made. The maple buffet, I'd purchased second hand, had a wooden roll top and three glass doors below. It protected some cherished glass ornaments along with my Royal Albert bone china set. I contemplated which piece of china to break and use as a weapon against myself. As I reached inside the glass doors my hand touched a favorite Royal Albert plate. My conviction waned. I put the plate down, slamming the glass door in disgust. The force left shards of glass from the broken door all around my feet. A sign, I thought, that I was supposed to finish the task of slashing my wrists. Picking up the sharpest looking piece of glass I pressed it into my wrist; not hard enough to cut through the skin though. With a quick motion, I flipped my right hand over exposing the top of my hand. I began cutting through my skin causing bloody ridges on the back of my hand. My screams were not from physical pain, more so, they were the agonizing realization that I was a coward who couldn't finish myself off. Cleaning up the droplets of blood and broken glass, I felt robotic and void of emotion.

When Ron got home and saw my hand bandaged, I lied and said the buffet glass just broke as a result of bumping the door; adding that it must have already been fragile or cracked. When questioned about my cuts, I concocted it was the shards of glass left in the door frame that I carelessly brushed against. He determined I didn't need stitches but that we needed to watch out for infection. I knew infection wasn't the thing to worry about; it was my lost mind that was the danger.

Tortured, is not a strong enough word to describe how I felt upon hearing the happiness of others. I did everything possible to stay away from people without alerting Ron that I was sliding down the bunny hole, towards tea time with the mad hatter and his crew.

At times I found myself around other people despite efforts to remain alone. In my social awkwardness, most would smile nervously and walk away in the middle of my sentence. Not knowing anything about current events and being too insecure to ask questions, I was a bore.

As if a game, every now and then someone would corner me and quiz my attention span. The ones that did this would ask or demand that I repeat back to them what they'd just talked about. It was most uncomfortable for me to hear, *"So Ann, what did I just say to you?"* or *"I just told you some highlights of my vacation Ann, can you tell me which one you liked the best?"* My inability to concentrate on their story might have appeared rude, yet my lack of focus was a symptom of the depression I had inadvertently fallen into.

Not to blame depression on all my lack of attention though, in fairness, I was easily distracted by watching others and mimicking their behavior. By copying other people I was able to forge fitting in with the group. When someone spoke to me, instead of listening to them, I'd busy my mind wondering if I should cross my arms and look interested or put my hands in my pocket to appear relaxed. Over the years I had memorized facial expressions, stances and short comments so I could fake my way through a conversation. My Self image was terribly distorted and these tactics became my way of coping. So knowing I still had to endure life, my biggest question WAS: HOW CAN I KEEP UP THESE PRETENCES?

My sadness deepened each time individuals would say things like; *"Why do you keep staring off Ann, what's wrong with you?"* or *"You look like a zombie, why don't you try cracking a smile?"* or *"You look so scared, what's your problem?"* and *"Why so quiet, I think there's something wrong with a person who's too quiet."* One very insensitive person said, *"You're such a bubble head, Ann, but your fun to have around as entertainment"*. One of the most painful comments came from someone I considered a friend, *"Oh no, the others aren't going to be able to come with us! That means it's just you. GREAT, how boring will this be?"* she said with a sigh.

People seemed to think it was their right to blurt out whatever crossed their mind. If they knew how unpleasant their comments were to me, I'm sure they would not have spoken like this. Then again some people don't care if they hurt your feelings.

Any unkind remarks toward me were a confirmation, of my own belief, that I was worthless. People who spoke harshly at me, their comments played over in my mind constantly. I believed them.

Chapter #4

DEMON DOG & JESUS COMPLEX

M Y MOTHER'S STABILITY OF MIND appeared to be consistent now, what a relief. Her sense of humour returned and her gentle way of enjoying life once again intact. As for me, I'd lost my ability to joke around and soon became a tyrant at home. Within this state of mind I also hid myself away from friends, most considered me a bit of a recluse.

A pep talk from Ron and seeing myself in a better light helped me find a wee bit of courage to start thinking about updating my work resume. Being pumped up with his reminders, of my past secretarial training and phone skills, motivated me to see beyond the four walls of home. Even though I'd had a long absence from office administration, I knew stewing and brooding around the house was going to be the death of me; literally.

I cleaned up nice and the first Company to interview hired me as file clerk and typist for their busy office. This job seemed to suite my personality as I could remain tucked away in the back office diligently typing and filing without being in contact with staff or clients. The hardest part of my job was socializing during break times. I often went for a walk alone during coffee or sat in my car to eat my lunch. Staff questioned my absences from the lunch room all the time. So I fibbed, telling them I had to run personal errands, in order to keep up on my family commitments.

The body, mind and spirit can only be out of sync for a short time before tell-tale signs of stress show up. My emotions bounced between insecurities and frustrations, with intermittent despair. How I managed to stay at my secretarial job in a downtown office, as long as I did, was amazing. I wasn't surprised when the boss got fed up with me taking too many 'personal' days off and asked me into his office. He basically fired me yet was kind enough to offer part time work. Even after reducing my hours from forty per week to fifteen per week, it became apparent to all that I needed to stop work altogether. Before long my anxiety was causing my body to tremble and loss of concentration made me incapable to function at my job. My feelings of inadequacy were now at an all time high.

After a lengthy hibernation in my house, a concerned neighbour contacted me suggesting I try Janitorial work. She convinced me I'd be mostly alone, good way to keep my body in shape and decent pay. As I agreed to apply for the job, she phoned the Owner and highly recommended me; and so, began my most unglamorous job of cleaning urinals at a pub. My hours of six o'clock through ten o'clock in the morning were perfect. On days the kids didn't have school I was able to bring them to work with me and enjoy their company as they helped dust, vacuum and tidy the Pub. It was through my kids that I soon began to laugh and be playful again.

There were a couple perks working as a janitor at a pub; lots of coins under the cushions and the occasional visit of a local dog. I guess this St. Bernard must have been used to getting tidbits from staff. He would often be sniffing around the back door, about seven o'clock in the morning, so I'd pop outside to give him a tummy tickle, scrap of bread and send him on his way. Knowing the rules well, no dogs in the Pub, I was careful about not letting this gargantuan dog inside. Wouldn't you know it though, oh yah this naughty dog barged right on into the Pub one morning; no big deal, until trying to call him outside. He would have no part of it as he pranced around the dance floor and trotted into the kitchen. Now this Bernard and I had been buddies for a while, outside that is, but I found out in a hurry he did not take kindly to people touching his collar. I thought St. Bernard's were friendly giants until *Cujo* tried to take a bite out of me. Fine, then, if you won't let me lead you gently out the back door, I'll try another strategy. It got down and dirty, me armed with a broom and determined I wasn't going to get fired over this stubborn dog. Seriously, this oversized fur-ball took the broom away from me and I jumped up onto a nearby table to avoid his revenge. Demon Dog figured he had the better of me but I had one more trick up my shredded sleeve. Jumping onto to the bar, where there were chips and cheezies conveniently stacked, I ripped a bag of cheezies open with my teeth and began tossing them onto the floor. Best way to sooth the savage beast, food. Gingerly sliding off the bar and stepping onto the floor, I slowly walked backwards towards the exit door. The whole way tossing cheezies just in front of me and praying there was going to be enough in the bag to get him right outside. It worked, out he went. Locking the door behind him, I knew that would be the last tummy tickle grumpy-pants got from me.

Things seemed to have gotten better and with my happier outlook on life I decided to take on extra work through cleaning private homes. Before long, I was working ten hours a day, five days a week as a Janitor and then going home to meticulously clean my own place. Obsessive would be a mild way of describing what I had become. Most nights I'd find myself climbing into bed after midnight. Even though I'd become excessive, this was the first time I felt pride in my ability and skill of cleaning. Damn I was good!

Working long hours and staying up late didn't tire me, in fact I became more energetic. It was like a continuous cycle of super human wakefulness. I slimmed down and became a chatter box. No more shyness.

All night long, I'd lay awake listening to continuous, rapid thoughts. It seemed real when I heard Spirit Beings giving me philosophical teachings; it never occurred to me that my mind was making it all up.

Convinced I was channeling advanced messages from the spirit world, I hauled out a small tape recorder and kept a voice record of all communications. Soon I was speaking into that microphone, not just at night, but also during my work day. Lack of sleep, poor eating, obsessed and self deluded I began sharing with others what seemed to be profound universal secrets. Had I known this was the onset of bipolar disorder, I would have asked for help, but to me it was exhilarating.

The infrequent times I came across the home owners that hired me, I'd engage them in discussion regarding spiritual awareness. My theoretical ideas were intriguing to most and when describing how I could channel God's healing energy, some of the people I kept house for, wanted an energy healing session with me. Apparently my behaviour seemed relatively normal to them or they would not have allowed such contact with me.

When providing a healing session, I'd invite the person to sit on a chair while I stood behind them. With my hands on their shoulder I'd quietly pray for their well being. Funny enough, all the people I provided healing sessions for acknowledged they were feeling waves of comforting energy moving through their body. They also told me their pain had either subsided or ended. Interestingly, the hands-on healing sessions were making a positive difference for the people I prayed over. When I was in sincere prayer, requesting wellness for others, my stability of mind was present.

For example, one such case, that proved an inexplicable healing, was witnessed by family members. Our Son, for many years, had endured a medical condition where skin tags grew on his eyelids. Every time the skin tags grew long, there was only one way to remove them; a doctor had to cut off the skin tags and then cauterized them. Although this was a simple office procedure, it was also an uncomfortable process for my child. The day came when Ron and I both noticed the new growth of skin tags had again gotten to a length that required another trip to see the Doctor. That night, while getting ready for bed, I humbly knelt down and prayed for God to remove these skin tags so that they would never again grow back and cause my Son to suffer. My trust and sincerity that nothing is impossible with God's love gave me the Hope that we might not need to book that doctors appointment.

When we woke in the morning, I prepared our breakfast and served it up. As I leaned over to examine my child's skin tags, I was astonished to see smooth skin with no skin tags present. Completely restored; healthy eye lids overnight! Those skin tags never returned it was a permanent healing.

After witnessing, the power of prayer to heal, Ron began trusting me to do hands on healing for the knee and foot pain he had endured for years. Within a few prayer treatments, his chronic pain was gone and it never returned.

So although healing sessions were verified by others, as legitimate healing taking place, my monkey mind was swinging back and forth like a chimpanzee stranded on a vine. During the times I prayed for peoples' health, my sincerity was such that my mind could get out of the way and I was able to *hold the space* for spiritual healing to take place. But, when I was no longer praying for healing, my stability of mind once again lapsed into irrational thoughts of grandeur.

When in grandiose thinking, I believed myself to be the Chosen One, sent by God, to save the world by raising everyone's consciousness. Yikes, who did I think I was, Jesus! Actually yes, I believed myself to be the female incarnation of the second coming of Jesus.

In my crazy-town mind, I thought it was necessary to keep my identity of being the second coming a secret; therefore, I didn't tell anyone I was Jesus returned to save them all. Too bad, because I'm sure that would have been a huge tip off for people to recognize that I was insane; thereby, getting me the psychiatric help I needed, sooner.

Chapter #5

INTUITIVE CHILD

I NTUITION AND SENSING THE SPIRIT World most certainly were not delusional experiences when I was a child. The reality was, at times, I truly knew things in advance of them happening. As a child I had a natural ability to empathize and even feel the emotions of others. I later found out this is called clairsentient, meaning clear feeling. No one paid much attention to my squeals of delight when I knew things. They were either busy with their day or not wanting to encourage what they thought was a child's fanciful imagination. It seemed they didn't believe me so I stopped talking about my 'knowing'.

Clearly I recall walking to my bus stop, early one morning, I might have been about twelve or thirteen years old. A sense of deep inner awareness and being a part of something bigger engulfed my perception. A knowing, that there is a living energy of intelligence that unconditionally cares for and embraces the world as well as each one of us. I knew then this consciousness was beyond my own.

At times my awareness of a Divine Spirit comforted me when I felt distraught from being teased by the popular kids at school. There were many nights I felt emotionally broken as a result of cruel bullying. You see I was an overweight, insecure, clumsy girl with flaming red hair. It was difficult bearing the brunt of nasty behaviour, yet, often a sense that it would all be okay flowed through me. Sometimes the presence of Love wrapped around me, I called this feeling God. It was as if this God-Consciousness was nurturing and encouraging me to remain kind no matter how others treated me. I felt peace from inside myself, when in touch with this essence of Love.

Talking to the few friends I had, about my perception of God, caused those kids to laugh and poke fun at me. I quickly learned NOT to talk about that either.

Another form of comfort came from my maternal grandma. With her, there was absolute certainty that I was loved and valued by another person. She and I spent one night together every weekend until I was about fourteen years old. We would watch Mayberry RFD, eating dinner from her fold out TV trays and sipping our coffee. Of course my coffee was mostly cream and sugar. It was during these sleepover visits I could talk to Grandma of my experiences and belief of God. She was always attentive and understanding towards me. As I got older, she once confided in me that her Mother had been very psychic and had even assisted the local police. She mentioned that psychic abilities can be a blessing or a curse and that it is not something to play around with. There wasn't much more I recall her saying around the subject other than my grandmother insisted I never use an Ouija board. She was adamant that it was not a game, but a very unstable method of contacting the spirits. She asked me to promise that I'd never use one.

As a senior in High School and later a student in College I had very little time to pay attention to my precognitive dreams, intuition and awareness of the Spirit World. My focus was on 'pretending' to fit in with others and studying to get a passing grade in school.

However, when I was in my twenties, I reawakened my psychic communications and they were confirmed by others to be accurate. One memorable experience of seeing a ghost was while visiting Ron's old friends who lived in an isolated, character home. As I walked through their kitchen, to find their washroom, I had a visual glimpse of a man in spirit *(ghost)*. I could also hear this spirit clearly talking to me telepathically. I felt uncomfortable in the presence of this Being and immediately went back to the room where my husband and friends were sitting. In my concern for what I had experienced, I blurted out to the home owners *"Are you aware there is a spirit man that lives here with you and he's not very pleasant. He seems very manipulative and is rather irritated"*. The couple looked at each other with an expression of horror and then said to me, *"Ann, did this spirit ask you to keep his identity a secret and not tell us he was here?"* I exclaimed, *"Yes he did and that's what I mean by he's very manipulative"*. They then told me they had moved from a place last year where this spirit man had been bothersome in their home. Up until tonight they thought they had left him behind in the other place. I never returned to their home so I'm not sure how they handled the situation, yet I'm certain they found a way to encourage the departed soul to move on into the light of God.

Another more pleasant experience happened when I visited some other friends in their home. They needed to find a flashlight to take with them and since it wasn't anywhere to be found, they were about to give up searching. Although I'd never been into their various rooms, I simply '*knew*' what room and the precise closet where they would find the flashlight. I enjoyed their shock and appreciation of my helping them.

Usually I felt comfortable with spirit communication, yet sometimes there were those exceptions where I was not. Such was the time when pregnant with our second child and I encountered an ominous Spirit. What made this spirit creepy was his less than friendly demeanor. Often times I'd see this young spirit man, appearing to be in his thirties, jet black hair, wearing a red plaid work jacket. He never spoke he'd just appear and fade off. I didn't feel comfortable with his presence and asked that he stop these visits. A couple years went by where I didn't see him anymore. But, as I got to know the new neighbour lady, she took me into her confidence and told me she felt afraid to be alone in her home because she sees a spirit man with dark hair, a red plaid jacket and he seems angry. Later I confirmed to her that I too had previously seen him on many occasions, she seemed relieved to know someone else had seen the same spirit person. It was a simple matter of asking him to leave, I told her, after that he no longer made his presence known at my place. She sent him on his way too, this time we both asked for the light of God to help him cross over to the Spirit World to be at peace.

To give an example of a precognitive experience; I woke one morning from an intensely, vivid dream. It was a vision of me in a bar, at a wooden table, across from a woman I hadn't seen in many years. In my dream she was telling me her husband had committed suicide and that she was adjusting well. Two days later, my husband surprised me by taking me to a local bar that had live music. I generally did everything I could to avoid bars, yet this time Ron convinced me to go in and listen to this great band. While there, I recognized the unique wooden tables, I'd seen them in my dream. Moments later I was actually sitting across from an old friend who indeed told me her husband had committed suicide and that she was adjusting just fine. The precognitive dream helped me to know in advance what to expect and thereby I knew what to say in this moment. I appreciated the psychic heads-up.

I bring these supernatural occurrences up to authenticate not just my natural ability to perceive the Spirit World, but every person's inherent capacity for accessing psychic abilities. It is my belief that every living thing has a sixth sense that makes it possible to perceive energetically.

With me however, there were emotional and neurological complications that turned my God given ability to perceive beyond the physical realm, into bizarre and horrific experiences at times.

Not yet aware of it, I was on the edge of discovering I had been passed the hereditary gene that was about to explode my bodies chemistry into severe, mental illness. It's not safe to mix Spirit Communication with any form of mental instability, I was about to find out the hard way.

Chapter #6

SELF DECEIT

A ROUND THE AGE OF THIRTY-THREE, my obsession with searching for spirit activity peaked. Thinking there were ghosts around and telling people I could sense spirits gave me thrills, making me feel special. Leaning heavily on the Spirit World to feed my confidence, I wasn't receptive to the consciousness of God within me. Far too focused on spirit people, foolishly I was ignoring my intuitive inner voice that was screaming at me to stop playing with fire. If you ignore your deep wisdom long enough, you'll eventually stop hearing it. In place of being in touch with the wisdom within me, I was being guided by pure egotistical deception. This deceit I experienced at the level of believing I'd tapped into my psychic gifts.

The authenticity of my psychic experiences became questionable in my early thirties. Even though some were true spirit contact most was nothing more than my vivid imagination. Due to the wrong thinking, my authentic nature was being held prisoner as I fooled myself using sprit contact to prove I was worthy. Undeniably people enjoyed my spooky stories and claims of psychic prowess, yet sadly their interest further prompted me to seek attention this way. Let me tell you, incorrect psychic readings cannot be done for any length of time without repercussions. Something has to give out. My intentions were good yet my deeper motives were fueled by a lack of self esteem and truth will always reveal itself. Some may call it karma I call it love in action.

For a while I was the *go to girl* for titillating chats about spirit activity. Love in action slammed that door shut when people began noticing my spiritual beliefs were becoming more and more bizarre. Claiming I could read minds and know the outcome of future events became quite disturbing to friends, especially when warnings of impending doom came out of my mouth. Needless to say I was not giving accurate evidence, at least not any more, by this point in time.

It was when I began hearing spirit voices talking to me that things got really splattered with poop, as it hit the fan. Once, while at work, I heard a woman's voice calling me a nasty, slanderous name. Assuming it had come from the only person in the room, my female boss, I proceeded to tell her off. Huge mistake, I almost got myself fired, but fortunately she had enough common sense to realize I'd had some sort of mental breakdown. A few days with time off and I returned to work, seemingly fine. Sadly, as the months flew by, my thinking descended into delusion.

A whole year later and my only companions had become what I called my spirit guides. Who needs live friends when you have spirits around you 24/7, to me, this felt much like I imagined loving relationships to be. Thinking I could see, sense and hear more clearly felt like I was in a heightened state of awareness. These Spirits, I thought I saw and heard, fed my need to be included in a group of caring friends. They were always there, providing loving kindness towards me. Only problem was, I didn't realize they were a fabrication of my own thoughts. True Spirit Beings, from Gods light, never distract a person from living stable lives; nor would they persistently be hanging around me. Unfortunately, I didn't know this at the time and so believed my own misconstrued thinking.

Here's the difficult part for Ron, in prior years he had witnessed my psychic accuracy and experienced my capability to channel healing energy. So when I became delusional and talked about psychic things, Ron wasn't hearing anything too outlandish, yet.

The difference between being delusional and fantasizing is that I had control over my mind when I fantasized and could instantly bring my awareness back to the present moment. With day dreaming, I knew it was make believe. But when in delusion, I would perceive imaginary things as real. The logic behind insanity is that the delusions appear so real, it negated any desire to even try to pull myself out of it. Whatever was in my mind was reflected or projected into the world around me. When this happened, unbalanced thoughts blended together with reality. Most of the thoughts within me were fear based, unhealthy, unresolved issues long past. So, no wonder my delusions were so negatively driven, everything around me reflected my upsets.

On the brighter side of my thoughts, were still moments of living in reality. This was when I would be focused on the present day; grounded and down to earth. When faced with difficulties though, back I would go into fantasizing. Oh how I enjoyed my day dreams. Being well practiced at making up fantasies, my creative imagination had no trouble seeing myself basking in the Caribbean sun while lying about on the deck of private yacht. Effortlessly I could make believe listening to exotic music while sailing over the sea. Even with my eyes open I could envision the emerald green ocean of the West Indies, when in fact I was looking at my own back yard. No harm done, I knew this was only pretend and could easily let go the self created mirage to return my mind to current life circumstances. A fantasy is a nice way to relax, pass time and re-energized. Yet in my case, I had become addicted to my pretending and began using fantasies to escape my responsibilities. In moderation, day dreams can be part of a healthy way to maintain balance. I had yet to learn moderation. Soon enough it was harder to find my way back to reality because it was so pleasant in my daydreams.

There were many lonely days I hid in my home while my family went out together. My inferiority complex hindered my desire to be at family functions. Fantasies occupied my time so I didn't have to think about dealing with my issues. On one of these occasions, with the family out of the house, I cranked the music LOUD and began to dance. That's all fun and fine, even good for the soul, but I began fantasizing I was a famous dancer and slipped into believing it too whole heartedly. Soon this fantasy got even more deluded when I believed a spirit guide was now dancing with me. I had one foot in fantasy and the other foot in delusion. If both feet ended up in delusion, it would be a difficult task to pull me back to real life.

What saved me from slipping into crazy town was an old friend who paid me a surprise visit. His name was Terry and he was a very tall, well built man, who had a strong foundation in knowing God. He was a man of faith and integrity. His five second appearance, in front of me, was enough to lift me into a stable mindset. Immediately upon laying my eyes on him I felt grounded and his existence reminded me to focus my thoughts on God's love. You see, Terry had died many years earlier. For some reason, beyond what I can perceive, Terry was able to reveal his survival to me. Five seconds, then his image faded away.

After the encounter with Terry, I had no desire to fantasize being a famous dancer and the pretend spirit dancer vanished. Instead I felt profoundly safe and loved, so I changed the music to something softer, to match my contentment. For a long time, after his spirit visited, I was able to face life's challenges and even enjoy being with my family and friends again. My self esteem and my faith in God reinforced. This is the way to know true spirit contact. The person in spirit only reveals themselves long enough to help you live in the present moment and they will leave you feeling a strong knowing of Gods existence. Then they go, so as not to distract you from living your life with both feet in the physical world.

Although my balanced thinking was intact for a long while, nevertheless, mental illness ultimately found its way back into my consciousness. Old habit was still too familiar. I hadn't put any effort into changing my thinking or creating new ways of viewing life. It seemed I had no control of my wandering, negative thoughts. In truth it wasn't that I didn't have any control, more so, it was that I didn't have any training or tools to help me do the inner work necessary. Had I accessed changing my thought process sooner, it's likely the mental illness may not have developed to the severity where I required psychiatric medication.

Incorrect thinking can be a slippery and dangerous slope, especially combined with chemical imbalance within the organic brain. I woke one morning seemingly normal and by afternoon my mind had created hallucinations and grandiose thoughts. No one knew I was tripping the light fantastic around the milky-way and that is the danger of psychosis. No one recognized I needed help!

Here is what I experienced:

While the kids were out visiting with their friends, Ron and I decided it was a good time to go grocery shopping. As Ron pulled into the parking lot, I told him my head felt dizzy and I wanted to sit in the car while he bought the groceries. Watching my husband walk toward the store, I noticed my dizzy feeling changed to a slight headache. Once Ron was inside the building I could see him moving around the aisles, as I sat patiently in the car nursing my now pounding head. Only seconds ticked by and suddenly my head throb cleared and I felt at ease, even euphoric. Sitting quietly alone in the car, I heard an explosive surge of air that sounded similar to that *'puff sound'* that a propane barbeque tank makes, when ignited. I knew immediately a fire had started in the undercarriage of my car! It would only be moments before the flames engulfed me. Right then, I saw thick black smoke billowing outside my car and heading skyward. Immediately, torrents of swirling, grey toxins began to creep up the sides of the doors and twirl up my passenger window. It was too late to open the door and run, I figured my destiny was sealed inside that car. Oddly, I felt calm and peaceful as I closed my eyes and listened to the roaring flames. I waited to feel the searing heat. Moments went by and I neither felt the pain I expected, nor did I smell the smoke. What was going on, I wondered, is this what it's like to burn alive, no pain? Curiously I glanced out the window only to realize the flames were extinguished and the smoke had vanished. As I looked out into the parking lot and saw many people strolling around, I wondered why no one had rushed to save me from the burning car? My hand rested on the door latch, fingers clenched around the handle until I found the courage to open the door. As my legs swung out and my feet touched the ground, I pushed my shaking body upright, then carefully closed the car door. To my amazement there were no burn marks or smoke stains. I gingerly touched the car, certain it would be hot, yet found the metal cool against my fingertips. I bent down to look under the carriage. It was clean. I wondered how this was possible. My wonderment suddenly ended as I felt a vibration of loving energy expand my heart center, lifting me into a sense of profound knowing. I believed a guide from the spirit world was whispering to me and reassuring me that physical death was impossible; because I was protected by the Angelic realm. With this belief in my mind, I felt a spectacular rush of vibrant energy coursing through my body. Freedom from all fear and feeling invincible. There I stood, outside my car in a busy parking lot and I began to spin, dance and laugh with wild abandon. Oh yes, in front of anyone who was within eye sight. I had no shame or concern over what anyone might think because I knew my purpose in life was to be savior of this world. I believed I was the next incarnation of the messiah.

By the time Ron got back to the car with his arms loaded with grocery bags, I was already seated back in the car and appearing normal. My imagined *spirit guide* whispered to me again that *I am to keep my knowledge a secret from everyone and act accordingly, so to fit in and not attract attention.*

Having slept well through the night, I awoke the next morning believing the burning car episode had been nothing more than a vivid dream. My thinking seemed to be back on track and any thought of being the *second coming of Christ* had evaporated for the time being.

Chapter #7

OFFICIALLY INSANE

I'LL NEVER FORGET THE YEAR my mental decline turned into a psychotic episode. It was 1993. Funny, how that sticks in my mind. I don't remember the year I received my first kiss from a boy, my first bike or even the year I got my first job. But diagnose me as mentally ill and that I remember? This was the year I turned thirty-five years old, I was in a fourteen year marriage and my two children were eleven and thirteen.

Probably the stress of preparing for a long drive across three Provinces to visit Ron's family played a part in triggering my first full blown break from reality. It was truly terrifying for me, zipping along in the car with four lanes of traffic. The mere idea of leaving my usual surroundings, where I felt a sense of control, was also daunting. Add the fact I was carrying the hereditary gene for bipolar disorder and I was like a hand grenade, with the pin already pulled out.

With Ron driving and suit cases packed, we sped off with our two kids for a three week vacation. The tension across my shoulders, tight jaw combined with the knot in my stomach was a constant reminder of the anxiety I was experiencing. Even knowing Ron was a safe driver didn't help me relax. The traffic roaring past us, the kids chattering in the back seat plus the static of the radio caused my apprehension to hit a new level of distress that I'd never felt before.

My head swirled with dizziness and my heart pounded as I clung to the seat belt, unable to speak. Then the trembling began to fill my body from the inside outward as my vision turned to black and white fuzzy dots. My mind raced with panicked thought that I was about to die. It was hard to catch a breath and that's when I let out a sudden scream of sobs that startled Ron and the kids. My tears and gasping for breath caused Ron to quickly pull over and get out of the car to assist me. Stepping out of the car I found my legs wouldn't work properly, I could only sit on the rough gravel alongside the road. It took a few minutes before my discomfort subsided and we were back on the road. Feeling depleted of all energy and petrified it might happen again; all I could do was sit hoping for the best.

After a couple days of being on the road, we were all filled up on fast foods, too much sugar and little sleep. Only minutes from arriving at my in-laws home, I burst into an emotional melt down. There I was in an out of control crying jag, nauseous and extremely cranky. The five to ten minutes it took me to catch my breath and pull my emotions together felt like an eternity. Acting like this in front of the kids caused me humiliation which worsened this experience for me.

Once we got to Ron's parents home, I was quickly put at ease by their down to earth, friendly hospitality. After welcoming hugs, much laughter and delicious homemade pie, we all had an early night. Now I was settled down and looking forward to meeting up with more family and friends the next day.

While Ron and the kids slept, I remained awake. All night long, there was a constant nattering of spirit voices talking to me. Off and on I could see spirit faces, of people long dead, floating in front of my open eyes. Considering it was pitch black in the room, I couldn't help noticing how illuminated their faces were. There was no fear of these departed Souls; in fact, I found them to be good company. When they vanished there was another form of psychic communication that began. This time I recognized the vibrant faces of people floating around the bedroom. They were all people who were currently alive and living near my home residence back in BC. They were all acquaintances from the Spiritualist Church. Even the Minister was there in the room with me. They were all expressing their happiness for me to be on holiday. One of them explained to me that due to my advanced psychic ability, I was able to see and hear them telepathically. They said anytime I felt bored or lonely I could call on any one of them for company. This felt real, I didn't doubt the validity of what I was hearing and seeing.

The mind is a powerful tool that can deceive or provide truth, but how do you tell the difference when your eyes and ears are confirming authenticity?

After Ron woke, he greeted me with his usual happy morning tone and gave me a kiss. He got dressed, washed and went down for breakfast; inviting me to join them downstairs when I was ready. Even though I had a sleepless night, I felt euphoric, overly confident and energized. I could remember the spirit communications I'd been having all night and wondered where the spirit beings had all gone now? Eager to join family for breakfast, I dressed quickly and headed for the top of the stairs. Passing by the old photos on the dresser, movement on one of the pictures spurred my curiosity. I stopped to look and remarkably could see the people in the photos waving their arms in effort to get my attention. As I leaned closer for a better look, they began talking to me. These little people, in the photo, were completely animated and I heard their voices. *Video photo frames had not yet been invented.* None of this frightened me, it felt natural and normal. I asked the people moving around in the picture frame if they were at peace and that's when one of them told me of a horrible fire they had died in. Upon hearing of this tragedy, it seemed I was instantaneously transported back in time, finding myself inside an old farm house. Immediately I was engulfed in flames, completely surrounded. Feeling the intense heat, hearing the roar of the fire and then gripped by the sadness of those that died in that fire, I managed not to panic. Within seconds I was back in Ron's parents Saskatchewan home, safe and standing at the top of the stairs. I didn't even remember walking away from the photos to get to the stairs? Deciding to go to the kitchen for breakfast, it seemed as if I floated down the stairs, without feeling my legs move. Effortlessly I found myself at the bottom landing, thinking; perhaps I've died and am now in the world of spirit? As I approached the breakfast table, all eyes were on me and I remember hearing Ron say, *"are you okay Ann?"* What a relief that Ron could see me because then I knew I was still physically alive. *"Yes, I'm fine"* was my reply as I took a moment to decide if I should tell him, his parents and my children of the experience I'd had with the ancestors who'd died in the fire. I wanted to tell them of the clear communication and seeing the people in the photos move, but my conscious mind convinced me they wouldn't believe me. Instead, I simply asked Ron's parents if anyone in the photos upstairs had died in a house fire. No they hadn't, was the response.

By the end of the day, I was mostly talking in rambling sentences that didn't make much sense to anyone else. As far as I was concerned I was passing on spiritual, universal wisdoms. While in this elated sense of perfection I believed myself to be in sync with the Universe and all its secrets. In spite of that, I'd have brief glimpses of reality which conveyed to me I was having strange thoughts. It shook me up, I felt confused.

At this early stage my mind was still flipping between real and false. Thankfully I had the presence of mind to take Ron aside and let him know I was going through questionable thinking. That's all it took for Ron to get me to the nearest Doctor office.

It was an odd feeling going to see a Physician, in an unfamiliar town, in a different province several hundred miles from home. Ron was a strong support for me as I met with the Doctor. He had many routine questions concerning my eating, sleeping and stressors in my life. Then the Doctor turned to Ron and asked what he has noticed about my behaviour lately. Ron talked about my moods shuffling between quietness, anger and crying jags on this trip, but he figured the stress of travelling had triggered me. Ron thought I was suffering from panic attacks. If he had thought about it, beyond our travelling, I'm sure Ron would have told this Doctor of my moodiness at home too. But he didn't. As for me, during this appointment, I was still out of touch with reality and unable to connect with my thoughts well enough to say what had been happening to me.

As I spoke to this Doctor about my views on spiritual beliefs, he became very interested to know more about my basic philosophy of life. I recall telling him there was an all knowing, all loving Intelligence that flowed within and around us all. My words seemed to flood from me as I expressed my comprehension of the continuous existence of our soul. The Doctor seemed intrigued by my outlook on life matters. Since I hadn't told him anything about how I'd seen spirit beings moving around in the photos; and I was no longer rambling run on sentences about the Universe, the Doctor concluded that I was fine. His diagnosis was lack of sleep as a result of anxiety.

He prescribed mild sedatives and gave me advice to get lots of rest. Before Ron and I left his office, the Doctor conveyed his respect of my beliefs with regards to spiritual matters. He told me he recognized some Eastern philosophy in my views and then he named some Authors, asking me if I had read their books. I had never heard of the Authors or read any books on philosophy. My understanding, of spiritual matters, was long within me, even since childhood. When Ron and I left the office my mind was steady and I felt reassured there was nothing for me to be concerned about.

That night, after taking the prescribed sedative, it still took a long time to drift off. While I lay awake, again I could see the faces of long deceased family members floating near the ceiling. They were smiling down at me radiating golden light. After finally dozing off, I slept soundly until morning.

Although I'm not able to recall all the details, I do remember waking and feeling like my body was merely a puppet occupied by some unknown entity. It felt like there was another person that had taken over my body. My mind was somewhere off in the distance watching the actions of my own body and hearing words come from my mouth, that were not my own. I internally screamed for help, but my body would not respond to my mental requests. Instead I became an observer trapped within my own body. It was horrible and I was terribly frightened.

Somehow, as the day went on, there came a time where I managed to force my consciousness to take back possession of my body. The sad thing was, the damage was done, I was now fully into my first psychotic break from reality. Completely delusional and caught up in elated bouts of mania, as I spewed peculiar notions. Miraculously, there was a transitory moment where I felt clarity and it offered me time to tell Ron my mind wouldn't think straight. I explained, quickly, my fear of the bizarre thoughts contaminating my mind. He admitted he'd heard odd comments from me and knew something was amiss. Within an hour, of asking for help, I had again escalated to erratic behavior. Ron quickly gathered our kids and explained to his parents I was having a mental breakdown and he had to get me home immediately. He helped them understand I needed my own Doctor who would know my past history and be able to diagnose properly.

It was a long drive home across Saskatchewan, Alberta and BC. We were on the road, only a short time, when I began hallucinating and seeing a demonic being running alongside the car. It's creepy form made my neck hairs stand up. This creature was the first truly frightening image I'd seen and it appeared to be real. When I first saw the creature, running as fast as our car, it seemed to be focused on the road ahead and not looking directly at me. Even though petrified, I stared at its hairless, boney, white body, oversized feet, hands and head. I didn't scream or tell my family because I didn't want them to become frightened, instead I prayed to God to keep us protected and safe from this evil looking Being. Right then, the figure ran off into the bush and I didn't see it again.

As we continued driving along, listening to the current song on the radio, while the kids played cards in the back seat, my thoughts moved into what felt like a heightened state of awareness. It seemed I was able to perceive several levels of existence happening simultaneously. On one level, I could hear the song playing on the radio and the kids chatting. On another level, the lyrics of the songs were giving me spiritual guidance and on yet another plane I was certain I could hear the inner thoughts of my children and husband telepathically. Then I perceived yet a fourth level where God and I were communicating as if in oneness.

Soon my experience changed and it felt as if our moving vehicle was in slow motion. Now, the sound of the kid's voices and drone of the radio seemed to disappear; as the voice of an Angel spoke to me. The Angelic Guide told me that I would be experiencing several years of mental torment and that I must trust that God's love would be continuously by my side. I received a warning, from this guide, that I would not sense the love of God during my time of illness. The Guide also told me that there would come a day when all will be well and happiness will return. I saw and felt the presence of this Angel. This spirit was a male, someone I recognized yet had never met in this life. When he told me he had to leave, I started to hear the radio and kids voices again. I became aware of the sound of the vehicle's motor and motion of the car. My surroundings were no longer in slow motion and I was again fully aware of the present moment. I could still see and sense my spirit guide sitting right there beside me. He was telling me goodbye and that we will meet again one day. My family had no idea I was experiencing this because I was quiet during this mind to mind communication with the Guide.

Suddenly I asked my husband to pull over to the side of the road. I believe it was the first sound I uttered while in the car this whole time of experiencing these levels of consciousness. He stopped the car safely and I jumped out. The Guide was still with me, I could see him standing on the shoulder of the road right beside me. I then felt the spirit guide reach out to me with his arms as he gave me the warmest, most compassionate hug. I felt safe and in the presence of God in his embrace. He then was gone. Suddenly, I realized I could hear the sounds of the kids complaining about wanting to get going. Ron opened his door, poked his head up asking if I was okay? Back in the car, driving across the Provinces, we headed toward home.

A short ways down the road, I began talking of the demonic spirit that had been running beside the car earlier. My common sense was nowhere to be found; I had no concern of my kids hearing me talk about such a bizarre thing. Ron knew he had to stop at the nearest hospital due to my unsettled state of mind. It was Saskatoon, where

Ron encouraged me to go into the hospital with him; as our two children walked solemnly alongside us.

As we crossed the parking lot, I spotted a single glove lying in the dirt and picked it up. I believed this was Michael Jackson's glove, who was a saint in my eyes, so I tucked it caringly inside my jacket next to my heart.

Once we entered the hospital, Ron was distracted by keeping a close eye on the kids as he looked for the admitting receptionist. I meandered off alone down a hospital corridor, in search of my hero, Michael Jackson. Roaming the Hospital for quite a period of time, I wandered in and out of wards. Chatting to patients with no sense of discretion, I said blessing over them, sent them healing rays of light from my eyes and told them to get up they are healed. Most patients were too ill to protest my bizarre actions, others humoured me and some merely shook their heads in disbelief. Eventually I found myself in a ward with about four beds, lights off and no one there. *Similar to the state of mind I was currently in; lights off and no one there!* I convinced myself this had to be Michael Jackson's room, so I sat on one of the beds believing he would soon return. With great expectation, I heard the room door open, but to my surprise it wasn't Michael who sauntered into the room, it was two nurses and a security guard. The next thing I knew I was in a little room with a wooden table and two chairs. I sat in one chair while the nice security guard sat relaxed in the other. During our time together in this room, I clearly noticed some movement within the wood grain pattern on the closed door. Faces of unfamiliar people, popped out of the wood pattern, staring back at me. Within seconds these talking heads started telling me the life story of the security guard, which I promptly shared with him. This tolerant man was getting a whole future prophesy from me and I don't remember the details of what I said to this security guard but I do remember him saying, *"what a beautiful future you see for me, I certainly hope your right."*

Huge chunks of my memory, regarding psychotic episodes, are not accessible to me. Only bits and pieces remain intact. Relying on Ron to fill in detail helps me to accurately describe what took place. I know from my husband that there were a team of Doctors who observed me and diagnosed that I was delusional. This team suggested hospitalization on their psychiatric ward. Ron insisted he did not want me admitted in Saskatoon and asked that they give me some medication to help me remain calm, until he could drive me back to BC. I was then given another prescription for a sedative and we were back on the road.

One vivid memory I carry with me, that I deeply cherish, is that of my Son and Daughter handing me two gifts. They'd purchased them at the Saskatoon Hospital gift shop. One child gave me a little troll doll wearing a nurse outfit; the other child gave me a cute little ceramic dog. It was their way of offering me support and love. As we continued our drive home, my guilt of not being a good Mom presented itself briefly, only to give way to my demented mind pushing me back into delusions.

We were getting closer to our province of BC and home, but it was getting late and Ron decided to rent a hotel room for the four of us. With the sedatives, I slept right through until early morning.

Something strange happened upon awakening and first opening my eyes. To me it seemed there was an evil entity trying to possess me. My head felt weighted down and my thoughts were foggy. Looking back, probably side effects of the sedatives? Along with feeling groggy though, there were also strange and violent thoughts swirling around my mind; disturbing thoughts. Try as I might, it was near impossible for me to think of anything pleasant or positive. This was bad enough but when I heard a grotesque and creepy voice screaming at me that it intended to kill me and trap my soul, I fought a mental battle to maintain my Self. This fight required me to focus every ounce of my sanity onto the desire of being a Mom to my children. It was through thinking of my kids that gave me strength to *hold on tight*. Truthfully, it felt like a war to win my own Soul. What I didn't know, until years later, is that severe bipolar disorder can cause strange thoughts that sometimes are frightening. To me, in that moment of torment, evil beings seemed the only logical assumption. During this waking nightmare, I had been laying in the hotel bed, on my side, with my back to the wall. The next thing I knew my entire body was flung, across two feet, against the wall. The flat of my back slammed hard against the wall and I lay crumpled in a heap on the floor; stunned.

Ron and the kids had slept through my ordeal. After waking my husband and telling him what had happened, he told me it was another hallucination. Begging him to believe me, to no avail left me feeling terribly alone in my fright. Wondering how that physically could have happened to me, occupied my thoughts as I changed out of my bed clothes. Having had a good sleep afforded me some sanity and I reconciled that either it was the intensity of my believing mind that may have caused it or perhaps an outside energy beyond my own? Regardless the good news is, having experienced this, I knew that nothing but love is real. Love lights the darkness and consumes all malevolence. Reassuring myself that I was fine now, the fight was over and my happy thoughts prevailed. Rather than go into fearful thinking, all I did was acknowledge that it happened, thought of caring for my kids and carried on with getting ready to head to the restaurant for breakfast with my family.

In the restaurant, after the waitress had taken our order, I abruptly had the thought that my Husband was plotting to kill me. Coincidently, just as I was thinking that, Ron got up from the table saying he was headed to the bathroom; but, instead he walked to the restaurant kitchen. I sat at the table, with our kids, watching him talk to our waitress. Upon seeing his actions, I was certain he and the waitress were old friends and he had just handed the waitress poison to put into my breakfast food. Even though we were two provinces away from our home town, my twisted logic created an elaborate scheme where the two of them had been in phone contact for months. My mind had me believing they were in love and Ron had brought me here intentionally to enact this heinous plan. It was quite a story line I had concocted in my head, sadly I believed it adamantly. Ron now headed to the bathroom, then came back to sit with the kids and I. The waitress then appeared and placed our food in front of us. Out of fear, I hesitated to taste anything. Then, reaching over I took a piece of Ron's toast thinking this was smart of me, he wouldn't have his own breakfast tainted. I ate it. Gradually I felt an aching heat move through my body, then dizziness in my head. I panicked thinking I'd been fooled and ingested the poison. I pushed my chair back from the table and ran towards the lobby screaming for help, claiming I'd been poisoned. The belief and fear was so great that I went into shock collapsing on the lobby floor unable to move. Laying there on the cold floor, I could hear someone asking; *"are you okay, what is your name?"* as much as I wanted to respond my body would not function and could not speak. It felt as if my consciousness had separated from my physical. No longer did I feel the panic of being poisoned. Now it felt as if my perception was calm and detached from the drama. From this place of inner peacefulness I could hear someone saying that the front desk had called for an ambulance. Within minutes I could feel my body being loaded onto a stretcher, placed in the ambulance and whisked off to the local Hospital. Once there, staff tested my blood and urine for any possible toxin levels. The Doctor observed me for quite a while and then suggested to Ron that I might be suffering from bipolar disorder or another form of mental illness.

My confusion over being told there was no poison in my body had me suspicious. Surely with me dropping to the floor in severe pain, unable to move, they would find toxins in me? Now I started believing all the Hospital staff was in on the plot to kill me. Next,

I became certain that it must have been Ron that threw me across the hotel room from my bed. My brain was misfiring all over the place and thoughts were disconnected. As spiritual signs seemed to jump out at me from magazines and hearing snippets of people's conversations, my fears were confirmed. I came to the conclusion they were *all* in on the evil plot, even the kids! Paranoia moved in and my last bit of remaining logic vacated.

It must have been pure hell for Ron to deal with this unimaginable lunacy from me. Bearing in mind he had two young children, pre-teens, to care for while Mommy fell from sanity. Instinct had me struggling with anyone who tried to subdue me, yet finally the well experienced Hospital staff managed to inject me with a strong sedative to help me relax. Thankfully they knew to do this, as it immediately went to work and I began feeling less frightened. The Doctors involved, encouraged Ron to have me hospitalized there but he wanted to get me to our home Hospital where my regular Doctor would have my past history. Now feeling like a bowl of jelly, Ron had no problem leading me to the car and pouring me into the seat. He had been given a new prescription for a stronger sedative that everyone hoped would keep me sedated, long enough, until arrival at our home emergency room.

Off we went again, me completely blitzed in and out of consciousness, as Ron did his best to remain focused on his driving. The kids had to endure witnessing their Mom in mental distress and their Dad doing his best to get us home without further incident. I can't imagine what that must have been like for Ron or our children.

The staff at this particular hospital phoned ahead to the General Hospital in my hometown, to alert them of our estimated arrival. They believed it was imperative for Ron to get me there straight away. Many more miles were yet to be covered plus a two hour ferry ride.

We finally arrived at our destination with Ron exhausted, kids upset and me oblivious from the heavy sedation.

This mental illness completely consumed my mind. I had no choice or control. You cannot think your way out of a psychotic break. It was heartbreaking for me to awaken from this insanity and recall some of what I had put my family through. I knew Ron was strong enough to withstand my lunacy, but I wasn't so sure our marriage would survive it.

Chapter #8

OFFICIALLY COMMITTED

L ooking around the emergency room I saw objects that are common in hospitals such as; panels of buttons on the walls, sprinkler heads on the ceiling and various forms of medical equipment. To me these objects were all hidden cameras that I believed a secret society, of evil people, were watching me from. Oh yes, conspiracy all around me, I was certain.

Even the staff at Hospital appeared to be demonically possessed, including my husband. I trusted no one.

While being moved to the psychiatric ward, my delusions had me believing I was going to be on the evening news for being the hero who ousted the evil society and saved the world. At times, when

Hospital staff turned their back, I'd look right into the lens of what I thought was a camera; winking and mouth the words, *"I know I am the Savior of our world, fear not"*.

To understand the logic behind insanity is to accept that the brain is a powerful tool. My perception of the world was based on what I could see, taste, hear, touch and energetically sense. So, I experienced a separate reality from the average person entirely because my brain was providing incorrect information. Electrical impulses were running amuck in my mind and I had no choice but to respond to what I observed. To me, everything I experienced was REAL.

After the emergency room Doctor spoke with my family Doctor they both agreed it was necessary to admit me into the psychiatric ward. Commonly this ward was referred to as *the fourth floor*. This was the first point in time that I had been given the official diagnosis of severe bipolar disorder.

Realizing they were committing me, in my-self deluded world, I believed God had placed me there so I could restore the mental patients to perfect health. My Divine assignment was to lead them out into the world to facilitate a new world order of Peace. In my grandiose thinking, I was the second coming of Jesus, in female form this time around. In my mind this was perfectly logical thinking, it felt real and very authentic.

As a nurse and orderly took me up to *the fourth floor*, I watched the nurse press the button on the wall beside the thick, locked door to the psychiatric ward. Upon hearing the buzzer and the sound of a latch bolt clunk, I was escorted through. The heavy door slid shut behind us with an automatic lock down to ensure security. This was not the first time I had been admitted through this high level security door. In fact, only two years prior I had gone through as a visitor, to see my Mom.

The first thing I noticed upon entering this ward is that everything from the floor, walls, ceiling and even the people, were in various shades of gray. I couldn't envision any colour. The nurse had me sit in what appeared to be a lounge, with the orderly, while she went off to do something. From where I sat my view took in the colourless staff members at a front desk area. Unexpectedly, while glancing around the room, I witnessed the most beautiful occurrence. Spectacular and vibrant colours began flowing through every item in the room. It was like a magical, invisible paint brush sweeping across everything. Pretty. With believing every person there were evil entities, I didn't say a word about what I perceived was happening. I remained quiet and docile so not to alert them that I was actually the Holy Messiah.

The following day, as I sat on the small hospital bed alone, I looked around to see another bed beside mine and a little two drawer table that was meant to accommodate personal possessions. There was no mirror in the bathroom, no lock on the door and I wasn't allowed anything sharp. With the strict Hospital regulations of the psychiatric floor, I had little use for the table with drawers. Just a change of clothes, comb, a toothbrush and dental paste was all I had and at this time all I needed.

It wasn't long before a nurse carrying a tray of test tubes walked into my ward, came up to me and said, *"Let me see your hospital bracelet"*. Taking my arm abruptly she added, *"Yup, you're Grace Ann"*. Without any warning she took my left arm, quickly tied a rubber tube around it and proceeded to unwrap something from cellophane. I saw it was a needle and asked her what she was doing? The nurse muttered that she was taking a blood sample from me. In her carelessness, she dropped something on the floor and exclaimed *"damn!"* then she picked up whatever had fallen and insensitively continued her task. This felt wrong and scary to me. The only reason I allowed her to do this was as a result of me telling myself to be calm and not struggle with her. It was when she took the alcohol soaked wipe, rubbed it over my arm then used her hand to wipe off the excess alcohol; that seriously troubled me. My logic knew that an experienced nurse would never contaminate a sterilized spot by using her hand. Her action translated to, *assassin in disguise*, in my paranoid mind. This technician was about to inject the needle and I protested. She ignored my concerns of her touching the now unsterile area of my arm. With her callous attitude toward me, I was sure she was part of a scheme to have me murdered. Believing I was Jesus, version two, didn't mean I couldn't be killed by the many malicious demons that were looking for me. That left me with one choice, get my ass out of there!

So not to alert her that I had caught onto her devious plot, I pretended my leg fell asleep and that I needed to stand for a moment. The second I was off the bed, I ran to the nurse station begging them to believe me that the nurse drawing blood was an imposter! The nurses at the desk insisted I let the technician draw my blood. I refused, so they held me in order to force me to comply. Trying to talk my way out of what I thought was a murder attempt, was not working. When you are steadfast to your belief of something, your body responds accordingly. My body went into a panic mode which caused me to thrash, scream and kick my way to safety. Next thing I knew my body was pinned to the floor by several staff and a Doctor was looking deep into my eyes telling me to calm down. Convinced they wanted me dead there was no reassurance by him telling me to be calm. This Doctor made it absolutely clear, in a gentle yet firm voice, that they would be drawing my blood for testing. He said I could relax and allow them to do so or they would hold me down and do it regardless. Heart pounding in my throat, tears leaking from my eyes, I moaned *"I don't want to die"*. Believing they were going to inject me with poison, I begged for my life. Out of options, no one to help me, so I mentally surrendered my life over to God and prayed that my soul would go to Heaven. A sense that God would keep me, swept through my mind and I relaxed. With that kind of authority on my side, I trusted the evil assassins could not destroy my soul. My terror was soon replaced with a feeling of peace, as the staff drew my blood. After they were done and let me up it was a relief to see I was still alive.

Come supper time, I was given a tray of food to take into the dinning area. There were four, maybe five, round tables where patients ate their meals. Taking a seat, my anxiety caused a panic surge through my body and I became alarmed when I lifted the lid off my dinner plate. Not understanding what the fear coursing through me was, again I imagined it was my psychic senses warning me that someone was trying to harm me. My insane logic told me that my imagined killers had laced my food with poison. One nurse gently encouraged me to eat but added if I felt it was poisoned, it's best to just leave it. She kindly asked if she could get me something else to eat. Her empathy spoke to my heart and my fear lifted. I thanked her for the generous offer but told her I felt safe to eat my original dinner now. It was in her relaxed attitude that I could sense she was not trying to control me, that helped me be at ease. Once my anxiety shifted, no more paranoia clouded my thinking.

A few hours later just when I thought it was safe to put my feet up, a man that was also a psychiatric patient sat down beside me and threatened my life. He leaned into my ear whispering menacingly, *"I could snap your neck and you'd be dead before anyone could stop me."* He pointed to the windows in the common room saying, *"You see those windows have no bars on them. I can take that chair, break the window and jump to the roof below; then onto the pavement and be gone before they see you lying here dead"*. I slowly got up and walked quickly to my room. Shaky, too terrified to call a nurse and tell what he'd said to me; I merely hid in my hospital bed and hoped he'd leave me alone.

That night, a different male patient approached me saying he was getting the nurse to lock him in his room. He warned me that a few patients were going to create a commotion to provide a distraction while one of them purposely hurt someone. I went to the floor nurse and asked to be locked in my room, but was told there were only two rooms on the psychiatric floor that would lock patients in. I did not have one of those rooms. I passed on the warning of a disturbance being planned and the nurse did not believe me. She merely scolded me and told me to stop thinking fearful thoughts. The more I pleaded for help, the more the nurse threatened to give consequences to my behavior. She let me know I'd be given an extra sedative if I didn't stop my rant immediately. Knowing already, from firsthand experience, that the staff was quick to hold me down and force me into submission if I didn't do as I was told, shut me up. Unable to let go the terror of what was coming, I had no choice but to walk back to the bed I was assigned and wait.

Twice a day a nurse came in and gave me medications; an antipsychotic, a mood stabilizer and a sedative. This particular night, I wanted to remain awake to protect myself. As the nurse stood beside me, I took my medications and swallowed. Fear caused me to be sneaky though and I hid the sedative pill in my cheek. As soon as the nurse left my room I spit it out and tucked it under my pillow. Most definitely, in my mind, a group of devious patients were coming for me and I wasn't going to be sedated.

Sure enough, in the wee hours of the night, I awoke to see a male patient starring at me from the doorway of my room. Chills of dread screeched up my back as I lay there quiet, pretending to be asleep. Peeking through the slits of my semi closed eyes and noticing he had walked away, I got up from the bed and ran to the nurse's station. To my distress, nothing I said convinced the nurses this creep was spying on me as I slept. In their opinion I was imagining it all. To my relief, suddenly one nurse noticed this man was actually walking the hall. As I turned around, there he was looking at me with a huge smile on his face. He acted confused about my fear of him, saying to the nurses that he was just up to use the ward bathroom because his room toilet was plugged. A nurse walked me back to my room. The moment she left I immediately pushed my door shut. That wasn't enough to help me feel safe, so I shoved the small side table against the closed door shielding myself from further psychological assault by this man. Although there was another bed in the room with me, no one occupied it, so I felt alone, not believed and unaided. Unfortunately, a nurse heard me rustling around and came back to my room. She forced the ward door open, sliding the table aside and exposing my tear stained face in the dimly lit room. She curtly explained they needed to look in on all patients, during rounds, so no closed doors were permitted. The nurse walked out heading back to her station, leaving me alone and terrified.

Left with no other option to protect myself, I grabbed the hospital gown which was tossed over the chair in my room and ran into the tiny bathroom. Lucky for me, being a small bathroom, I could securely tie the gown to the door knob inside and the other end of the gown to the towel rack, bracing the bathroom door closed. Then I climbed up on the sink counter, knees tucked up to my chin, crying. The stress of waiting to be brutally attacked kept my body trembling.

Unexpectedly I heard a phantom voice, within my mind, telling me to sing *"This Little Light of Mine"* an old and familiar hymn. So I nervously began singing out loud;

> *This little light of mine, I'm going to let it shine*
> *This little light of mine, I'm going to let it shine*
> *This little light of mine, I'm going to let it shine*
> *Let it shine, let it shine, let it Shine!*

Within one verse of that hymn, not only did I stop crying but also I was able to untie the gown from the door handle and climb back into my bed. Still singing, I continued into the second verse and by the time I got to the fourth verse, my reassurance that God would protect me from any harm was a strong hold in my heart and I'd fallen fast asleep.

The mind most certainly can be our best asset, if what we believe is positive and then we take action based in peacefulness.

The next morning while eating breakfast with the other patients, the man who had threatened me once again came close and whispered in my ear, *"I see you sleep sitting up"*. He was letting me know that he did walk back to my room to peer in and was now trying to get his kicks by upsetting me. This time I didn't feel afraid of him as I allowed the words to *This Little Light of Mine* echo within my mind. Feeling safe through focusing my thoughts on love, kept me strong.

Interestingly, before the end of this day, this threatening man had a psychotic melt down and had to be placed in a straight jacket, locked into a room where he waited for security to have him removed from the ward. He ended up placed in a larger facility that could handle his aggressive behaviour. Relieved he was gone yet dumb struck realizing the nurses had not believed me about his antics. Could I blame them though? Not really, because if I struggled to know the difference between delusion and truth, how could I expect staff to trust my wavering mind.

Shortly after being in Hospital and thoroughly saturated with psychiatric medications, I began realizing I did not have special abilities to read minds. It became painfully obvious that I was not Jesus, reincarnated, either. The medication was stabilizing my chemistry and clarity was returning to my mind. This was helpful on one hand yet devastating on the other.

There I was, obliged to admit I was actually just another patient with a mental illness. No poison meals, no evil beings possessing the staff, yet truly there had been the real danger of the male patient threatening violence. So how was I to discern the difference between reality and chemical imbalance?

Now I just wanted to go home, as the bleak sadness filled me. Worse of all, my Doctor confirmed I had a mental illness that required medication for the rest of my life. Great, I was officially insane. Knowing there was no way for me to control the chemical imbalance within my body, I reluctantly submitted to the medication.

It took a while, but with perseverance and a combination of group therapy, medication and support from family I started to regain a sense of identity. My depression moved from hopelessness to despair through to acceptance of an illness that carried an age old stigma.

Just as I was almost ready to leave the ward and go home, a new nurse walked into my room. She took a look at the small bouquet of flowers sitting in a plastic vase on my bedside table as she quipped, *"I don't know why people bring you flowers, all it does is encourage you to feel sorry for yourself and think it's okay to be in hospital. It's not like you're sick, and the last thing needed is for others to reward you for being here"*. The rest of the day was hell for me, the crying and self hatred returned. I believed this nurse to be right, that I didn't deserve flowers or anyone's sympathy.

Later in the day there was a staff change, a nurse I'd come to be familiar with was on duty now. When she saw the change in my mood, she wondered what had happened that knocked me backward. I didn't tell her straight away, instead I mumbled about not being worthy to have friends bring me flowers because I was just wallowing in self pity. When in the vulnerable mind set of mental illness, I tended to think all professionals were correct. Soon enough she helped me express my confusion over what the earlier nurse had said to me. Thankfully, she was able to get through to me and judging by her response, I'm certain the day nurse would have been spoken to regarding her one-dimensional thinking. Fortunately for me, the current nurse's understanding got my thinking back on the right track.

The truth is family and friends often show their love and support in the form of gifts. The more compassionate nurse helped me let go my feelings of self contempt and realize fully that flowers brightened not only my room but served as a reminder that someone cares about and loves me.

Painfully, I came to learn, there are disgruntled people working in positions of authority where they do not belong. On a more positive note, there are many highly trained, empathetic professionals, working in positions where they know how to help patients heal. My appreciation of them is deep.

Chapter #9

WHY ME?

I T TOOK QUITE A LOT of time, pouring over my past and scrutinizing my own behaviour, before I could accept my diagnosis of mental illness. This hereditary and severe illness stole my personality and my whole identity. The feeling within me was one of being in a void, nothing to cling to as far as perceiving myself. Mostly I could only see myself as a mental patient, someone who is ill and unable to function like the rest of the *normal* people. When the chemistry in my brain spiked it caused the electrical circuit of my brain to misfire; for me, the plunge into the depths of insanity were brutal.

Knowing my Mom and I both had the same genetic illness, terrified me. My worst fear was having possibly given this hereditary disorder onto one or both of my kids. Then I considered; what about any possible grandchildren? A sweep of nausea churned in my stomach as I blamed myself for unknown, future possibilities. Most days and nights were spent crying, curled up in a ball on my couch or bed. The household was taken care of to only a slight and basic level, that's all I could manage through this phase of depression.

The Doctors told me, with the severity of my condition, I must remain on medication for the rest of my life. At my young age of thirty-five there wasn't a more devastating sentence. Not only was I shame riddled but also struggling with the stigma of mental illness. The general community, meaning most people, view any form of mental illness as the person being untrustworthy and damaged goods. When people found out I had a diagnosis of bipolar disorder, it was my experience that the majority of them treated me differently; they kept me at arm's length.

Along with stigma struggles, there was also the very real concern of medication toxicity damaging my internal organs and putting my body at risk. Why me, was the big question at this point in time. Why Me?

After a short time, it was evident that medications were benefiting me. The three prescribed were; lithium a mood stabilizer, risperidone to relieve psychotic symptoms and ativan as a sedative to help calm my anxiety. This combination of pills needed to be taken daily.

Regardless of the proper medications in my system, the illness occasionally broke through and I endured bouts of manic euphoria, paranoid delusions, severe depression, ghastly hallucinations and panic attacks. This left me unable to rely on my thinking or medication. Mostly I was much like a Zombie, point me in the right direction and tell me what to do.

Commonly, I was unable to focus my attention long enough to even read one page of a book. For a while I couldn't maintain my attention span to complete simple tasks or hold a conversation with anyone. On top of these mental disruptions I also endured flu like symptoms as a result of the side effects from the medications. Then the weight gain. I went from a trim 125 pounds, right up to 195 pounds. My hair became dry and straw like, breaking off, leaving a mess of unhealthy, dull frizzy hair.

One day, having got up the courage to go into a mall shopping, I stood outside a store looking into their display window. Hearing someone walk up behind me, I turned around to see a woman I'd never met before and she appeared to be about my age. She gave me a wink and said, *"You must be on some strong medications too, huh?"* When she walked away I noticed that her hair was dry, thinned and frizzy; similar to my own.

After a lengthy time, five almost six years, on the medications I developed uncontrollable hand tremors. The embarrassment of lifting a cup to my mouth and having the shakes, spilling liquid over the rim of the cups, was demoralizing. Even just sitting quietly, my hand tremors were obvious. I began folding my arms, tucking them into my pockets or holding my hands under a table to hide the irrepressible shaking. Speaking to my Doctor about this didn't help much, as I was told it was a symptom of known side effects.

There was a person, who didn't know me very well, that sarcastically laughed and asked me why I was so nervous? I just looked down toward the floor, unable to tell them it was not about nervousness. The medications had several side effects, this was just another one. I was so ashamed of this that I preferred people to think I was nervous rather than know I was mentally ill and on psychiatric medication.

Shame also made common daily routines grueling. Like the time I braved walking to the post office. It was my habit to calculate what time of day would be most likely NOT to see anyone on the street or in the post office. What a stress filled ordeal it was for me to be in public. Sure enough I miscalculated this particular day and there were many folks headed to pick up their mail. Some people were degradingly obvious as they stared at me and when they realized I was looking back at them they'd fumble a forced smile or just quickly look away. I hated being known as the mentally ill person in town. One friend, who remained close to me, used to tell me it was just me *thinking* they were staring at me. That was equally hard to deal with because my friend would not believe me. O-well-O-well-Oh, I'd repeat to myself in a sing song way. It seemed to cheer me slightly while I swept my hurt under the carpet and carried on.

There were acquaintances that talked to me as if nothing was different about me, but then there were the oblivious ones who actually spoke louder and slower to me; as if I were unable to understand their words. Some friends drifted out of my life, no longer interested to be around me. The few that accepted me, without judgment, I was thankful for. At first, for a long time, my feelings were hurt because I thought I'd done something wrong by people walking away from me. Ultimately I learned that people didn't walk away because I was a bad person; it had only been about their discomfort with their own feelings towards me. I'd done nothing wrong, bad or disrespectful.

After some reclusive time at home, I was ready to venture out into my neighbourhood again. Feeling it was unlikely to see anyone out on the street this time of day, I decided to walk my dog through the quiet residential area. A woman, I'd not met before, was in her yard tidying up her flower garden. Once she spotted me her friendliness was apparent as she struck up a conversation. I was grateful that she was a talker because I wasn't. Very soon into her monologue, she uttered a heartbreaking comment, carrying on about the crazy bipolar woman who lived nearby. Her perception of (in her words) the 'nut job' was that *she* shouldn't be allowed to live in the neighbourhood because there are children around and they could be in danger. Listening to her fume about the odd behaviour of the mentally ill woman triggered my shame, bringing me close to tears. Here I thought she was talking about me without realizing who I was. When she called the bipolar woman by name, I then understood it was not me she was referring to. My anger then swelled. Although I wouldn't defend myself, my valor came in defense of another person. I simply stated, *"I'm sorry you feel that way about her, I know she must be suffering terribly because I too am bipolar. We're really not monsters you know, I even have children of my own that I am capable to look after".* As a result of expressing myself, I didn't walk away angry. I felt compassion for her embarrassment and reached out to her by saying, *"Its' okay, you have no way of understanding mental illness if you haven't experienced it yourself".* I then carried on walking my dog, feeling a bit happier that I had perhaps raised someone's awareness in consideration of bipolar disorder.

Over the many years of digesting psychiatric medications and suffering the misery of bipolar episodes, I noticed my hair thinning rapidly. Eventually the top of my head was almost bare, leaving a two inch wide strip of baldness. No bangs grew anymore so I also had a receding hair line. Not an attractive look for a woman. To top it off, due to my expanded weight, I wore frumpy clothes trying to hide my fat body. Even my 5'7" tall frame took on a shorter appearance because I became stooped with rounded shoulders. During family gatherings there had been a few photos taken of me from time to time, but when I came across any of myself, I tore them up and got rid of the pieces. It was awful seeing images of myself looking overweight, balding with hunched shoulders.

Mental illness changed me physically from being a tall, slender, pretty red head with green eyes and clear complexion to Bozo the clown, all before I turned thirty-nine years old. I learned to use hair spray to secure a comb over. Even at the young age of fifteen my daughter had a natural gift with styling hair and a substantial knowledge of hair products. In her capable hands, what was left of my natural hair was at least restored to a healthier sheen.

With time, I eventually got on the upward swing, having reached acceptance of my new look and feeling compassion towards myself. I'd finally grasped the truth in recognizing that other people's judgment had nothing to do with me. With this in mind, I let go of my resentment towards the ones that had made ignorant statements to me. Really they just didn't know any better. I believe Marianne Williamson wrote; *"We must all learn to see human behaviour as one of two things; either as love or as a call, for love."*

Having a handle, on my experience with bipolar disorder, I again asked the ultimate question; *Why Me?* This time my emotions felt at ease because now I had an answer: Why not me! Regardless of the unique challenges faced through dealing with mental illness, the blessing was that through the difficulty I was spiritually maturing. Learning to master my own mind and trust myself again.

Chapter #10

THE RELAPSE

I T FELT GREAT AS I started seeing myself as wife and mother once again. This gave me a sense of identity that I had been missing. Resigning myself to a life of simplicity cooking meals, cleaning house and helping Ron with his construction business; I no longer tried working outside the home.

With being alone most of the time I relied on journaling my thoughts to keep a sense of connectedness to life. Through writing I was able to deepen my inner awareness and frequently find solutions to my problems. As I wrote down what was troubling me, eventually I'd get to the answers to resolve concerns.

Remaining stable minded for a lengthy time tricked me into honestly believing I would never again suffer another psychotic episode. The medication was helping me tremendously. Group therapy was creating a safe place for me to talk about my experience with the illness. I had bi-weekly individual therapy sessions with my psychiatrist, which helped me deal with emotional fallout. My family and a few close friends rallied around me in support. I ate balanced meals, got regular sleep, exercised and appreciated my life. Yet through all this, to my surprise, the next episode of bipolar disorder was more devastating than the first one.

During a public gathering, where spiritual music was being played for the purpose of worship, it became apparent I'd slipped into delusion. I sang loudly and danced erratically. In my mind, I was a skilled singer and dancer. As I swooped up to people, trying to make them dance with me, I was met with cold stares. People's jaws dropped as eyebrows lifted while they watched my out of control dance and off key screaming of made up lyrics. My family and friends were not with me at this event so there was no one to stop me from disturbing the peaceful gathering. It played out with me eventually leaving, feeling like I was the Christ incarnate. Mania can be a fun place to live, when you're in it; different story when you wake up realizing what you did.

The next day I convinced myself I'd just momentarily got caught up in the enthusiasm of the music. I persuaded myself to believe I really didn't do anything unusual, I was just being free and happy. Denial is a great place to hide out for a while and it afforded me the luxury of feeling I didn't have to tell Ron what I did.

Within a few short weeks, after my singing-nut-dance episode, I again went into a delusional state that was most dangerous. No one close to me realized my mental decline had gone into psychosis again. So, no one stopped me from loading my two kids into our family car and driving off one frosty, snowy winter day. The near accident happened when I had driven down the curvy road about two miles and then decided to spray the windshield with wiper cleaner. The cold air immediately froze the windshield spray and I couldn't see a thing! My thinking was that Angels were keeping the car on the road even though I could not see anything past the frost. To me this was a test of faith and I could only pass by allowing the Angels to guide me safely. My poor kids had no choice in what their Mom was doing. The road was curvy, the car was travelling at top speed and I couldn't see out of the windshield. I just drove blindly. Thankfully, there had been no oncoming cars at the time and luckily the normal setting on the heater was enough to clear the frost, just slightly, for me to see I was about to run into the culvert on the wrong side of the road. Had I not turned the wheel quickly, we would have crashed. The kids saw the near miss, yet they had no idea I was in psychotic episode.

One night, not long after the car incident, the hallucinations began again. It was Christmas break so Ron and I had allowed both our kids to invite a friend each to sleep over. Being in mental decline is not always detectable by people close to me, I appeared balanced of mind. We had eaten dinner, watched some television and even chatted, while the kids enjoyed board games. The kids stayed up late talking while Ron and I went to bed early. Sometime after midnight I awoke feeling a spirit person shaking me. I opened my eyes and saw flames blazing through our master bedroom. I screamed at Ron to get up! Fire!!! I ran from our bedroom and woke our two kids and their friends. As they sleepily rousted from their warm beds I pulled them down the hall and yelled at them to GET OUT OF THE HOUSE NOW! As I forced them out into the cold winter night, with at least a foot of snow on the ground, I frantically grabbed coats and shoes from the closet shelf and threw them into the snow bank. All the while I barked orders for the kids to get into their shoes and coats and go farther away from the burning house. Get onto the street I yelled. I could smell the smoke billowing around my shoulders and head, so I ducked down under the smoke and headed back into the house. I called to Ron, terrified he was unconscious from the fumes. Out of the dense smoke I saw Ron walking towards me. He was asking me why I was warning the kids of a fire. Apparently I was the only one experiencing the fire and smoke.

Poor Ron had the unsettling duty of calling the parents of the two kids that were sleeping over and after hearing I had gone berserk, thinking there was a fire, those parents were more than happy to pick up their kids at two in the morning. Me, I remained in an altered state where the house was still on fire. Ron, dealing with parents and their kids, didn't notice me trotting off to the next door neighbours. Thumping on their front door screaming *fire* woke them and trusting I was sane, they agreed to call 911, emergency, to get the fire department immediately. By the time Ron comprehended what I'd done, it was too late; the fire truck was already blaring it's siren up our street. Decked out in fire gear the team of responders thoroughly searched our house for signs of fire. Of course they found the house to be in good order and safe. By now, with the flashing fire engine lights, some of the neighbours had come out of their homes and stood on the street. Curiously they peered in our direction, trying to figure out what was going on. Soon enough the fire truck shut off the flashing lights and quietly drove away. With nothing to see the last of the on lookers went back to bed. No matter what Ron said I would not believe him that there had been no fire. For me, there was no doubt that there had there been a fire, I saw it with my own eyes! The worst part was I figured the reason the fire department couldn't see the fire is because it was now hidden out of view within the walls. There was no freaking way I was going back in our house or allowing my children and Ron to go back in because I knew when that fire hit our oil furnace there was going to be an explosion. Our kind hearted neighbour saw Ron's plight and understood I was off in another episode, so he offered us to stay in his spare room until I settled down. Accepting this assistance was difficult for Ron, but he knew my deluded mind was inconsolable. Doing what he thought was best, Ron pretended to go along with my paranoia; we all settled in at the house next door to ours.

By morning I had completely lost any ability to discern between reality and delusion. Ron was able to calm me by promising a drive to Hospital. In my mind I believed the Hospital was where I could get doctors to prove to Ron I was sane. When in the car with Ron a *knowing* came over me; He was going to murder me. With no doubt, I felt certain he had stowed an axe and shovel in the trunk to dispose of my body. That drive was a nightmare for me. In my silence, fear racked my mind. As we drove towards Hospital, Ron took a turn off the main road to go to a friend's house. Ron told me he had to drop off a work related document for this man. My heart raced because I thought he was conspiring with his friend to kill me. My mind scrambled for an escape route before it was too late to save myself. This unexpected detour fed my paranoia and I panicked. Jumping from our almost stopped car, I ran to the front door of a house and banged on it. Through my loud hysterical screaming for help, the owners opened their front door and let me in. Since I was terrified of Ron and claiming he was going to kill me, he was forced to stay away from me. The home owner drove me to Hospital while Ron followed behind in our car. Looking back, I can't imagine the dismay Ron must have felt during my paranoid accusations toward him. The only reason the person helping me didn't call the police was because he knew my Husband and that it would be highly unlikely Ron would do me harm.

Yet again admitted to the psychiatric ward, the medications I'd been on previously were adjusted. During this two week stay in hospital, I was mostly sedated while the stronger medications did their work in stabilizing my body chemistry. Rest and nutrition along with therapy sessions helped me regain composure. Having time to reflect on what happened during my recent mental break down, I wondered how this could happen to me again. How could I believe the lies my mind fed to me? How is it that I was able to see, hear and even smell things that did not exist? There was no hope in me that I would ever be able to trust my own mind again. Beaten down and feeling numb, I succumbed to depression again.

Some of the more helpful staff in Hospital encouraged me to rest easy and feel safe. The psychiatric ward offered crafts, art time, pay phone access and once a week the patients prepared a meal in the kitchen together. We were not allowed to handle knives, so a staff member provided that part of the preparation. I felt insulted at first. It took me time to get my head around the staff not trusting me with a sharp object. Okay, I could see their point, after all, when delusion set in there was no way to think your-self out of it. Besides, I didn't trust my mind so how could I expect staff to?

A heartbreaking truth for me was the realization that I had absolutely no control over my thoughts, at times. Will this ever end, I wondered. How can I live life without feeling joy, peace or even a tiny fragment of trust in my own mind; considering death was a fleeting thought, yet more so, I wanted to live. My family loved me and this I didn't doubt, with them by my side I could manage.

While still in Hospital, there came a time I started feeling more grounded and capable. My concentration was better so I asked Ron to bring in my binder of inspirational quotes that I had collected from well known authors. There was one particular poem that gave me a sense of hope. Feeling like other patients might enjoy this poem too, I approached the nurses' desk asking them to check the poem out and if they thought it was appropriate, perhaps they might post it on the bulletin board? They read it, they liked it and they posted it.

The name of the poem is *Each Day Brings A Chance To Do Better* written by Helen Steiner Rice. Due to copyright legalities in which someone does have the rights to this poem, I was not able to obtain permission to reprint it in my book. Yet, I can say this poem is about how we sometimes will wish for another chance to have a fresh beginning and wipe out our mistakes. The inspirational message goes on to encourage us to make a brand-new start and that it is as simple as holding strong to our desire and keep on trying with all our heart. There is always a chance to start anew if we want it!

The next day I was expecting a visit from the resident Psychiatrist and I knew he was close to sending me home. Figuring if not today, for sure tomorrow I'd be released. Smiling at the Doctor as I took my seat across from him, I listened to his official comments based on the nurse's report. It was a shock to hear I had to stay longer. The nurses had written in their report that I was displaying manic behavior again. They stated I had insisted they post, on the bulletin board, a poem I had written and that I believed it would make the other patents well. Upon hearing the Doctor say this, I protested explaining that is not what happened. The more I disputed what the nurses wrote about me the more he disbelieved me. Adamantly I stated that I'd never claimed to have written the poem nor did I say it would make patients well. Of course he didn't believe me; I was manic in his eyes. Had I've known those particular nurses were capable of misconstruing truth, I would never have suggested they consider the poem for the bulletin board. In their defense, I will add, perhaps there had been a shift change and communication got mixed up between staff. I don't know what happened but I do know their inadequate report of what took place directly affected me having to stay on the psychiatric ward longer than I needed.

This report, by these nurses, also stated I was seen everyday pacing the halls, acting too happy, up too early and using the pay phone before 7:00 a.m. Agreeing that I was walking the halls every day to get exercise and concurring that I felt happier these days because I'm not depressed; I admitted getting out of bed around 6:30 a.m. and getting dressed for the day because that is my routine at home. Yes, I told the Doctor, I'm on the phone just before 7:00 a.m. because my husband *asked me* to phone him before he leaves for work. The Psychiatrist simply dismissed my effort to reason with him and explain why I was doing those things. In my frustration and upset with this nonsense I finished off my defense by asking him to please believe me that I was stable now. He shook his head, saying I'm sorry but you'll be staying a few more days until your moods settle down. He began telling me that my behaviour was clearly leaning to anger and if I escalated further he would give me a sedative. I felt stunned and fearful of him. In that moment I understood the kind of power the staff in Hospital had over me. I shut up immediately.

When Ron came to visit me, I told him of this ordeal concerning the Hospital staff. He spoke to my Doctor and explained that the only exercise I could get was pacing floors on the ward and indeed everything I had described, regarding my routine at home, was true. Once he had the Doctor understand I only made those 7:00 a.m. phone calls as a result of Ron's request, my behavior was no longer perceived as manic. Ron's opinion was valued. Common sense helps me appreciate why the Psychiatrist had a hard time believing me. When in an episode I could be very convincing and come across as making sense, even though I'd be in the throws' of the illness. Yet from my point of view, as the patient, it was frustrating to undergo this kind of incorrect observation by medical professionals.

Thankfully, I was released from hospital without being held longer. It was through Ron explaining the normalcy of my behaviour that made the difference. Now being of sound mind and on adjusted levels of medication didn't mean I was out of the woods, as far as self esteem issues go. There was a huge dip in my self confidence, not a fun place to be. Thinking it was okay to confide my feelings with someone I knew, I told her how utterly hard it was to get through each day. It wasn't comforting to have her reprimand me, saying I was lucky I had a husband that supports me and kids that love me. Then she told me I had nothing to complain about considering many people go through depression without anyone there for them. She told me I should *'get over it'* and get on with my life. I suppose she thought her lecture would push me forward, she was mistaken; instead it shut me down further.

Coasting through life thinking I better not complain anymore and taking my medication, I stayed at home. I'd resigned myself to the fact that there wasn't much more horror I could go through, I'd experienced it all, I thought.

On the upside, my resolve was strong; this was an illness within my body and I am not an illness, I am a human being.

Chapter #11

BOOT CAMP COUNSELING

LTOGETHER THERE WERE THREE PSYCHOTIC episodes that landed me stays in Hospital. The in-between episodes were not always obvious to others, if my demeanor was quiet. Bouts of psychosis could often be mild enough that I managed them without hospitalization. Regardless, the end result was me occasionally stuck in a tormented mind, without professional assistance.

One such unnoticed episode had developed to a crescendo over a period of weeks and ended in a near tragedy. It started out with me hearing messages from the spirit world, though television and radio. It was as if the actors and radio announcers were speaking directly to me. At first this communication seemed pleasant as if they were commending me on my highly developed psychic abilities, then these seemingly spiritual messages turned to warnings of upcoming danger. These impending messages of doom terrorized me and for days on end I would wait in fear for the perceived future danger to come.

Convinced that eventually the forewarnings would happen, my body went through unbelievable stress. The kicker was these imagined spirit voices, from media sources, were also telling me I had to keep my knowledge of tragedy coming, a secret. If I warned people it was my belief that I would cause more harm to the world by tipping the balance in favour of evil forces. So I suffered in silence.

Soon this psychotic episode moved into visual hallucination where I thought I saw a man dressed as a cowboy standing in the middle of a road I was driving on. As my car moved closer to him I slowed down and could see he had raised his hand and folded his fingers to give the impression he was aiming a gun at me. I drove right past this sinister character and could feel his eyes boring into the side of my head.

To take a moment out and talk about hallucinations seems important at this point. Just so that the reader understands that some of what happened through my mind, conjuring false images, indeed was nothing more than hallucination brought on by chemical imbalance within my brain. Yet, I believe at times there perhaps could have been some truth to the things I was seeing. For example, the cowboy I talk about who I saw as pretending to point a 'finger' gun at me. Maybe there really was some freaky man dressed up being foolish in the middle of the road and my psychotic mind made it personal to me? I don't know to this day if he was a living person or if I was imagining him because no one was in the car with me to verify it? One thing for sure, the more outlandish hallucinations are easy to look back on and know for certain that they were induced by the mental illness. The other thing I'll say about hallucinations is that they were really just projections of what was going on in my mind. During this time in my life I carried many unresolved issues and fears; the psychosis reflected my own consciousness out into the physical world. Now back to the episode I was talking about!

Travelling down the same road, about fifteen minutes later, I drove by a paving construction crew. My window was down and I heard the flag girl call out, *"lock your doors Ann they're coming for you soon".* I couldn't believe she said this to me and how did she know my name, I'd never seen her before.

Where ever I went, for days on end, it seemed there was a conspiracy where strangers were warning me that someone was coming soon; to hurt me.

Within an episode I rarely spoke out loud, that meant if people were around me they would have no way to understand I wasn't thinking clearly. It was my certainty that if I spoke out loud the evil society hunting for me would be able to track me. All my bizarre notions were silently tucked away in my own mind. The rare times I reached out to people, while in my delusion, it was my belief that I could safely communicate with those people using telepathy. In my mind, when I called psychically for help, the person I reached out to became involved in my conspiracy and yet the person didn't have a clue they had become part of my loony-tune story line.

The climax to this ongoing psychosis happened when I was at home with Ron and one of our kids. Through a series of coincidences, such as hearing the sounds of people running outside our home and then hearing the plunking of our piano keys from the basement, when no one was there, convinced me intruders had broken into our home. Upon hearing the piano keys tinkling, the only possible scenario in my mind was that the intruders were trying to lure us down stairs to investigate the piano sounds and then kill us. *Little did I know it had been our cat falling off the bookshelf onto the piano keys!* I begged Ron not to go into our basement to investigate, but he did anyhow. While he was gone, I panicked and tried to get my teen to follow me to hide in the master bedroom. My kid would have nothing to do with my paranoia and chose to stay in the living room. As I entered the bedroom, looking for a safe place to hunker down, the chemical imbalance caused me to believe I could hear men walking towards my bedroom. Sudden terror ripped through me and my panic escalated to fight or flight. Thinking they were coming to murder me, I chose fight mode. I clamored to get the gun locker key and get to Ron's hunting rifles. Successful in grabbing a rifle, I was unable to find the bolt and ammunition as a result of Ron's diligent efforts in gun safety. Hearing the men's footsteps approaching and me with no way to protect myself I did the only thing I could think of. I crawled into the back of the bedroom closet holding the rifle aimed at the open doorway. My heart pounding, I could only hope the sight of the gun would be enough to scare the men away. It was within seconds of sitting in that closet that a man appeared through the doorway, had my gun been loaded I would have surely pulled the trigger out of sheer fright. I was not in my right mind. Thankfully I couldn't find the bullets because it would have been my own husband I would have shot. It was Ron that came through that doorway. There were no nasty, sinister killers in our home. The only thing that had happened was my crazy brain misfired and created a series of sights and sounds that did not actually exist, other than within my head.

As bizarre as this behavior sounds, I was not admitted to Hospital because I appeared settled down and genuinely stable right after. Ron had no idea I was prepared to fire that gun, he assumed I was just scared and using it as a prop to make myself feel safe. Therefore, Ron didn't know the depth of my psychosis and I was incapable of telling him.

To me, things felt normal and everyone around me just thought I was a bit quirky. No one considered I was in another episode of mental illness.

Not having yet thudded against rock bottom, there was still more challenges waiting for me. One such trial involved a self proclaimed spiritual counselor. He was a blessing in one sense and a rude awakening in another.

Before elaborating on the self affirmed spiritual counselor, let me give some previous history of my religious background. It definitely has some bearing on my ordeal.

For many years, I'd briefly visited a few different Church denominations. In some cases I did try to conform by attending bible studies. That only served to change my view of a loving God into the idea of a punishing God that I began to fear. So I stopped following along with groups that forced man made religious doctrine through threats of eternal damnation. Although I ended my affiliation with certain Church groups, I was able to continue respecting the individuals for their strength of faith and dedication to adhere to what they knew as God's will; but, they seemed to think I was less than them for not accepting their belief system. I was written off as a lost cause which led to some Christian friends ending our friendship. Where's the love, I wondered?

It eventually became the Spiritualist Church where I felt most comfortable. Their philosophy and image of God were similar to mine. Most people there were kind, compassionate and nonjudgmental. They practiced mediumship and hands on healing which were spiritual abilities I was comfortable with. One of my favorite things about the Spiritualist Church was the sincere respect they held for every other religion.

As much as I felt at home in this Church, I remained withdrawn and sat in the very back row so I could leave the service before the fellowship started.

My occasional psychotic fracture from reality, sometimes lasting weeks, caused me to stop attending this Church, periodically. But when I did attend the Spiritualist Church, I anxiously awaited the time in the service allotted for hands on healing. There were six stools and beside each stool was a person who would invite God's healing energy to flow through them and then place their hands, gently, on the Sitters shoulders. I sat for healing almost every time I attended Church. I felt in alignment with God when receiving healing and always felt better for having done so. Before long I was staying for fellowship. How enjoyable it was to feel so accepted, even though I was very quiet and awkward.

So now that I've provided some history of my spiritual beliefs, I'll go back and describe how I met a fellow who accredited himself as a spiritual teacher and counselor. It was at the end of a Church service where a man, I'll call Lester, approached me. He told me he sensed I was clairvoyant and invited me to attend his mediumship development circle. Thus began what I refer to as my time of spiritual boot camp and it was harsh.

Accepting Lester's invitation to psychic development proved to be interesting. I was one of five participants and once again, I was able to perceive accurate and provable spirit contact. It had been a long time since I'd allowed myself to consciously open to the spirit world in this way. Being on medication seemed to keep my chemical imbalance somewhat stable, so I trusted it was okay to delve into spirit communication once again. Little did I know my mind was still under the influence of; poor self esteem. The biggest difficulty was my very naïve nature and vulnerability to the opinions of others. Simple comments from group members began to upset me and soon enough I stopped feeling comfortable being there, so ended my participation.

Lester, who was leading this group, was sorry to see me go. He asked me to consider having sessions with him as my Spiritual Counselor. He portrayed himself as a counselor, energy healer, medium and philosopher. I'd never seen a *spiritual* counselor before and jumped at this new opportunity. Although I understood Lester was not a professionally trained, therapeutic counselor, I placed my confidence in him. He suggested we meet once a week and offered in lieu of cash I could do his paper work for him, this seemed like a generous deal to me.

In the beginning sessions were all about him getting to know my background, my fears and what my thoughts were around spirituality. Over a period of time I noticed he'd subtly correct me and drop in his beliefs about spiritual matters. By the time I had seen him, for almost a year, I felt dependent on him. Sadly I did not recognize his inexperience or my fragility, until the hurt was done.

Sometimes Lester made suggestions that were helpful to me and other times, his ideas stifled my creative desires. During one of our sessions, I enthusiastically told him I discovered the public library had spiritual cassettes by Wayne Dyer and other popular speakers. I was happy knowing I could borrow them. He became defensive with me and insisted that I borrow *HIS* tapes and he then showed me several drawers full of Spiritual information from his channeled messages. I didn't question why he did not approve of me going to the library and listening to the well known speakers. In my feeble minded state, I did as he wanted. Looking back now it's painfully obvious how intimidated I felt around Lester.

Another session, I expressed to him my intention to make my own set of spiritual wisdom cards. I told Lester my passion was ignited as a result of noticing the birds and small furry animals in the forest, while on my walks. I shared the details, excitedly, including how I'd been keeping a journal of the various animals I'd seen and how I'd written what each one represents to me. In my process, I was for the first time, tapping into my own positive creativity. This kind of thinking was most important as it kept my focus in a highly motivated, positive flow. Lester had his own agenda and immediately shut my creative juices down. He stated, why would I even do that, why change the wheel it's already been invented. When I asked what he meant, Lester told me there are too many positive affirmation cards out there already. I felt crushed and under his thumb. I never did follow through on my fun idea. Instead I felt the depression seeping back in.

Yet another session with him, this time I discussed wanting to learn a skill I could do from home. My thought was to look into massage therapy and perhaps see about taking some training. Lester told me I was not cut out for that, he said it required a lot of physical strength and I'd have to know all about the skeletal, muscle and nerve system of the body. He instructed me on all the effort and work it would take and years of training. When he was finished pointing out how hard it would be for me to develop massage therapy skills, I felt depleted and hopeless. He had succeeded in convincing me I wasn't capable.

If I had more self esteem, I would have told Lester to piss off and then gone on to try my hand at new ventures, but I wasn't quite there yet. It was much later in life that I figured out that it's okay to stand up for myself. It was also much later down the road before I learned that integral counselors are supportive, encouraging and never manipulate their client.

Many sessions went by, several months worth, in fact almost a year. Why did I stay, mostly because I saw myself as insignificant and him as the authority over my life.

While in sessions with Lester, eventually I became perpetually sad. Ron pointed out to me that he noticed my emotional state going downhill. I still wasn't capable of putting two and two together and recognizing this so called counselor was at the root of my discouragement. So what do I do, yikes, I go to my next session telling Lester that Ron has noticed my sadness increasing. Lester then managed to convince me that I was living with an angry man. Where was he getting this from, I wondered? He then pointed out all the things I had said during the course of our sessions and when he fed it all back to me, I had to agree, some of my complaints didn't hold Ron in a bright light. With Lester directing my focus onto everything I had previously said that I didn't like in Ron; soon the day came when I told this spiritual counselor I was going to leave my husband. That's about the time he told me I was wise to leave Ron and that he could help me work out a plan of action. He also clearly stated that he would not accept any responsibility for my decision. At least Lester was honest, but suddenly I felt duped by him, I was sure he had been coaching me toward leaving Ron.

Thankfully my incorrect perception of Ron cleared, before I made the biggest mistake of my life. My reasoning mind got through to me and I had a private chuckle recognizing it was actually Ron who was living with an angry woman, not the other way around.

Now that I was catching on to Lester's coaching style, I made a decision to finally end my sessions. We met at his place, as usual, and while he was making tea in his kitchen for us, I stood beside him and gently said, *"Lester, I appreciate all the help you've given me over the many sessions we've had, but I know it's time for me to end coming."* He acknowledged what I'd said and agreed maybe it is time to stop sessions. In his next breath, he suggested we begin healing sessions where he could do energy healing on me. Why I agreed to this I'll never know. Perhaps I still held onto the innocent notion that he could help me and I decided, against Ron's advice, to forgive and forget the blunders of past sessions.

The weekly sessions continued with Lester now in the role of healer and teacher. Long story shortened, after I listened to his negative view of psychiatric medication combined with hearing of his anger toward the medical profession doling out pills under the pretence of helping patients, I concurred he must be right. It was then I decided to stop taking my medication, after all, I also believed Lester's energy healing had completely cured me of all hereditary mental illness. When I told him of my choice to end medical treatment for bipolar disorder, he applauded me for my courage and at the same time made it clear that he would not accept any responsibility for influencing my decision to finish psychiatric medication. I agreed it was my own conclusion to do so.

It was my choice to end medication abruptly and my responsibility alone, that I agree with. Yet, my decision was made as a result of his coaching me. Not to lay blame anywhere; just saying when a person is weakened emotionally they become easily pliable to ideas discussed.

Had Lester encouraged me to consult with my Doctor or Ron before stopping medication, I surely would have done so. Figuring all the support I needed was in my coach, my tossing away medication remained quietly between the two of us. It was actually a case of the blind leading the blind I think? Me, still unbalanced in my life and he had zero understanding of the repercussions of what can happen when a mentally ill person drops off their medication.

Off medication just over a month and all still seemed well. As I sat across from Lester, he handed me a cup of black coffee, while he continued with his, lengthy, spiritual lecture. I'd only had a couple sips of my coffee before I started feeling light headed and then the room started to spin. I reached for another slurp of my coffee hoping it would clear my head, but to my surprise, as I tipped the cup to my lips, I saw there was a lump of dark green disgusting sludge, stuck on the inside of my cup. It was in process of dissolving into my coffee. I would never have seen it if I hadn't tipped the cup at a certain angle and happen to glance in. Upon showing Lester the deposit on the cup, he acknowledged seeing the green lump of mud, but didn't have a clue what it was. I noticed how rapidly he grabbed my cup out of my hands and rinsed everything down the sink. Before he could pour a fresh coffee in a clean cup, I went from light headed to seeing white and black speckles before my eyes. Considering the possibility that he might very well have poisoned me, I ran directly into his bathroom locking the door behind me. Now sitting on the bathroom floor, head between knees, trying my best to stay conscious; my breathing became constricted and a sense of suffocating enclosed me. Lying on the floor, I prayed for relief. Within seconds of lying flat out, my breathing became normal and the light headedness subsided. My fear took over and all common sense disappeared as I deemed he intentionally poisoned me.

During the time I spent in his bathroom, intermittently he would knock on the door asking if I was alright. I would scream at him to go away and leave me alone. When feeling strong enough, I carefully opened the door and peered out. He was standing by the door with a blanket. To me it meant he was going to wrap my body in it, to dispose of the evidence. I asked him to call an ambulance for me, which he discouraged. Feeling shell shocked and not certain what I should do, panic took over again. Pushing past him and running outside onto the rain soaked patio, seemed like a good idea. Sock feet with no coat, I got to the edge of the deck and was about to jump the two foot drop onto the grass and run toward what was, ironically, the mental health clinic. I heard Lester's voice behind me saying *"Ann stop, wait"*. It took every ounce of mental strength to stop and turn to face him. In that moment I changed my mind about running and instead chose to face my fear of him. Brushing past him, I walked back into Lester's home, put on my shoes, coat and grabbed my purse. Without a word, I calmly walked to my car and drove myself home.

At home I recounted this frightening experience to my husband. Ron reassured me that Lester would never poison me and gingerly broached the subject that perhaps I had been in a mild episode of delusion. He didn't know I was off my medication, but because I did know, I suspected it very well could have been a mental breakdown. Yes, truthfully, there had been a nasty sludge in my cup of coffee and it could have triggered an allergic reaction but I was now sure that Lester had not purposely exposed me to that. I agreed with Ron that it would be best to keep an eye on my behavior, more closely for a while. I still didn't divulge my secret of being off my pills.

A few days later, having gathered my composure, I respectfully ended my sessions with Lester; by phone. He simply said *"if that's what you want"*. Then he told me he had a psychic link with me and said he would know how I was doing anyhow. His attitude seemed unfriendly, stern and that frightened me. I did my best to put my thoughts on my home life but felt uneasy that he actually stated he could telepathically watch me. Who tells a person they will know how you're doing because they have a psychic link with you, that's just creepy!

My experience, with Lester, taught me to pay attention to the behavior of others and walk away quickly if I feel uncomfortable with them for any reason. Truly every decision I made was my own responsibility; yet my defenses were down due to the fact mental illness had diminished my ability to discern. I'm sure this spiritual coach I involved myself with believed he was the finest of them all; yet for me I prefer coaches to be more conventional in their approach. I know now there are specific characteristics I watch for when hiring a spiritual coach or professional therapist.

1. I always check the Counselors credentials. Just because they say they are trained does not mean they are skilled

at counseling. Not every person who hangs a 'counseling' shingle on their front door step is competent.

2. It's important for me to feel a rapport with the Coach. I need to feel comfortable, encouraged and supported by them.

3. I find it helpful for a Coach to ask open ended questions and listen to my answer without judgment. A skilled professional will help me surface my own answers. They will also encourage me to take easy steps towards the healthy changes I have decided on.

4. For me, a sure sign of a competent Coach is when they do not disclose their personal upsets towards any topics. In my opinion, a capable Coach will empathize without revealing their personal opinions.

5. My thought is that the Coach works for me and respect needs to go both ways; becoming a team seems to work best.

6. A skilled Coach will welcome hearing what my beliefs are so he/she can more fully understand where I'm coming from. A Coach doesn't try to convince me that my beliefs are wrong and theirs are correct.

7. I consider proficient Coaches as ones that insist you see them from one session all the way up to possibly eight or ten sessions at most. The reason for this is to protect the client from becoming dependent upon the Coach. My experience has been that Coaches will often require ending for at least two months before coming back for more sessions. This encourages the client to put into action what was discussed in previous sessions.

Psychiatric care is different and often requires longer treatment.

Within a few days of putting a stop to all contact with Lester, I learned the hard way that ending psychiatric medication, abruptly, was a very bad idea. I was slammed into yet another distressing brush with paranoia.

Hitting the bottom and bouncing off the rocks was no fun and harder yet, this time, I had no medication in my system to help me regain foot hold.

Through delusional psychosis, several bizarre visions haunted me including the image of Lester floating around my ceiling, spying on me. My hallucinations didn't just stay focused on him though. This psychotic break took me into the bowels of hell with sights of extremely horrific images. Seeing grotesque, depraved creatures was alarming. It completed freaked me out seeing these beasts because they appeared real. Of course my body reacted to what my mind believed and so it responded to my thinking by shutting down my natural bodily functions; one of which was menstruation, it stopped for months and various parts of my body held painful tension.

It was through Ron's good judgment that I ended up in Hospital a third time. He had no way to fully comprehend the extent of my psychosis, yet his keen senses alerted him something was wrong; my actions were not congruent with my words. Mostly, I appeared to be functioning in my usual habit yet at times he saw expressions cross my face that were disconcerting to him.

The ramifications of hastily ending my medications, proved to be the most grueling mental battle I ever faced.

Back on the psychiatric ward of the Hospital I began more counseling sessions, this time I went back to a highly skilled, professional counselor who was a good fit for me. What made her a good fit was that she actively listened without interjecting her beliefs onto me. As she would brain storm with me, helping me come up with my own ideas to improve my life, she never suggested I follow her advice. She conscientiously would ask me which of our collaborative ideas did I like the best, if any.

With proper levels of medication back in my system, group therapy and a supportive husband, I was soon out of psychosis. Carefully finding my way back to being a wife, mother and individual was daunting because I felt my spirit was broken after this most recent battle with mental illness. Pretty much, I had given up any hope that I'd ever have freedom from psychotic episodes. Take my medication and deal with it, was my thought. I vowed to never again attempt getting off psychiatric medication.

Despite my bleak outlook, something significant was about to happen that forever changed my life, for the better.

Chapter #12

GOD, PLEASE HELP ME?

Fine, a life of antipsychotic medication didn't seem so bad when I considered the alternative; grotesque hallucinations. Perhaps I'd be able to keep my head above water and at least survive.

There was a woman I met, along my recovery road, who knew very little about mental illness. One day she invited me to tell her more about how I cope with bipolar disorder. Upon sharing some of the ways I manage, in her blunt manner she said, *"Oh you're lucky, you have family to take care of you. All's you have to do is take your medication. It's much harder for me, although I don't suffer from mental illness I'm a single Mom and have to do everything on my own. I don't have a husband to take care of me the way you do."* I've always taken into account that every person has their individual challenges they face in life. Not one being harder than the other, just all having their own unique hardship. I can't imagine being a single mother facing the difficulty of financially supporting a family, alone. It must take a special kind of courage and determination not to mention stamina. My hat goes off to her for being able to successfully raise her children and maintain the financial burden alone. Yet, her comment saddened me that she wasn't able to comprehend my ability in having taken responsibility for my life.

This wonderful woman, whom I admired, actually thought I was lazing about taking medicine while leaning on my husband to take care of me. What she had no concept of was that no other person can walk through the mental darkness to find the light for you. Yes, people can hold your hand to support you through psychosis and professionals can help with certain prescriptions, but the individual suffering mental breakdown ultimately has to master their own mind. The patient has to apply effort, to become well. Friends or family can only support the process from a distance.

My gratitude is a constant towards the many family members, friends and professionals who did everything possible to keep me safe from harm and encouraged me while I was ill. In the same frame of gratitude, I hold myself, knowing I was willing to face my demons and lay them to rest. Any person that is involved with a form of mental illness, whether they be the one afflicted or the one observing the mental decline of a loved one; both are equally affected by the challenges that ensue.

Depends really, doesn't it, on which side of the street your standing. No matter the position, the grass is never greener on one side more so than the other. I've had the experience of being on both sides of the street; as an observer watching my Mom suffer bipolar disorder and then as a bipolar patient myself. I can honestly say, both positions have their challenges, one place is not easier than the other, just different.

Over past years I'd put much effort into becoming mentally well, such as; surrounding myself with inspirational material, skillfully replacing negative thoughts with positive ones, nutrition and exercise. Then there were the many classes I attended; anger management, self esteem, communication and of course the many hours of counseling sessions. Even so, it seemed parts of my memory were blocked at times. Strangely I could easily recall some of the menacing episodes I'd suffered; but, coping skills I'd learned along the way were often oblivious to me. The closest way to describe this by-product of the illness would be what I imagine amnesia might be like. At times I had the impression of being in a black hole of nothingness. After talking to my Doctor about this I learned stress, chemical imbalance, medications and depression can cause memory lapses and feelings of being dim-witted. This felt good hearing the reasons why, but didn't stop me from still going through the muck of it all.

Having spent much time in past counseling sessions, groups and classes; this time I wanted to simply do what I could on my own.

My next strategy was to write the various coping skills onto recipe cards and carry them in my pocket or purse. This way, I could always access those tools learned, regardless of the lack of my memory recall.

One of my favourite tools was the recipe card I carried around, with the affirmative reminders such as;

» *This too shall pass and things will feel better soon.*

» *God hasn't gone anywhere so be patient and trust.*

» *I am safe because God has my back.*

» *Vulnerability is not weakness as it takes courage to expose your Self.*

» *Love is all that is real anything less will soon fade away.*

» *I am filled with Gods essence just like everyone else.*

» *We are all equal and all worthy.*

On another recipe card I'd written the Lord's Prayer;

Our Father which art in Heaven, Hallowed be thy Name.
Thy Kingdom come, Thy will be done on Earth as it is in Heaven.
Give us this day our daily bread and forgive us our trespasses,
as we forgive them that trespass against us.
Lead us not into temptation, but deliver us from evil.
For Thine is the Kingdom, the power and the glory,
forever and ever. Amen.

This Prayer always comforts me.

Yet another recipe card carried reminders of what I wanted to be devoted to. I got this idea from Iyanla Vanzant's book titled *Until Today.*

» *Today I am devoted to acknowledging the good things that I am.*

» *Today I am devoted to living a guilt free life.*

» *Today I am devoted to shining my light without complaining about the darkness.*

» *Today I am devoted to telling the truth about the realities in my life.*

» *Today I am devoted to becoming aware that I am okay as I am.*

I would choose just one, devotion, then throughout the day would re-read that devotion and allow it to settle over me.

There was another card that helped me tremendously and it wasn't a recipe card. I came to have this *'other'* type of card through a stranger who knocked on my door and I found the courage to answer. Oh yes, I knew he was a Jehovah Witness come to convince me to accept his religious beliefs. As I peeked between the mini blinds of my bedroom, I could see his shinny black dress shoes, leisure suite and the brief case he carried. This particular day I didn't care if he was going to pressure me about religion or not, I was so absolutely distraught with loneliness I only wanted some human contact. Opening the door as he knocked and inviting him in, I remember thinking it strange that this man did not have a partner with him. Right away he handed me a pamphlet and began his introduction. He could hardly get a word in edgewise as I sobbed and dripped tears all over his pamphlet. In his wisdom he pulled out his Bible, opened it and pulled out a post card. Upon handing it to me he explained that the post card had been his grandfathers and he confided to me that the picture on this card had always given him hope. He then asked me to look at the picture on the card and tell him what I thought of it. I stopped crying as I scanned the drawings of various animals; bunnies, tigers, elephants, mice, lamb, lion, humans and many more species. I told him I felt peaceful and comforted looking at these images. With that, he asked me if I'd like to hang onto it for a while, maybe it will help me remember there is hope for us all, he said. This stranger at my door genuinely cared about my emotional pain and he proved that through giving me his treasured post card that had been his Grandfathers. Many years later I was able to properly thank this kind hearted soul and give back his Grandfathers post card.

Cards helped me remember, when my mind faltered. I further helped myself remember by cutting brightly coloured strips of paper and writing positive affirmations on them. Then placing several of these strips of paper on mirrors, walls and my bedside table; displayed for me to view every day.

Another way to help myself was by tape recording my own voice repeating affirmations, later at night I often drifted off to sleep listening to some lovely declarations to the sound of my own voice. Thankfully I owned headphones, so not to disturb Ron's sleep.

Once, a close friend who was suffering from depression, confessed to me that her use of positive affirmations were nothing but a useless waste of time. She exclaimed angrily, they don't work! I encouraged her to write affirmations that she believed in. If you write or tape record positive statements that you simply do not consider at all truthful, your mind will reject them. Some suggestions I offered, that aided me, were to use wording such as;

» *I am in process of...*

» *This or something better...*

» *I am willing to accept the possibility that...*

The language you use is most important. I lost contact with my old friend yet I trust that she found her happier mindset and has now created greater joy in her life.

As Peter A. Cohen said, *"There is no one giant step that does it; it's a lot of little steps"*

Over the passage of time though, it seemed I had gone backwards in my emotional and mental health. Another mind phart and more depression slipped in.

I began wondering if my old friend had been right all along; perhaps positive affirmations don't work? What was going on in me that I felt so awful, again! Even my pocket cards weren't helping much these days so I got rid of them. Bad move. Here I had come to a misery hurdle and didn't realize that following my coping skills were more important now than ever.

Okay so I kind of learned the hard way, in addition to taking lots of little steps towards mental health, I also needed to be diligent and consistent. I gave up too quickly.

What I hadn't figured out at this point in my life is that I'd been trying too hard on my own and not allowing myself to rest easy in God. Geez, I didn't really even know what *rest easy in God meant* during this stumbling block. I'd soon experience it though and that's the best teacher of all; experience.

This mental obstacle that impeded my happiness was not letting up! Now that I was back on proper levels of medication, vowing to never again go off my meds, I endured life. By this time, I often queried Gods existence as I called to mind the many times I'd been tossed around the mental roller coaster. At times I felt, if there was a Divine Intelligence, I must have been deceived by it or ignored. After all, I had believed God was healing me, only to discover I remained ill. What's up with that, I snarled to myself.

Nevertheless, as they say, all things happen in God's gracious timing. My turn about, freeing me from mental illness, came in an unimaginable way. It started out as an unrelenting, feeling of dread that wouldn't release me and I could see no reason to continue this horrid existence. My body felt like an aged arthritic woman, with a damaged spirit. Talk about falling off the wagon, all those fabulous tools to maintain a positive mind, gone-d-gone! I had lost my way. I thought, a life time of psychosis, depression and now physical pain was the only thing in the cards for me. I tried and I failed. No amount of classes, groups, therapy or Spiritual healing was getting me out of this unhappy existence. So with that dreadful thought, I walked down our basement stairs and opened the tiny closet door. This closet was a small storage spot under the stairs. I climbed in, laid down on the cold, cement floor and I pulled the door shut. There was only me, alone in darkness, praying for death. I just wanted some relief from my tormented mind and aching body.

Within minutes, a delicate feeling of someone lovingly hugging me, gave me a slight moment of reprieve from my anguish. My awareness of this spiritual presence; gently moved me towards renewed hope. Then words formed in my mind and I spoke them out loud, *"**God, Please Help Me**"*.

These four words, said sincerely, changed my life quickly and permanently. It wasn't so much the words, it was my surrender to hand over my entire life to a Divine Intelligence separate from my own consciousness; a higher power. Hope and faith returned to me and I considered it was as a result of honestly hitting what is often called, rock bottom. That is the only place where sincere, humble trust in God could have been found, for me anyhow.

The experience of *resting easy in God* was now felt, and I was never to forget it. This place of surrender was different from any other prayerful state I had ever known. When you land on rock bottom, there is nowhere else to go, except to curl up into God's Graces.

I quietly sang a hymn that popped to my mind, *"I'm pressing on the upward way, new heights I'm gaining every day, still praying as I'm onward bound: Lord Plant My Feet On Higher Ground"* .

With enthusiasm, I pushed open that closet door, pulled myself up from the cement floor and walked up the stairs toward my computer. As I sat in the chair and opened my email, I saw there was a random inspirational note from a website I had subscribed to. It was an uplifting blurb referring to a 380 degree turn around bringing peace to a world issue. A few days later I walked into Church and as I walked by a couple of women chatting together, I overheard one say to the other *"never fear because a 380 degree turn around is coming"*. Unquestionably I knew these 380 degree references had nothing to do with me, yet I decided to spark my hope and amplified it by telling myself I can turn my life around 380 degrees with God's help. The 380 degree term became a mantra to me for a while and that positive mind set helped me to overcome my inherited illness.

"God Please Help Me", remained my simplistic prayer for a long time. This prayer was not asking God to change my circumstances or give me material things to make me feel happier; it was a prayer asking God to **CHANGE ME** so that I could love myself, be free from fear and be at peace. Whenever I thought of those four words, I felt as if a huge Universal **YES** was being said right back to me.

Finally that day had come, where I rested easy in knowing God's love. I surrendered. Now, until you've hit that tough place of inner pain, you might not be able to understand what I mean by I surrendered. It means I directly admitted I could not do life on my own, but that I could trust a higher power to be in charge over me. Giving up my will to rest easy in God's, enabled me to stop fussing and simply BE. Admitting defeat is a place of absolute willingness to believe there is a power, a creator that has all intelligent knowing of what's best for you. More importantly it is a location, within your core, that wants to make the best possible choices for your own well being. You have to yearn for that care so much that it causes urgency or a feeling of passion that fuels you into action; mentally, emotionally, physically and spiritually. By the way, when I say *you have to yearn for that care or feel a passion that fuels you*, even crying from the pit of your soul while reaching for the Divine Holy will get you the help you crave.

The wiser part of me, which I understand as my stilled, inner voice, held me securely so I could take action on two easy things. One, keep taking my medication, two, keep praying. I almost forgot;

there was a third thing, make up more pocket-cards and use them consistently. Keeping my mind focused on positive things helped me stay in touch with the essence of God within my Being. From that place I experienced life as a sense of adventure because I knew God was in charge; not me.

For sure, if you want God's help you have to meet half way. My part was to put in the effort to keep my thoughts focused on the positive. So, I fearlessly tossed aside all doubt, created some new affirmations on recipe cards and they worked excellent for me:

» *Taking medication does not mean I am ill, it means I am in process of realizing perfect mental health.*

» *I am in alignment with God's will and I easily know what my best choice is in any situation.*

» *All circumstances are coming together to support my health and well being.*

» *The intelligent, loving consciousness of my higher power is in charge, not me.*

» *This challenge is helping me develop wisdom and insight.*

» *The creator knows my heart and the heart of all others, therefore is helping us all to find a peaceful solution.*

» *Everything in my life has and always will be for my benefit, there are no mistakes only wisdom gained.*

» *There is no hurry; all things come in God's time not mine.*

» *There is no shame in anything I've ever said or done, I did my best in that moment.*

» *I take responsibility for all my actions that may have harmed others and know love, will gently guide me, to make amends.*

» *I thrive and enjoy all aspects of my life knowing God is really in charge of this universe.*

» *Even though this feels scary, Love will give me the strength and courage I need to press on.*

» *Even though I slip up now and then, I forgive myself because at the core I am a good person.*

I had to make right choices to be able to follow God's will for my well being. It wasn't always easy to follow what that wise inner voice nudged me to do. Geez, the first thing on the agenda was to stop eating sugary and processed foods. Now I was feeling an urge to eat meats, veggies, fruits and grains; the old food groups had been candy, breads, fried food and Chinese food.

This is not to say, that after I established good eating habits, I didn't indulge on occasion. Even to this day I believe chocolate is a food group all its' own.

After a while another nudge came and I stopped watching dramatic or violent programs. It was a choice that was easy to make because I truly wanted freedom from mental disruption. I stopped watching soap operas, no more TV court cases, even talk shows were off my list of viewing due to the drama. I stopped watching the news too. What came into my viewing pleasure were inspirational movies, motivational speakers and nature shows. I found terrific TV shows that taught cooking, art, pet care, gardening and decorating. I figured I'd hit the gold mine of great entertainment. Even my music choices evolved. Although I still listened to old time rock and roll, blues and jazz; I began including sounds of nature set to soft instrumentals and gospel. When I did my housework I cranked the Gospel and to soak in a tub or head off to sleep, I loved nature sounds. My reading material changed from Ann Rice's Vampire Diaries to Illyana Vanzant's One Day My Soul Opened. I went back to books by Wayne Dyer, Doreen Virtue, Deepak Chopra, Louise Hay and so many more! Every night I listened to motivational cassette tapes with headphones strapped to my ears. Eventually cassettes became obsolete and I progressed to CD's. I found if I wasn't mindful of my choices it was rather easy to slip into bad habit. Again consistency, effort and diligence paid off.

It wasn't long before I figured out why, in the past, I had been drawn to watch violent, dramatic shows and read brutal stories in books. It was due to my chaotic, fearful mind acting as a mirror for that drama and aggression I was compelled to watch. As I changed my mind to view life as safe and peaceful, my movie and book choices reflected that same theme.

The more I learned about myself the sooner yet another nudge in the right direction would come. This time the wise guidance urged me to stop journaling my complaints and upsets and start writing in my journal what was going well. My writing took on a whole new level of positivity. Even when I did have a challenging upset going on, I would journal the problem and then keep on writing until the solution emerged. My initial upset might be written as a rant to begin with, but soon thereafter, I'd get to the perceived peaceful solution. If I couldn't find a solution I would pray *'Please heal that part of myself that feels angry towards this person and help me to forgive'.*

The inner prodding, the nudges, always showed up one at a time, so not to overwhelm me. Mentally, I filled my mind with uplifting affirmative thoughts. Oh yes, positive affirmations do work when you combine them with prayer and stay consistent.

Physically I took action by eating nutritiously, walking, adding colour to my clothing choices and slept at least seven hours a night if not eight.

Emotionally I kept a journal to acknowledge my feelings and I reflected on my writing for the purpose of seeking insights and solutions. I talked openly with Ron about what was going on within me.

Spiritually I maintained a prayerful mindset that kept my awareness on the loving universal consciousness that was separate from my own yet also a part of me. Love, is what I focused on. My world changed rapidly as I paid attention to my thoughts. Along the way I began hanging out with spiritual-minded people; positive, integral, responsible and compassionate.

If you're not sure whether the thoughts you mostly think are positive or negative, have a look around and notice who you are spending time with? If your *thinking is stinking* you'll be in the presence of like minded people. The *light and lovely* thoughts you hold will create just that in your life; more light hearted moments and lovely people to share them with.

Chapter #13

BRUSHES WITH THE DIVINE

THE ONLY REASON I COULD now trust my own mind and act on my inner nudges was as a result of daily, sincere prayer. A short prayer in the morning allowed me to be reminded and feel into the presence of Love. When going to bed, another short prayer to forgive myself or others for any perceived mistakes and most importantly my prayers were filled with everything I held gratitude towards. The beauty is, most every night I'd fall asleep while contemplating what I was grateful for. In keeping with honesty, some nights it was not easy to think of one thing I felt grateful for. You know, those days when everything seems to go inexplicably wrong. On those nights I'd thank God that I am alive and able to breathe the air. Thanking God also that I live in part of the world where I have enough food, shelter and clean water. Thanking all the people in my life that have shown love

to me in one form or another. I found there was always SOMETHING
I could feel appreciation for, even when I was feeling discontentment
with problems that seemed to crop up now and then. This prayerful
mindset, in the morning upon waking and at night before sleep, was
an absolute daily routine. For me it had to be in order to stay within
balanced, correct thinking.

After a brief morning prayer, then I went about my day focused
on what I was doing throughout my day. This was a discipline, in the
beginning, that required my constant attention. My previous habit
was to allow my mind to wander onto worries, concerns and upsets.
Half the time my mind was elsewhere, caught up in past dramas and I
missed out on the current moment. Too many times I'd caught myself
walking through a lush, green, beautiful forest path and realized my
mind was so immersed in past things that I had missed seeing the
plants, squirrels and birds along the route. Reminding myself that
even something that happened thirty minutes ago is in the past, my
time is *NOW* and *RIGHT NOW* I am enjoying this gorgeous walk. If
I was with my kids, I kept my mind on current activities with them
in the same manner; with the thought *right now* I am with my kids.
If I was doing dishes, my moment was all about what's going on in
the kitchen. That was my time to think about grocery list or plan the
next meal. *Right Now* I am in my kitchen for the purpose of nurturing
myself and family through cleaning, cooking or planning meals.
While driving the car my full attention was on the road, scenery and
thinking about where I was going and why. Living in the place of
RIGHT NOW makes it easy to listen to my *inner gut knowing* and
follow positive nudges; I was living with both feet firmly planted on
mother earth.

Paying attention to wise guidance that sprouted from within me,
became my new normal. After you discipline yourself by following
an easy and enjoyable routine, very quickly there is no further need
for the habitual exercise. Commonly it's known that after thirty days

of committing yourself to a new habit, it becomes a natural part of you that no longer requires work to maintain. Imagine this; when you practice a discipline and if you keep it up for thirty consecutive days, you've now created a new *groove* in your mind. Your thoughts will automatically go to that *new groove* because it's the easiest path to follow.

Maintaining attention on my present moment was a huge part of my road to wellness. Forging new grooves on the pathways of my mind was another tremendously helpful way to create more joy within me.

Feeling a greater sense of joy, as a result of my new outlook on life, something quite remarkable began happening. I noticed many synchronistic moments where positive outcomes for my Self and others were happening. One such happenstance took place during a time both Ron and I were concerned about finances. We didn't know when the next job would come through and our conversations had taken on a flavour of bitter mustard greens. As we walked down the hallway of our home together, complaining of the lack of money, we both saw something fall from our ceiling and land directly in front of our feet. It was a coin, a dollar coin to be precise. Astonished that this could happen, I picked up the coin and stated it must be a reminder to acknowledge what we do have and quit talking about lack. Feeling amazed, grateful and inspired; Ron and I both remained confident that all our true needs would be met. Sure enough everything fell into place. There really had been nothing to worry about, jobs came, bills got paid on time and we were provided not only enough work but also more than enough abundance in all areas of our lives to enable us to flourish. There was even enough to share with others!

Here is another astounding experience where a five cent coin helped a friend and I put financial troubles into perspective. While sitting in a local coffee shop, sipping our tea, my friend shared with me his desperate financial situation. Not knowing if his rent could be paid for the following month was causing him much stress. As a means to encourage him I told him what happened to me a few years before hand. It was during my own financial depletion where I'd pulled a five cent coin out of my pocket and stated to the Universe *"I am financially secure because I have money in my pocket"*. Soon thereafter my husband and I got work and our financial burden ended. My point was to remind him that by making a strong positive statement like this, it can help ease the anxiety while you get back on your feet. My friend seemed unimpressed by the story as he got up to get a refill and I followed to get another pour into my cup as well. Okay, here's the thing, upon walking back to our table we saw there was a shinny nickel sitting on his chair. I didn't put it there, he didn't have a nickel to put there and no other customer was anywhere near our table. The outcome, he tucked that shiny five cent coin into his pocket with a huge smile on his face and then exclaimed, *"I am financially secure because I have money in my pocket!"* My friend ended up having enough money to pay rent, have food and right around the corner he was again thriving doing the type of work he loved. Cool, fascinating how these things can happen.

These brushes with the Divine helped me end any deep seeded doubts and surely know there is a Universal, life force of intelligence, that is evolving each one of us. The beauty is, this consciousness I call God, is helping us evolve whether we care to recognize it or not. To me it's like this; God sees you even though you might not see the Universal Spirit.

One such perfectly timed miracle was when a new book found its way into my hands, *The Four Agreements* written by Miguel Ruiz. Agreement number one, take nothing personally. Two, assume nothing. Three, always do my best and four, be impeccable with my words. Another new level of joyful peace came into my life.

Someone 'upstairs' knew I needed simplicity to concentrate on. Sometimes miracles show up in common ways, yet profoundly in Divine Timing.

Another God send was when a person I barely knew gave me two free tickets to go see a motivational speaker. He was virtually an unknown and I would never by choice have paid for tickets to go. To my surprise it was through this man's inspirational lecture, I was given another helpful tool to influence further success in my wellness. He encouraged the audience to let go of judgment, stop manipulating and stop blaming others. He claimed if you did this, miracles will follow. He was right, I purposely applied the three suggestions and miraculously all difficult people vacated my life. The difficult people didn't physically walk away they departed as a result of me no longer seeing them as difficult people. Get rid of judgment and you'll feel acceptance and tolerance towards others. End manipulation and you'll see that there is no one being resistant in your life anymore. Stop blaming others and you free people while empowering yourself.

Think about it for a moment. Our only enemy is what we ourselves perceive to be the enemy. What I've come to accept as truth is that I have the power to eliminate all perceived enemies simply by changing my own thinking around the person or situation. Anyone behaving contrary to love is merely screaming out for love. Understanding this frees me to feel compassion towards even those that act out with cruel or aggressive intentions. They no longer are viewed as my enemies. Having stated this; if people in my life continue behaving in ways that make me uncomfortable, I leave! I leave the room or I might leave the job and most certainly I leave the relationship if there is continued abusiveness. People do not become my enemy if I choose to walk away; I love them from a distance so that I can maintain a healthy mind, body and soul.

In the past, my habit was to manage the mental file cabinet I kept in my head. When I woke up each morning, in order to maintain that imaginary file cabinet, I'd have to remember the people and every wrong I thought they did me. Keeping these thoughts, held in mind, was similar to having a littered mess of several stacks of paperwork as high as the ceiling scattered around my room; talk about mind clutter. There is nothing more disabling than keeping track of who has done you wrong, it's downright exhausting. Forgive so that you can let go and open up more room in your brain to hold onto the happy events of your life.

Someone said to me years ago, when something nice happens to you 'red flag' that memory and go back and revisit it often so you'll never forget it. As we age, we'll only have those memories we hold fast to that will keep us company!

Many occurrences of synchronicity proved God was conspiring to help me. Such was the case when I was driving along a deserted road on my way home and discovered a very old, mangy, mud caked, midsize dog wandering lost. Try as I might to find his owner it was soon discovered that he had been abandoned to die alone. We decided to invite this old doggie to be part of our family. After a visit to the vet, some antibiotics and a bath, turned out this fella was a pure bred duck tolling retriever, very rare breed.

Within days we noticed our other two dogs were taking a dislike to our new family member, which caused much stress all the way around. We felt our best choice would be to find a good family to foster him till his end days. Ron and I decided we would offer to pay on-going vet bills if it encouraged a good home for this elderly dog. Well, not only did we find a perfect family to adopt this sweet natured Duck Toller, but they happened to live on a farm and had veterinarian knowledge and access to medications. These wonderful people not only gave this dog proper medical aid but also tender affection to ease his golden years. The miraculous continued; those people hired Ron to do some building for them and the woman was a local artist who taught me much about nature and new ways to perceive it through art. Yet another level of happiness entered my life.

God in action or you might say Love in action; to me they are one in the same.

Now, this doesn't mean God wipes out our challenges, illness's or tragedies. What it does mean is that Divine Intelligence allows us our own choices to behave any way we want. The Divine Holy knows we will eventually learn what works well and what doesn't in our lives. Some call it cause and effect, others say Karma and I've even heard it referred to as good luck or bad luck. No matter what term you put to it, ultimately, we and we alone are responsible for what we create in our lives. If we ever feel our choices just aren't working out for our best, then we can invite Love to step in and help us *come on up out of the muck*. What that does is give us a hand up, when we sincerely want that help. I exercised my *free will* by asking God to please help me. Then I took action on the opportunities provided me.

ACTION; staying in our sadness or giving up will not make our life better, we must put one foot in front of the other and move towards what we want. Leaving Crazy-Town required; letting go of my garbage, packing my bag with clean clothes, holding God's love and walking towards joy through making better choices in my life.

In describing my life journey that brought about mental wellness, I mention God throughout. I do my best to convey not a religious tone, but a Spiritual or Natural quality. Sometimes I've seen how even just the word *God* brings harsh memories for some individuals and shuts them down. If this be the case for you, maybe substituting the word Love for God will help. That's really what I'm saying, God equals Love.

There are many ways to understand God; equally a number of ways to call that Holy essence by. Words do not always do justice to what we are trying to say, tolerance is important, especially if you are leading a group. Here's an example of how my words spoken in a simple prayer, triggered the group facilitator. This particular group was focused on noticing Divine synchronicities and Gods healing. The facilitator asked me to say the closing prayer one night and when I said;

Dear God, please will you correct our thoughts so that we are truly in alignment with your Divine Consciousness. We pray that we go out into the world, knowing our minds are inspired by your Loving guidance. Amen."

Upon hearing my prayer, the facilitator jumped into the center of the group as she exclaimed, "WE DO NOT NEED OUR MINDS CORRECTED!" Being reprimanded this way initially felt disrespectful and it embarrassed me. Within moments though, I comprehended that her resistance to my prayer did not mean I had been bad or wrong; it simply meant she had a different view of prayer. Knowing this, I excused myself from attending the group and found one that was more similar to my own expression of spirituality. Brushed once again by the Divine, this situation perhaps was necessary to show me how far I'd come in raising my Self Esteem; there was a time I would have beat myself up if I met with someone's disapproval.

It was Lao Tzu, the father of Taoism; that said *"If you correct your mind, the rest of your life will fall into place"*.

A dear friend who's known me a very long time told me that he envied me because of my strong foundation in faith. He further explained that I am never alone because I have the awareness of this loving presence in all things. I couldn't help wondering if my friend stopped believing in Love, whole heartedly, because of all the devastating hurt that had happened in his life? Possibly some part of my friend believed that God didn't hear his prayers because his troubles persisted. My heart ached for him. Sadly, like me, perhaps he had to hit rock bottom before the surrender. One thing for sure, I was certain, the Divine was brushing all over him except he couldn't see or feel it due his mindset.

Through earnest prayer, paying attention and purposely looking for opportunities to better my life, I found them. Some of these prospects were quite obviously of my own doing, yet, some things were straight-up God in action. To me, those miraculous, unexplainable events proved to me that a more advanced consciousness was at work in my life.

Seeing something phenomenal often enables us to fully believe; except if you've been in a psychotic episode laced with hallucinations. The flow of life occasionally accommodated me by having other people see the same amazing things. Such was a time when Ron and I were walking our dog along the regular exercise route. Most cars were considerate as they drove past us, slowing and providing a wide birth. About four feet in front of me I noticed a bright, florescent pink paper lying on the side of the road. A car, coming too close to us, breezed past and took my attention away from the neon paper, so I walked right beyond it. Interestingly, heading home an hour later, that same bright paper was catching my attention again. This time we stopped, I picked it up and discovered there was writing on it. In large, bolded letters it read:

One Free Danish – One Free Coffee – One Free Loaf Bread.

Also, it had the name and location of the Bakery offering this gift. The bakery was located in a different town from where I lived, only a thirty minute drive. Here's the miraculous part; the prior week I had taken a friend to a bakery in that same town and purchased her a gift of, Danish, a coffee and one loaf of bread. Holy-Guacamole, not only did I go and enjoy those free items; but because my friend lived in that town, I also had another great visit with her. Now that's a tangible or should I say tasty experience of being brushed by Divine.

Chapter #14

HAPPENSTANCE

T HROUGH THE SEVERITY OF THE bipolar illness that had previously tormented me, I had learned a lot about the workings of my own mind. Who knows, perhaps my life purpose has been about mastering my own mind all along? No more did I view the severity of bipolar disorder as a curse or punishment, now that I had befriended myself with warts and all, I graciously appreciated the blessing psychosis had been as a teacher for me. I was a more compassionate and wiser person for having experienced mental discord.

My only regret was of missing so much of my children's lives. If I could have done things differently, I certainly would have cried out to God sooner and thereby become well that much quicker. Then again, I console myself knowing I did the best I could at the time. There was no road map for me to follow back then.

With stability of mind and mental health now my new normal, amazingly I discovered at times I could still see spiritual guidance from things outside myself. Snippets of conversation, television or radio comments, words from books; all these sources were providing accurate, helpful, spiritual guidance. The big difference, from the time these sources used to cause paranoia, is that now-a-days all the messages were proving to be true and uplifting. These messages were springing up periodically and helping me make better choices to create a healthy balanced lifestyle. The one thing I had done differently, since bouts of psychosis, is that now I was steadfast with my intentions always on the light of Love. So naturally my thoughts projected outward were simply mirroring back to me the positive way I now saw the world around me.

To explain further, what I mean by outside sources giving me spiritual messages, I'll describe a scenario that took place between Ron and I. We were having a heated discussion, actually it was a full blown argument, when I unexpectedly heard an Actor on television say his line, *"know your priorities and choose your battles wisely"* at that very moment our two dogs went into a teeth gnashing war over a toy. As I continued bickering with Ron, I couldn't help noticing I was standing directly in front of a wooden carving of the Indian god named Ganesha. This particular god represents family values and is often prayed to for removing relationship obstacles. Instantly, my thoughts pulled together a helpful message from the combined; TV actors scripted comment, my dogs fighting over a toy and family values statue. What occurred to me is that this battle, with Ron, was similar to the dogs squabbling over something small. Immediately I gave silent thanks to myself and the Universe for alerting my senses to pay attention to deeper wisdom. The outcome to our squabble was both Ron and I apologizing to each other and warm hugs shared.

I understand why I was able to perceive a wise message from that particular series of happenstance. The combination of an actors' line, dogs fighting and statue of Ganesha were all just going to happen anyhow, but, because I had been in the daily practice of seeking wisdom through prayer; I had trained my subconscious to be on the alert for peace and solutions. Therefore, my keen senses grabbed onto what was going on around me that would help me focus on resolution; rather than have the arguing escalate.

Aha, so, there is the answer to some past paranoia! When my own mind had been centered on fear based thinking; I was attuned to 'hearing' 'seeing' and 'sensing' things that were equally fearful. It seems obvious to me that our own mind can either be a weapon against ourselves or a powerful tool to create wellness within ourselves. Our own thoughts determine whether we use our minds for our own benefit or not. Oh yes, the choice *IS* ours.

Creating a new positive groove for my mind to tread on, it had become natural for me to pick up nuances around me that supported encouraging messages. It's because of my mind set; my habit of looking for goodness is well established.

This did not happen by wishful thinking, my skill came about as a result of my effort applied. I intentionally changed my negative views to affirmative thinking. Let me tell you, I was prepared. My pocket cards were filled with heartwarming lines and I was on the ready to replace gloomy thoughts with happy thoughts.

I know I've said it before, but feel it can't be said enough, my desire and dedication for my wellness was only possible through God. I could not have done it alone. God did not miraculously, spontaneously heal me; more so, it was by calling upon God I was supplied with the courage and inner strength to choose love. The Universal flow of love provided many opportunities for me that was truly miraculous and at times spontaneous, yet I still had to *choose* and take *action*.

God helps those who help themselves; I consider this a very true statement. You cannot remain idle and expect your life to change for the better. Choose and take action.

Thing is, due to my experience with mental illness and having recognized spiritual messages both in and out of insanity, I've come to also accept this; *nothing has any meaning other than what we ourselves place on it*. The reason I believe that statement holds truth is because when I used to struggle with paranoia, all synchronicity lead to messages of fatality. Now that I have a more positive outlook on life all synchronicities lead to wise, spiritual messages of guidance. How we translate happenstance, coincidental moments, depends on how we view life in general.

To move on into another way I receive spiritual guidance I'll bring up the topic of intuition. Here's an experience I had that might convey what I mean by intuition. One day, I went to the apartment of a woman I had just met. As I sat in her kitchen, chatting with her, I noticed she was sitting next to the kitchen counter where there was a very long and sharp carving knife. My heart began to thud and a feeling of dread swept through me. I had the thought that she was going to grab that knife and stab me. Now, many times in my past, due to bipolar episodes, I'd gone into delusions and paranoia so I didn't really trust my own intuition at this point. I knew what to do though. I internally prayed, *"God, correct my thinking and align my thoughts to be in your divine truth and guide me"*. I then felt calmly inspired to say, *"sorry, I have to go, can I talk with you another day?"* I then immediately left her apartment. As I climbed into my car I wondered if perhaps I had over reacted, yet felt relief to be away from her. Several weeks later, this same woman phoned me and confided she suffers from schizophrenia. That day I left her apartment abruptly, she admitted she had been in a paranoid episode and felt terribly afraid of me. She considered grabbing a butcher knife off her counter to protect herself from me. Upon hearing this I was glad I didn't panic and run from her home; that could have caused her further distress. Instead, through calming my fears with prayer, I knew exactly what to do. This incident, to me, is a good example of paying attention to intuition. Oh yes and a good example of what to do if you doubt your intuition; simply pray for wise guidance.

Besides intuition, I also experience moments of one-to-one communication with people in the spirit world. Making a statement like this might either stir readers to assume I'm still residing in *Crazy Town* or be comforted because they too have this natural ability. Either way, based on my own encounters, I'll share what I feel to be truth. It seems to me that those of us, who do communicate with spirit people, need to be especially of a healthy mind or else we risk contaminating accurate spirit contact with our nonsense. If you are not stable minded, most likely, as I did, you'll twist the context of the spirits message to suite your own story line. When my balanced thinking and restored health was in place, spirit contact became provable through evidence given. This is something I maintain to this day, accurate provable evidence is a must or I will end the spirit contact. My intention is to help people through mediumship not confuse them with unverifiable messages. Since I know all too well, how deluded thoughts can distract and detour us off into La-La-Land, it has become imperative to have substantiated proof.

Some people have approached me saying that they think mental illness is caused by demonic aggressors from spirit, tormenting me. It's a big subject and I'll address it, but only in brevity. It is my understanding and belief that there are many factors in place to determine our state of illness or wellness. Like it or not, scientifically, living in the material world we are susceptible to hereditary factors through our genes and DNA. Then there is location, location, location.

What are you ingesting through foods, air, water, soil and many other physical variables? What is your state of mind, how have you been treated throughout the years? Not wanting to go on and on, I'll shorten it up by saying;

As far as I'm concerned my mental discord was mostly a result of fear based, unresolved issues and stress filled thoughts that triggered the inherited gene that caused a flood of brain chemistry to cause an electrical misfiring within my brain. Simple terms: a case of emotional and physical imbalance.

Although at times I was hallucinating seeing creepy, scary entities, they were merely reflections of my inner fears being projected outwardly. My confidence, empowerment and sanity returned once I figured that one out. Less than loving spirit beings are not to blame for mental illness. We must empower ourselves by understanding that whatever thought crosses our mind, no matter where it comes from, we alone are ultimately the ones who choose to believe that thought or not.

To be clear, I'll repeat; the spirit world did not torment me. My own thinking caused suffering. I am a firm believer that I am responsible for any thoughts that cross my mind, no matter where they originate from. Ultimately, I have the final say whether I choose to accept any thought as truth.

Back to the subject of talking with spirit people, it's my understanding that people who have crossed into the light of God will present as gentle, loving, supportive and never tell us what to do. Loved ones from the Spirit World know not to interfere in our lives. They respect that we need to live life with both feet planted on the ground. Below is an experience I had, that might get across what I mean.

One early evening while in conversation with a friend, he said something to me that I found completely insulting, even degrading. I told him off and walked away. While in my home, feeling angered about his rude remark, I suddenly became aware of my Aunt sitting in a chair across from me. She had died several years previously. I saw her image clearly, yet she was transparent. My Aunt telepathically told me that I was mistaken, in truth this man had been teasing and did not say anything rude or insulting. She further encouraged me to continue daily prayer and seek wisdom. She was only there for seconds and gone. There was no doubt that this spirit communication with my Aunt was a blessing. So, I followed her suggestion and prayed for guidance in how to proceed with this new information. God spoke to my heart, through a strong urging, to go back and ask this man precisely what he had said. I did that and sure enough this friend explained to me what he actually said and meant. It was shocking to find out I had indeed heard him wrong. Thanks to the grace of God that my Aunt was able to get through to me and encourage me to repair a long time, dear friendship.

The level of comfort is reassuring, knowing that I can at least trust God's guidance to get through to me, when I pray then listen. Much appreciation goes out to those souls from the other side who occasionally take the time to encourage us.

I used to think so much nonsense that my mind-chatter wouldn't allow me to get past my own thoughts to hear my wise voice of common sense. The only way I know to turn off the *Monkey Mind* is to put my full attention on thoughts of love.

It really helped me to contemplate God, Saints, Angels, and of course Jesus. Doing that immediately got my thinking straight and thereby caused me to feel centered and down to earth.

I'd noticed, since my prayer *'help me'*, I never again experienced psychotic episodes. That was in 1998. In recalling that memory of being huddled on the cold cement floor of that basement closet, it was my darkest time. Ironically, during that dark experience, the moment where I felt another Being wrapping me in love fortifies my faith in God to this very day.

Although psychosis was now a thing of the past, unfortunately I still had mild depression at times. Perhaps I hadn't had enough sleep, or there might have been stressors triggering me; regardless of the cause, I soon learned what helped me cope through my unhappy mind and that was by holding onto hope and faith. Reminding myself that God was still there even if I couldn't feel that presence of love helped me. This eased my gloominess and soon it passed.

Many may not know this; Mother Teresa herself spent many years unable to feel the presence of God, Jesus or the Holy Spirit. In her courage and dedication to this world she bolstered herself to keep on being kind and helping others, through sheer faith. Certainly I am not comparing myself to the magnitude of love that Mother Teresa showed in her life time; my intent is to encourage us all to remember that it's okay if we are not able to feel the presence of love all the time. More importantly we must be kind to ourselves and others regardless.

Early one Sunday morning, I awoke feeling forlorn. After wrapping a robe around me I walked out to the living room and turned on the Television. By chance, the TV channel was on a Christian program. The Minister invited people to ask Jesus to come into their hearts and restore them. Since I was still feeling rather crappy I figured why not? With sincerity, I quietly knelt down on my living room carpet, folded my hands together placing them near my heart and said a prayer.

"Jesus, I know you lived on this earth yet I don't know the truth of your journey. I trust and love you, so please Jesus, will you now enter my heart forever and help me be completely well. Restore me."

I didn't see any visions or feel any loving beings in the room with me. But I did feel good about myself for being able to talk to Jesus, straight up like that. I trusted He could hear me. This was not a religious gesture. What I had done was with absolute humble sincerity and *I believed* Jesus would help me.

After a lengthy period of time, I noticed something outstanding; my struggle with depression no longer existed. Mine was not an instantaneous healing. It was more a changing of my mind that happened through continued, prayerful intention. I developed a strong desire to be well and maintained a strong faith. Inviting Jesus into my heart was an important step in the right direction.

Wonderful as it is, not battling with mental illness, I certainly was not exempt from emotional based feelings. That's just part of being human, we have feelings. My emotions are at their best when kept within the realms of healthy expression. When I'm happy I show it, when I'm not pleased I show that too. When I'm down right angry I do my best to express it respectfully, without blaming others, yet I'm a work in progress and do on occasion slip up. Having come from a family where Dad would often be loud and aggressive with his temper, I have to continuously keep myself in check, or I too easily slip back into bad habit. The good news is I'm much faster, to respond gently, than I used to be!

These days, instead of acting on upsets and staying mad for days, weeks or years; if I have a disagreement that leads to anger, generally I will have resolved my feelings within anywhere from a few minutes to a few hours. That's quite an improvement from the long time grudges I used to hold. Back a few years ago, there was nothing wrong with my memory when it came to holding resentments. It was far too easy for me to call up an old argument from decades ago and start right back in on my upset as if it just happened in the moment. What a relief that I don't maintain that file cabinet in my head anymore, I can't remember the last time I went to bed angry. Poor Ron, I used to keep him up until three in the morning if that's what it took for me to feel understood. I am not so hard on him anymore; I've learned to use better communication skills and patience.

Humans are certainly complex on many levels. My opinion is that it's best not to sternly analyze your own or the behaviour of others. Just notice where you are at with your feelings, making it a habit to check in with yourself. Then find your path of peace, follow what feels harmonious and loving. In addition I like to follow the KISS method: *Keep It Simple Sweetie.*

Chapter #15

THORNS, TREES & ROSES

THE SIMPLICITY OF IT ALL was that the secret to my good mental health started at the level of my thinking. It was apparent that my prayers combined with contemplation upon love and quietly listening to my inner wisdom, became my road map out of Crazy Town.

If concerns, doubts or worries got in my way of the present moment, I immediately turned those concerns and doubts over to my faith in God. My motto became; *I Now Let Go and Let God.*

An acquaintance brought my attention to a marvelous short meditation. She encouraged me to close my eyes and imagine a garbage bag slung over my shoulder containing all my upsets. Most often, I perceived my garbage bag to be grossly enormous and bulging with unwanted issues. Upon having a feeling for the size and shape of the garbage bag hoisted over my shoulder, it was then time for me to entrust the Angels to lift the hefty bag off my shoulders. I would then take a moment, with my eyes closed, accepting that those Angels had indeed whisked the garbage bag off and given it up to God. To seal the deal, I repeated these words to myself *"now that I have handed my burdens over to God, there is no longer any reason for me to dwell on them. I know a peaceful resolution is happening for all involved"*. This visual, meditative prayer, always comforted me and when I handed over my problems this way, I always felt calmer and noticed the worries were quickly restored to peace.

Before long I had enough proven experiences that showed me beyond a doubt, that if I reacted to upsets, I only fed into the chaos and made things worse. Trusting that God knew everyone's heart and knew what was best for us all, gave me permission to stop judging what I thought people needed. In doing this I was able to relinquish all attempts to control situations. It felt fantastic to be free of the self imposed burdens. *Let go and let God!*

By the way, letting go is a lot easier than most people realize. Just think about it; what ever happened, even two minutes ago, is over and finished if YOU don't go back and keep rehashing it. Get yourself doing something fun and turn your upset over to the Divine. Then trust that everything will fall into peace soon enough, without your assistance.

Now as for deeper wounds from past interactions, try this; *Revisit the past hurt, for only a few brief moments and the whole time you're doing this, search for what wisdom you learned from that challenge. What insights? How does that past scenario benefit you now? Then focus on the valuable things you learned from that painful event; turn that bad memory into a memory filled with benefits!*

For the sake of your sanity DO NOT FOCUS ON THE HURT. It's like driving a car. If you are behind the wheel, cruising down the highway, you have to be looking through the windshield in order to stay safely on the road. Oh but yes, a good driver will glance into the rear view mirror in order to know what's going on behind them. Here's the thing, if that driver keeps on staring into the rear view mirror they will crash! Glance into your past, bring forth the wisdom and focus back on your present moment.

Recently I found out something incredibly interesting that helped me put another piece of my mental puzzle into place. I came across, by chance, a YouTube presentation by Dr. Caroline Leaf. She talked about her scientific research that proves your thoughts create pockets of chemical deposits in your brain. Now here's what interested me; fear based thoughts show up in the brain as what looks like thorns and peaceful thoughts create bursts of a different chemical that show up in the brain looking like full branches of balanced trees. It's kind of a cute twist on words having this Doctor with the last name of Leaf, huh?

To share my understanding, of Dr. Leaf's information, a little deeper; the thorns (pockets of chemical) we create within our brain by holding anger, worry, frustration, resentment, etc. stays there until we change our fear based thought. Those chemical thorns have the potential to cause illness so it's for our benefit to eradicate them. It's not hard to transform thorns into beautiful trees. I'd been doing it for a long time and didn't even realize it. To begin, if you are holding memories of upset, you can call up that memory of discord and seek out the wisdoms, insights and benefits learned from it. In doing this, you will have turned that negative memory into a positive one. That thorn releases its pocket of chemical and is aided by the injection of a healthy chemical responding to your new outlook on the old memory. You now have transformed a thorn into a healthy bushy tree, in balance.

While since I'm talking about thorns and trees in relationship to creating a healthy mind. I have a very appropriate experience to share. It started out with me searching my home library for a book to read. I pulled out one called, The Pleiadian Workbook, authored by Amorah Quan Yin. After quickly scanning through it, I wondered why this book was in my library. Definitely not my cup of tea, I felt. A bit more browsing through this book and my attention rested on page 102. This chapter discussed the concept of *clearing with roses.* It was a bit of a lengthy read and even though I loved the way the author described using images of roses to let go of painful memories, it got too boring for me and I closed the book putting it back on the shelf. Decidedly, I felt there was no need to learn about clearing with roses since I had several methods of releasing old wounds already in place.

It was close to noon when I arrived at a local restaurant to meet an old friend for lunch. While chatting about daily routines, my very psychic friend pipes up and says, *"Oh Ann, one of your spirit helpers is here and has a message for you"*. Sure I say, let's hear it? To my utter surprise she tells me this spirit wants to encourage me to go back and read that book about roses. I had not told my friend anything about that book I had just scanned through! Immediately after lunch, my friend and I went and bought a dozen of my favorite roses, pink. I promised her I'd read the chapter on clearing with roses and get back to her with regards of what the process entailed.

After a long read about clearing with roses and how to use boundary roses, I began doing a very simple practice called *'blowing roses'*. The quick and simple instruction is to sit quietly where you will not be disturbed for at least fifteen minutes. Start with prayer to get a sense of God's presence then close your eyes and imagine a beautiful rose, in full bloom, floating about six inches from your face. You then recall any people, places or things that have upset you, placing them gently into the center of that beautiful rose. Once you have included all that you want to, within the petals of that rose, you then envision the rose closing its delicate, velvety petals around those issues and people. Once you see the rose as a closed bud, you imagine gently blowing the rose as you think about it floating upwards into Gods love. You stay focused on the knowing that God will assist all concerned for the best possible outcome. This meditation must be done with loving intentions. This rose meditation I've described is slightly altered from the *Pleiadian* book description, just to keep it short. If you would like to know more variations on this rose meditation the above mentioned book is very informative.

Keep in mind please, I have not read any other parts in this particular book, so I'm not advocating the books message, since I don't know what its fully about.

Deep appreciation and gratitude goes out to the spirit helper that managed to get my friends attention over lunch; thereby alerting me to go back and learn the rose meditation. It proved out very helpful for me. Later on over the years I began sharing this method with others, who were actively seeking a happier life and this particular method of *'blowing roses'* was equally helpful for them too.

As long as I'm on the subject of thorns, trees and roses I would like end this chapter with the well known reference of the garden within our minds. It goes something like this:

In the floral garden within our minds we must be diligent in pulling the weeds so that they do not take over and strangle the beautiful flowers.

Chapter #16

HEEDING THE HUNCHES

To BE CANDID, I REALLY don't fully understand the mysteries of the mind and especially don't know how the mystical world of spirit activity, occur. What I do know is that I am a truth seeker and although I have some beliefs that I adhere to, I am not holding so tightly to those beliefs that I'm not able to accept new information and thereby easily change my mind accordingly.

Someone once said to me, *"keep an open mind, but not so open that your brains fall out"*. I agreed heartily with them.

Earlier, I talked about intuition, synchronicity and spirit communication and gave examples of what I meant by each. It's amazing to me how much we probably miss by not placing our thoughts on higher ground. I've learned to make positive thinking a habit, yet even so, I don't always pay attention to valuable forewarning. Being human I am a perfect example of not being perfect. Then again, who knows maybe in our imperfection we are perfect. Enough with the play on words, I don't want to lose sight of the case in point.

Now here's a prime example of ALMOST missing an intuitive warning. I took my car in for a tire rotation. The mechanics at the shop removed my car tires, rotated them and put them back on the vehicle. I assumed, being that they advertised themselves as tire specialists, that they had tightened and checked all the bolts holding my tires in place. I paid the bill, got in my car and drove across their parking lot feeling a big time discomfort in my tummy. As I was approaching the four lanes of speeding traffic on the highway, my tummy turned to a knot and the hair on my neck prickled. Then the thought came, *just pull over and check those tires.* My conscious mind convinced me I was just nervous because I was about to merge with rush hour highway traffic; so I made the mistake of ignoring my intuitive feelings. Thankfully, my inner knowing wasn't going to allow me to get hurt without one last effort to encourage me toward safety. As I pulled onto the highway and got the car up to the 90 KL speed limit, my body trembled and I felt fear. Not knowing what the fear was about I naturally tamped the brake gently and got the car slowed down. Other drivers glared at me annoyed, as they sped by, but I knew I had to drive slow and stay on the outside lane. Within seconds of slowing the car, my driver side back tire fell off! Since the vehicle was slowed, I was able to manage the car to a safe stop without smashing into other vehicles. There was severe damage done to my car, yet no one was harmed.

Greatly comforted and impressed by the many ways I am guided to make wise choices. For example, the *light of love* got through to me and dimmed my fear when I was ready to use a tire iron on the guy that forgot to tighten my tire bolts. That lucky man remains uninjured as a result of me making yet another wise choice.

There is a common saying that refers to 'cutting yourself some slack' and I put this into action when my vehicle tire fell off in rush hour traffic. A wee bit of verbal manure, slipped out of my mouth during my fright. Knowing my words were nothing more than a knee-jerk reaction to my shocking experience, helped me release any self judgment.

If we strive to be mindful of our thoughts, good on us YET please remember to 'cut your Self some slack"! It is not healthy for us to obsess over being flawless in thought all the time. In fact, being too hard on ourselves may even lead to feeling disappointed and eventually giving up trying to be reasonably mindful. Perfection is not the goal. Peace is the objective. Learn to be gentle on yourself while doing your inner work.

Moderation in all things helps us maintain balance in all areas of our life. Eating sensibly yet indulging in treats occasionally is one way I more easily stay on a nutritional path. Exercise is important to me, in order to feel strong and remain flexible but I know myself well and I will only keep up a physical activity if I enjoy it. As it turns out walking is my favorite way to keep up my muscle tone, agility and release stress. I did try workouts that my friends liked and pretty much their routines did not hold my interest. If you don't enjoy your workout, you won't keep up on it, so do your own thing. Another favorite part of my day was dedicated to prayer and meditation. This nurtured my spirit and helped me balance mind, body and soul. I've heard it said that every thought is a prayer, true I suppose; however the form of prayer I refer to are my intentional, focused thoughts on love.

With balanced living you'll have your feet planted firmly on this physical earth, where we're meant to be in this life. Moderation of all things is Key.

What a fabulous feeling, tossing the blankets off myself around seven one morning and feeling rested. Eating breakfast with Ron and discussing the fun side of life, while we entertained new possibilities on our horizon. This was a whole new way to converse in our household. I liked it, a lot!

It was nearing the end of 1999 and my life had unfolded into one of unwavering balance. I had read various books on spiritualism, self help, true life stories of inspiration and my home was filled with angel cards in pretty much every room. Beautiful crystals were placed caringly around rooms and decorative candles adorned table tops and bathtub. I'd taken up an interest in Feng Shui therefore I took care to give away or sell anything that I felt discord towards. There were many ornaments, pictures and even clothing that reminded me of unhappier days, so I let them go and replaced with items that enhanced the atmosphere in our home.

One piece of clothing that now held sad memories for me was a black, thread bare sweater. During my depressed years, it was all I ever wore and to accessorize it I added black socks and black pants. To say goodbye to this sweater, that had provided me a sense of comfort for years, I held a purposeful '*letting go*' ritual all by myself, while in my laundry room. In case anyone might be interested to know the steps to my goodbye ceremony, here it is:

Step one; I washed and dried the sweater with a sense of gratefulness for all the years it had served to provide me a sense of comfort. I contemplated the memories of feeling security within the old familiarity of that sweater.

Step two; once cleaned and dried, I neatly folded the tattered sweater, placing it into a paper bag. With appreciation I then rolled the bag up as small as it would roll.

Step three, I laid it gently inside the garbage can and said goodbye dear friend. That was it, closure.

As much as that sweater had been an important part of my dark and melancholy years, it was time for a much needed change. My happier mindset required a more colourful clothing choice to match. To begin my new wardrobe I made a modest purchase of three pairs of florescent socks; green, pink and yellow. They became my signature look for a while. Soon I moved on to the more traditional subtle colours, but not before I had buckets of giggles with friends as they teased me about blinding them with my brightly lit feet.

Next bit of fun I had was in creating a vision board. Browsing through old magazines and family photographs gave me more than enough material to arrange on a two foot square cork board. When I finished creating my hoped for future, on this board, I sat back admiring it for a long time. Soon it found a place on a wall within my home.

Glancing at my vision board now and then helped me maintain a focal point on what I wanted to create in my life. Eventually it got tucked into the back of a closet and pretty much forgotten about. Interestingly, over the course of only three years, all but one of those dreams on that board came true. The one remaining vision on my board is currently in progress; this book, written thirteen years later.

Not to keep anyone wondering, I'd like to share what was on my vision board that became realities:

> » I created more fun and laughter with family members.

» New friendships formed with positive, uplifting people.

» I began meditation classes and eventually facilitated my own group.

» After developing my healing and mediumship abilities, I provided public demonstrations.

» I became a volunteer in the community raising money for Heart and Stroke Foundation; Spiritualist Church; Counseling Agency; Hospice Society.

» My mental health was fully restored.

» I realize my dream of becoming a lay counselor and after training I assisted individuals, couples and facilitated groups through a local Counseling Agency.

» My fear gone, I became a public inspirational speaker.

» A home based wellness room complete with loaning library afforded me space to provide healing sessions for others.

» Very significant was the magazine photo of a healthy dog, which was posted on my vision board. My dog, who suffered from severe canine arthritis, was fully healed and able to walk again. Our Veterinarian was shocked upon seeing my dog's recovery because earlier he suggested we consider euthanizing her, since no medication or surgery would help her now. By the way my dog, a Rottweiler, was only four years old when diagnosed with hopeless arthritis. She lived a ripe old age of twelve and although she got a bit stiff in the rear end, she was able to trot up and down stairs right to the end of her life!

» I think it's probably okay now to also tick off the 'Writing a Book' that had been on the vision board – I trust within the next six months this one will be published.

Fashioning a *Vision Board* combined with applying effort to take action on what you want; creates amazing results.

Later I'll talk more on how I was able to expand my comfort zone and live my life fully. Along the way, even though I had successfully become mentally healthy, I still needed to face huge learning curves. Challenges are necessary, in my opinion, to help us stretch out and encounter new experiences.

For now, I'll go back in time to near the end of 1998; this was around the time I felt a burning desire to write about my recovery from mental illness. I hadn't yet actualized my vision board dreams, but one thing for sure; I absolutely had realized that it's possible to have a joyful, peaceful life coping with mental illness. This spurred me on to write a ten page article on my experience as a person managing with severe bipolar disorder. Although I was still taking psychiatric medication, I was able to view my journey as a huge success. I had learned how to deal with my illness and I valued the help of medication.

The article described, from a patients view, what it felt like to struggle with assorted forms of psychosis. Then went on to say how I overcame the stigma and depression. I have to say, this article was in rough form. No editing which meant there were spelling and content errors throughout. But, it was written with depth and honesty. I had one intention, one single prayer, "*God please let this writing of mine reach someone who will be helped through reading of my experience.*" Then I posted it on my webpage.

Soon after posting my article on the internet I received an email from a woman who happened to come across it while searching for information on mental illness. She was a psychology student doing her thesis and she wanted to interview me for further research on the topic of her essay, which was on mental illness. Having someone interested to know more about my experience with bipolar disorder was very healing to me. After she interviewed me, her request was to take a printed copy of my article to her College instructor. Thrilled by her suggestion, I held no expectations as I agreed and handed her a copy. My only thought was that perhaps someone will be helped. To my surprise I received a call from the College Instructor asking me if she could use my article as a teaching aid in her class. I choked back tears as I gratefully gave my permission.

It was five years later, 2003, when I got a phone call from a long lost friend. She was now taking a College level psychology class and during one of her classes the Instructor had read an article written by a psychiatric patient. My friend said it was like déjà vu to her because what she heard sounded just like my experience. She asked me if I had anything to do with that article. Through tears of happiness, I acknowledged it in fact was my story. She then told me; over the past years the College has been using my article to help students understand and develop compassion towards people struggling with mental disorders. This was a prayer answered for me. Others were benefitted for having known of my experience. I was hugely benefitted as well, another level of healing deepened within me as a sense of connectedness to life was realized.

To jump forward in time, it was around the year 2010 when I phoned the College to see if my article was still in use? Twelve years had gone by. The instructor who had been using my story in her classes had retired some years prior, taking the article with her. The new Teacher was not aware the article had ever existed. Not terribly surprised, I politely thanked the Dean for her time. It took me a moment for my mind to grasp what the Dean was saying; I was expecting a goodbye and to my astonishment she was inviting me to come as a guest speaker for the current psychology class. When I accepted it was like a whirlwind and suddenly I found myself in front of the class. Admittedly, I felt a tad nervous. To my relief it was a small gathering that afforded me the comfort of an intimate sharing.

I enjoy writing, it's much like time travel; so back to 1999 and I'll carry on where I left off. This year happened to trigger several intense emotions within me. I could never have known what unimaginable joy was in store, but first I had to suffer the unexpected death of my Dad.

Chapter #17

CHANGE HAPPENS

L IFE SO FAR HAD BEEN a journey of mental and emotional proportions. Familiar with several forms of psychiatric therapy and various spiritual beliefs, I noticed similarity between the two. Psychology is all about mental health treatment, performance enhancement and self help. Spiritual beliefs also seek to improve our mental health, enhance our performance and self help. As well, both are dependent upon the individual taking responsibility for their own thoughts and actions.

There is one certain distinction between psychology and spiritual beliefs; spirituality acknowledges the existence of life after the death of the physical body where psychology doesn't. That difference caused me some difficulty in speaking with my therapists. Being diagnosed as mentally ill and then trying to talk about spirit activity and communications with the unseen world, was awkward. It was painfully obvious that I wasn't being believed.

Can you imagine sitting in your psychiatrists office saying, *"I see dead people, well actually they are very much alive except they live in a spirit world. Oh, but they can focus their energy and occasionally communicate with physical people."* The saddest thing was when I would attempt to prove to my Doctor that I could connect with people in spirit and then fall flat on my face. It seemed when I was stressed and trying to prove myself from a place of worry, no accurate communication took place.

Pretty much, I learned to keep quiet about my natural abilities of sensing energy and seeing spirit beings. After coming through the whacky hallucinations brought on through Psychosis; I could understand why I was not taken seriously by Doctors.

For the longest time I shut off my psychic side and that was easy since I no longer felt a desire to communicate. I went through a period of time where I felt it was pointless and I even held some blame towards the spirit world for not complying when I needed them most.

Finally, the day came where my instinct kicked in and my desire came back. Being cautious, I only allowed *loved ones* from spirit to have communication with me; never would I dare randomly invite any spirit being to come close. To me it was much like going to town and coming across several strangers, I wouldn't open my car door and invite a total stranger to hop in. For heaven sake, who knows what kind of a person they may be. A person I knew and liked, yes of course, they I wouldn't hesitate to invite. Same thing with spirit people; I would only invite the ones I knew were in the Light of Love.

Not to leave the impression I did lots of communicating with spirits during this time of my life, because I didn't. More important to me, at this time, was living fully present in the physical world. Participating in life became fun instead of frightening. The realization I had a long ways to go in order to heal some wounds, was more my focus and intent.

In years gone by, I used to think my purpose was to heal others, but not once back then did I consider I firstly needed to get a grip on my own perception of the world. *Heal thyself and then you'll be able to assist others*, echoed in my mind.

A great suggestion was passed my way. My brother-in-law, Garry, gave me the name and phone number of his favourite acupressure therapist. So appointment made and off I went to the big city for my first session of body work. I was enthusiastic to try this modality to facilitate my healing. Upon arriving to the therapists home studio, I was invited to walk through the large hall, turn right, walk past the library and go on into the therapy room; where I was told I would see the massage table. Removing my shoes in the foyer and hanging my coat on the available hooks, off I went to wait for the acupressure therapist. Down the hall, turn left, wait turn right, nope I think it was left... turn... Oops nope... go back right—AHA—found it! There it was, the massage table. Oh my goodness, I'd never seen such a huge massage table. It was covered with a beautiful shade of burgundy cloth and lined with a wide, intricate wooden frame. As I climbed up on it and laid down, I wondered why there was no step stool to make it easier to boost myself up on the table. I couldn't help noticing how hard and uncomfortable the surface of the massage table was, no padding what so ever. Then it crossed my mind, how the heck is the therapist going to do acupressure with me on this broad table, he'd never be able to reach properly. To my disappointment there wasn't even a pillow or blanket. Right then, in walked the therapist and he did his best to stifle his laughter as he said, *"Mrs. Carlson, this is the billiard room, I think you'll find the massage room much more comfortable."* Oh no! I'd climbed up and laid down on his pool table.

So much for turn right or left, just point me to the nearest exit will you? After letting go my embarrassment, I noticed how skilled this therapist was and he truly helped me reach a new level of wellness. Better yet, from then on I knew the difference between a billiard table and massage table.

Speaking of healing, one Sunday service the Minister said to the congregation, *"How you behave here and interact with other members is generally how you will be in your daily life outside these Church walls. Ask yourself, are you holding your love back from others or are you willing to reach out?"* She caused me to contemplate a moment and have a look at where I was with my behaviour. It was through looking across my recent past that helped me recognize that although healing was still needed in some areas I sure had come a long ways.

Firstly, I acknowledged some good changes I had brought into my life. Such as, instead of sitting in the very back of the Church so I could leave without anyone talking to me, now I was sitting up close to the podium. Something else new, that I felt good about, was realizing my early arrival to Church so I could help set up chairs; then, staying after the service to have fellowship. It was with contentment that I acknowledge to myself that my answer to the Ministers question was, *YES, in my daily life I was doing similar by initiating new friendships, planning dinner parties, reaching out to help others in various ways.*

My calendar was filled with things I loved to do; tai chi, swimming, attending theatre, helping elderly friends. I definitely had lost fear of living and now had become part of the world in a way that I had never experienced before. Had I not taken time to think about this, I might have missed feeling so pleased with myself. I'd certainly come a long way.

Having found my strength and feeling empowered from the inside out coincided with the alarming loss of my Dad. He suddenly died January 21, 1999.

Exactly ten days before my Dad's death, one of my kids told me there was an odd message left on our answering machine and that the call display on our phone showed it had come from my parents' number. Ron and I both listened to that taped message over and over again to be sure our ears were not deceiving us. The recording actually sounded like a distant, ghostly voice, just like the movies sometimes portray. The voice was that of a man with a strong English accent and his precise words were, *"He died so I picked up his soul and led him"*. Although some of my Dad's ancestors were English, there were no relatives nearby that had an accent, we were certain no one would play a joke like that anyhow. We knew it was an authentic spirit message, we just didn't know for sure who was about to cross over into spirit world. Of course, I had my suspicions and said to my husband and teen, I wonder if my Dad is okay? He was only 72 years old and in relatively good health so we didn't feel there was a concern. Well, ten days later my Dad did die of a massive heart attack, at home in my Mom's arms. During our deep grief of missing Dad, we were also comforted by hearing this spirit message; it reminded us that Dad would not have been alone in his transition to meet with God on the other side.

Three months after Dad died, I was again faced with death of a loved one. This time it was our young and beautiful golden retriever. She was hit by a car and died three days later. Tragedy, grief, unwanted change and it was my spiritual understanding and faith that helped me to accept.

At the same time there were financial burdens, accidents and teenage crisis. All genuine difficulties I had to face. Through my strength of faith, I took all in stride and attended to situations without mental illness creeping into the mix. I felt humbly grateful for my recognition of a Divine Consciousness that I could draw strength from.

Having a healthy outlook, even through loss and times of grief, allowed me the serenity to simply feel into whatever honest emotion surfaced. It wasn't too long before I was back in stride again, enjoying the life I had. Missing Dad, missing my dog and yet appreciating my loved ones that were still physically with me.

On the track of the physical, I noticed one day that my physical appearance changed once again. So subtle, that I barely noticed except one day while passing by my own reflection I saw a beautiful image. I was no longer stooped over with rounded shoulders, the excess weight was gone and the most beautiful expression adorned my face. Even my hair had taken on a healthier look; what had been frizzy, brittle hair was restored to a soft, healthy sheen. The one thing that had remained was the balding on top my head, considering the years of psychiatric medication I wasn't surprised.

I affirmed the benefit of medication and felt thankful in how it helped me. The medication in my system adjusted my chemical imbalance which afforded me steadiness of mind, so I could do the inner work necessary to recover. For this reason, I continued taking medication without complaint or worry. I'd seen that psychiatric medicine did not get in the way of my spirituality nor did it hinder my physical activity level. In fact, through my positive mindset, my energy was always steady.

Even though this medication was known to have a side effect of weight gain, I discovered that through prayerful mind, my will power was amplified and it was easy to eat sensibly and keep physically active. No weight gain was the result.

Along with my appearance, most of my life, I had an unsightly condition on the back of my right hand that also crept up my wrist. It looked like a rash of raised red bumps that Doctors were unable to remove and no prescription creams helped. This was the year I decided to pray asking God to remove this unsightly condition. Over a period of weeks, I also asked two spiritual healers to pray that this condition heal.

After all three of us invited *Divine* healing; those raised red bumps that had been with me for many years were completely gone!

I appreciated the physical healing that took place, but I was confused as to why some things heal and other ailments don't. I came to the conclusion it was best to simply ask for restored health on any matter and let it come about in its own good time, without judgment or question.

Another pleasant difference in my life was that I no longer needed to have visits with psychiatric staff and didn't attend any more mental health classes. The Doctor had switched my medication from Lithium to Valproic Acid (Epival), due to Lithium becoming toxic in my system. Being on lithium, for a long time, caused several side effects; one result was hand tremors. Once the mood stabilizer, Epival, was introduced to my system the tremors subsided. Since I no longer suffered psychotic episodes I was taken off the antipsychotic known as Respiridone. With good sleep habits now in place, I was also taken off sedatives. I felt much better on just the 1000 mg per day of Epival.

Giving up my limiting beliefs, giving up the need to control everything, giving up excuses, giving up complaining, giving up living my life to suite other people's expectations; kicked the door wide open and allowed great joy to fill my life.

Change happens to us all. It's the natural process, evolution of all things. Some change brings joy, other change may bring sorrow and many varied emotions in between can often surface. Three words helped me ride the wave of change. Those three words are; acknowledge, accept and arise.

Acknowledge; truthfully what is going on in the present moment.

Accept; that this is now the new normal.

Arise; knowing your sorrow over the change is a healthy expression of your sincere feelings. Comfort within, will soon return.

Chapter #18

DIVINE TIMING

I T WAS IN JANUARY OF 2000, nearly a year since my Dad's passing, when I began entertaining the thought that I might not need medication anymore. It seemed to me that I was not just managing the illness or in remission, I had a feeling that the hereditary mental illness was no longer a part of my body or psyche. What stopped me from decreasing medication and attempting to end it altogether was the very thought; what if I'm wrong.

The memory of haphazardly going off my medication only three years prior, then experiencing the worse psychotic episode, was still fresh in my mind. At this point, I felt I had a lot to lose. Having finally achieved a level of confidence and self awareness I was not willing to put at risk. My Grandmother used to always say, *"When in doubt don't"*. I had some doubt so I didn't mess around with my medication. Well not this year anyhow.

Refocusing my attention onto my accomplishments, I decided to take a break while I had some alone time and mull over the many different aspects that helped me move out of mental disruption. Sitting by my window seat, deep in thought, the dark blue lid of our hot tub caught my eye and beckoned to me. Why not, I figured, as I poured a small glass of wine and walked out to the tub and lifted the lid off. Pushing the tub button, releasing jetted air streams from several locations under the water caused the churning swirls of crystal clear water to create soothing sounds from the rising bubbles. With the cold brisk air of January brushing my bare shoulders, it felt decadent, as I melted into the warm water. I reveled in the feeling of water massaging all tension away. Taking a sip of wine from my glass, I reflected on my success of mastering my own mind thus far. The feeling of celebration as I enjoyed the moment seemed significant. I had a feeling my life from this time forward would be different. Perhaps it would be better and much more adventurous. Raising my glass of wine, all by myself in the hot tub, I said out loud, *"Cheers Ann"*.

Only six months later, in summer of 2000, my life did become better and more adventurous! While sitting on my patio with a friend, enjoying her company, I shared with her my secret yearning. As I described my desire to find a way to help others, who are suffering from mental difficulties, her encouraging smile hinted to me that she wanted to tell me something. I passionately stated, *"I wish there was a way I could become a counselor and assist people in their recovery"*. My friend couldn't contain her comment any longer as she told me to watch the local newspaper advertisements. She went on to explain that once a year the Government subsidized Counseling Agency in town offers a College level, lay counselors training. Her support of me was deeply appreciated, she pointed out some qualities she saw in me; compassion, experience, gentleness and sincerity. One last piece of information she passed onto me; there is a fee for the training yet the Counseling Agency will cover my costs as long as I will commit to working as a counselor in their Agency for two years to pay off the course.

Divine timing! A week later I looked in the local newspaper and there it was, the advertisement for counselors training at this Agency. My concern was, with a history of mental illness, the Agency could not accept me as a counselor. I decided to check it out regardless and what a happy surprise when no one asked my medical history. So onward I proceeded.

It seemed all the potential trainees, including me, found the process of even just applying to take the lay counselors training intense. First we had to attend the free orientation lecture hosted by the Counseling Agency. It appeared the professional therapists were looking to weed out people that were not serious about dedicating themselves in developing counseling skills. There was no doubt in my mind that I fit all their criteria and since they still hadn't asked any of us about our medical background, I advanced to the next step.

After filling out the Counseling Agencies application form and handing in my resume, the staff must have liked what they saw because I got a call back for an interview. The trainers were very adept interviewers and even though I knew they were scrutinizing me, I felt at ease with them. Now that they met and talked with me, they decided to phone the three people I named as personal references. That was a challenge for me to choose people that knew me well enough to know I was now undeniably stable. I chose well, all three attested to my integral, responsible and compassionate nature without revealing my diagnosis of mental illness. I hadn't asked them to keep it quiet, I trusted what needed to be said just would be.

It took about a week before the Agency called to let me know I was approved for the three day pre-training sessions. The three days were a prelude of what to expect in the full six month counselors class. It was also a means for trainers to discern who might not be ready for this type of training. All twenty-six of us were told up front there were only twelve seats and that not all of us will be invited to continue onto the full course. Being professional counselors, the trainers used discretion and wisdom so that if we didn't move into the full training at least our self esteem would remain intact.

When the three days of training finished, my emotions got the better of me and worry set in. Knowing better than to put too much importance on one thing, didn't stop me from getting far too caught up in whether I'd be asked to carry on with the training or asked to end. Many long walks through nature trails, while I waited to hear from the Agency, helped me release some stress. A few days went by before I received a call inviting me to participate in the full counselors training program. I was delighted to embark on a whole new chapter in my life. I hadn't felt this kind of enthusiasm before, to me it was a dreamed of opportunity that might end up with me assisting someone else through their journey.

The counseling training turned out to be much more that merely learning active listening skills and open ended questions. We were often video-taped during classes and required to watch ourselves on tape to notice our habits. Upon seeing myself chewing gum on video, I stopped that unattractive habit and never went back to it. I noticed I did a lot of head bobbing when I listened to people and what's up with that comb over hairdo; I had to laugh at myself. Ultimately, as much as I detested seeing myself on film, watching the footage helped me cultivate better habits. The thin, receding hair however, I had to accept as is.

Ironically, a few days later while grocery shopping I noticed the check out woman seemed to be about my age and she had absolutely the most beautiful smile I'd seen. Due to her happy demeanor and friendliness, I almost missed the fact that she was balding and had sparse whips of hair patches across her scalp. She was an awesome role model for me. Walking away I reminded myself that she has the right attitude. Hair or no hair, I was going to be my happiest self possible.

At times the counseling classes were emotionally deep for us all. I suppose the trainers designed the course with this purpose in mind; to surface left over unresolved hurts. It was apparent to me that I was just a bit, well okay, a LOT more emotional than the others. Fortunately, I had the ability to ground myself and reign in those emotional bursts quickly. Still, I couldn't help wondering what the trainers might think about my occasional, emerging tears.

Every few weeks, each participant was required to meet the trainers for an individual evaluation interview. Upon my second evaluation meeting one trainer pointed out the potential she saw in me to become a counselor; but, I was assured if I were to continue in this training, I would need to bring certain issues to a close. Those issues were; guilt of not having been a good parent and becoming emotionally charged when speaking in front of the class. So there it was, now I knew how they felt regarding my demeanor in class. This feedback spurred me on and helped me explore new levels of myself. More than anything, I wanted to unfold my abilities to help others and blossom into my full potential.

Immediately, wasting no time, I sought out healing sessions through my Church; this gave me a combination of prayer support and being able to talk privately with a trusted source, about my issues. Mostly I was holding onto the belief that I had been a terrible influence on my children, guilt of not being there emotionally for my kids when they needed me. One thing for sure, I had come a long ways from the frightened woman who used to believe I was a victim and everyone else was to blame for my hurt. Now, I was able to own my past choices, take responsibility for my past actions and admit where change needed to happen within me. Talking with a spiritual healer, who had a good set of ears and common sense, assisted me to find my own solutions. End result, I accepted that I did the best I could as a Mother who was suffering from mental discord. Reminding myself that presently I make excellent choices and I am a loving parent to my children NOW.

As luck would have it I was able to participate in spiritually based workshops, in my community, where the facilitators had some very advanced counseling skills. One of my favourite methods, that helped me most, was the sacred speaking circles. Who ever held the talking stick could share their inner most feelings without interruption from others. This technique helped me hear myself and reconnect with my inner core. My authentic, calm self soon found her way back into the world.

Through these spiritual workshops I met a Native Elder who invited me to attend several sweat lodges through the aboriginal community. My new friends welcomed me by means of their actions, their respect and compassion towards me.

I felt loved and connected through fellowship to a community of people who carried ancient wisdom to all they embraced. I immersed myself in a deeper understanding of my inner feelings and came away with a sense of gratefulness for who I am and who I share this world with.

Quite remarkably, my personal healing sessions, the workshops and private life easily flowed around maintaining my ability to participate in the counselors training classes. Each of my activities seemed to enhance and compliment my other interests.

Not to sound flippant or dismissive but to quickly acknowledge what else helped empower me:

- » I hugged trees while appreciating my own connection with nature.

- » Sunk my bare feet into muddy river banks as part of a cleansing ritual.

- » Climbed nearby mountain to enhance my physical, mental, emotional and spiritual levels.

- » Attended Native sweat lodges for purification, prayer and strengthening my spiritual bond with God.

- » Jumped into an icy river to increase vitality, energize and stimulate physically.

- » Sat cross legged on the earth while meditating.

All of these freeing experiences created a strong feeling of valuing My Self as is. In a world that often promotes competitiveness, judgments and criticisms, it's best if we do everything we can to ensure we remember our true core authenticity. Letting go the need to be accepted by others according to their standards gave me permission to follow my own heart.

Soon I understood why I had been so emotionally charged, when speaking in front of a group of peers, during the counselors training sessions. It was a result of not feeling worthy. After speaking freely during spiritual workshops, sweat lodge and with Church healers; expressing My Self easily, soon became natural. My confidence in tact and emotions balanced, I settled into a contented feeling that remained with me.

Still absorbed in the counselors training, perhaps three quarters of the way through, I was called in for another evaluation. This time the trainers acknowledge my personal growth. They saw I had resolved my parenting guilt and emotional eruptions while speaking. Most importantly, through seeking to heal my wounds, I discovered there is only this moment that is real, everything else is only a memory. Knowing this puts my entire life into proper perspective.

Nearing the end of the counseling course and thinking about my progress, I saw clearly how easily I could attain anything I put my mind to. It's just a matter of following through one small step at a time. Setting aside insecurities and learn by doing. In a way, I was quite childlike in my approach; innocent, gullible, sincere, enthusiastic, gentle. Into my forties, I no longer saw myself as stupid, unworthy or mentally ill. What some people might take for granted, because they always had good self esteem, was like gold to me. To feel the love for myself with imperfections and all; is such a blessing.

There was no doubt in my mind that I was ready to take my seat beside people who wanted to talk about their wounds and surface their answers.

In 2001, I went to my final counseling class and last evaluation interview. When I heard the counseling Supervisor invite me to be a part of the Counseling Agency team, a smile spread across my face and my heart expanded with happiness.

Within me was pure thankfulness for my life, I appreciated every person and situation because I knew none of this would be possible if it weren't for all my teachers. I consider every person I've ever met, my teacher.

Then a concern crept in, disrupting my contentment, again I wondered do I need to tell my Supervisor that I am on psychiatric medication? The second I told this truth, the Agency policy would require me to leave. It's not like healing from a broken bone, that's visible. Healing from mental illness was something different and especially that I still took medication. So I stayed in the closet a while longer because I was sure they would not believe me; that I was completely mentally well.

Chapter #19

HOW CAN I HELP?

AVING COMPLETED THE TRAINING AND now a lay counselor in sessions with individuals, I was like a duck to water. Of course, even when ducklings are learning to swim they need guidance. At the Counseling Agency we had a strong team of professionals, so I never really felt alone in the room with a client, even though physically I was. Often, after a session, I'd debrief with a professional Therapist. This helped me see where I could improve on my skills and also acknowledge what I was doing well.

Through my genuine respect of all people, no matter their background, I developed a keen ability to see through to client's strengths. This made me a good helper in sessions and my willingness to attend regular case conferences, with other counselors, only excelled my abilities.

Soon enough, I expanded my comfort zone by attending the Agency meetings. This educated me on policies, protocol and formalities of how a meeting is run and I more fully understood the inner workings of a counseling agency. It was quite scary for me to sit through these meetings initially. Insecurities jumped into my head and I had to be firm with myself to let them melt away. By allowing and moving through my fear, of not knowing my place at the meetings, I soon felt more at ease. Although awkward at times, I learned how to express myself during these meetings, with practice. Learn by doing, became my new motto.

Now that I was settled into the Counseling Agency, familiar with their policies and seeing clients regularly, my social skills developed. That used to be the hardest part for me, socializing. There were still occasional times where I felt uncomfortable chatting with colleagues because I wasn't up on current events and couldn't discuss what I'd been up to over the past several years. If I disclosed my previous bouts with mental illness, I imagined their jaws dropping. It was my guess, if I were to describe how I overcame paranoid delusions and psychotic episodes; they'd appreciate my story and then have to ask me to leave the Agency. With a twinge of sadness, I kept my greatest accomplishment a secret. On the upswing though, it didn't take me long to figure out that I could talk about my current interests. Turned out the other counselors and I had a lot of pastimes in common; gardening, pets, and hiking, just to name a few.

Comfortable with clients, enjoying the camaraderie of staff and friends propelled me into a life of unimagined, thoroughly enjoyable experiences. I had never once in my life realized how relaxing it was just to show up and be ME. Once you make up your mind and focus on what you want, the Universe opens wide to accommodate.

Like the gentle unfolding of a rose, my consciousness increased and greater joy filled that space.

I never thought a lot about where I was headed or what the future held for me. Yet I did pay attention to how I felt in the moment and thereby did my best to follow what seemed the brightest path. This was not necessarily the easiest path though, mostly the well lit path required physical exertion. This reminds me of one of my favorite old movies; *The Wizard of Oz*. Although the main character, Dorothy, followed that golden-yellow brick path, she had many mishaps along the way! Totally, I relate to what Dorothy did in that movie. Similarly, I followed my golden-yellow brick road, faced many challenges until I finally realized that the way home is not *just* on a physical path; it's the total connection between our heart, mind and soul. At the end of the movie, Dorothy has this revelation and 'clicks' her heels together while wearing her ruby red sparkling shoes and says, *"there's no place like home, there's no place like home"*. Miraculously, as she focuses her thoughts inward upon the love she feels in her heart, she opens her eyes and is safely home again. The moral of this movie is cleverly revealed through the character Glinda (the good witch) as she says; ***"You had the power all along my dear."***

Hilariously, during one of the Counseling Agencies Christmas parties we did a joke gift swap and the gift I received was a pair of ruby red slippers with sparkling sequins all over. Of course the person who gifted these ruby sequined slippers to me had no idea of the significance they held for me.

There is no place like home and HOME is located within your heart center. Clicking your heels together and repeating, *there's no place like home*, in a simplistic way can be called a prayer. It is the **INTENTION** that helps you get centered from within. Pretty much that is why I consider Prayer to be the Key; you are setting a clear intention. Then, once you understand you can trust Gods guidance to ignite you from within, you are strengthened to take responsibility for yourself. It's empowering yourself, when you surrender to the intelligence that is greater than you.

At this point in life, my intention was strong, clear and focused. I simply wanted to know how I could be of assistance to others throughout my day. I wanted to be kind, generous and encouraging; therefore I was. By leading my life this way, I never wanted for anything. I always had plenty of work that I enjoyed and abundance flowed in all areas of my life. My attitude kept my sight on living life humbly and in this peaceful mindset, I felt deep gratitude towards all aspects of my journey.

Just to be specific about what I mean by *being of assistance to others*, I am referring to using my various abilities to encourage others. Important point; when you are seeking ways to be of assistance for others it doesn't mean you are willing to be at anyone's beck and call. Nor does it mean you are feeling sorry for anyone. Feeling sorry for people, weakens them. Whereas empathizing with people strengthens them. Sympathy is when you see someone as weak, frail and unable to fend for them-selves. Empathy is when you feel compassion for the person and you may even be able to relate to their particular challenge; yet you see them as capable and strong enough to surface their own solutions.

For me being of assistance meant; I will do my best to encourage, support, offer my skills or bring laughter to or even just smile at someone to remind them they are not alone in this world. I believe every person has all their own answers buried inside; as a helper my job is to assist them to *mine* their own gold. There was bonding between myself and others yet I was not attached to them. Bonding brought personal closeness that felt respectful and remaining detached allowed me to keep from being drawn into anyone else's drama-story. To remain detached from peoples harrowing stories required me to see their strengths and wisdom. I also had to trust that they'd ultimately come through their personal challenge, intact and wiser for having had the experience.

Here's a perfect example of how I paid attention to where I might be of help and how it actually changed my own life for the better too. While walking up the stairs to the Counseling Agency, to see a client, I noticed the Secretary yet again busy beyond what a normal human would be expected to do. I wondered to myself, how can I be of assistance? Instantly and without question I walked behind the desk, as the other phone line rang and picked it up saying *"Good morning, Counseling Agency, Ann speaking, how may I help you?"* My previous secretarial training came flooding back and the staff noticed my confidence behind the desk. From that point on I was hired to work behind the front desk on busy days and as a fill in for the secretary when she went on holidays. I loved it because I was doing everything I enjoyed; seeing clients, doing front desk work and during my personal time, I began exploring spiritual energy healing once again.

In my past, most of my adult life, I'd felt the benefits of inviting Gods healing energy in, to restore my own health. Often I'd witnessed and experienced how profoundly Universal healing energy had assisted others in their wellness too. We are all vessels for channeling healing. I keep in mind that I merely *hold the Space* through intentioned prayerful mindset and in this sincerity, healing energy flows through all present. There are many ways of facilitating healing to happen; such as, a Mothers kiss on a child's hurt, or a Father's strong arms embracing his frightened child, a strangers gentle words spoken to a person feeling alone, a neighbour offering fresh baking. However you focus love towards another living soul; that is sending God's healing energy. The crucial recipe to be a healing channel is easy, natural and free to everyone. Here are the two ingredients required; compassion and intention.

Prayers that invited restored health; were a natural craving for me. You don't need to take a class or read books to learn how to access your natural healing abilities. It's as easy as feeling compassion for someone and then using your intention to invite Universal Love to assist. When laying my hands over a person, during a spiritual healing session, I seemed to always feel heat, coolness or vibration moving right through my body; especially my hands. The confirmation of valid healing came when I and others experienced the injury or illness restored to health. My curiosity peeked and I wanted to find out more about this amazing thing we call healing energy.

Although we do not need to take classes to develop our healing abilities, there are situations where you would seek out formal training. Such was the case when I wanted to participate in the Church services as a spiritual healer. In the participation of a Spiritualist Church service, there are specific accepted methods of hands-on healing that must remain consistent for the simple fact of maintaining the integrity of the organizations beliefs. The Minister and Church Board of Directors also need to confirm that each healer is authentic. Knowing this, I took the Ministers healing classes so I could understand the prescribed method for spiritual healing within the Church. After completion of the healing classes the Minister invited me to partake in the services, alongside several other healers. So on Sundays, six of us would take our place, standing beside seats, where anyone at the Church Service could sit to receive hands on healing to aid them. It was with humbled appreciation that I participated this way.

Weeks had gone by and through accessing my healing abilities on a regular basis, my capacity for channeling through prayer, deepened. I also learned how important it is to only see health for anyone I'm supporting in their healing process. As healers we must be able to see the best in people when perhaps they can't see it for themselves.

Now that I was consistently active as a conduit for healing energy, I began offering healing sessions from my home. I noticed that most people having session with me wanted to express their inner most feelings. My counseling skills were not only an asset, but a necessity to really be present with people. I was able to listen and relate to the person while helping them consider their options for bettering their lives. Soon, I was encouraging other healers to learn some basic counseling skills, even if just through books. Some were inspired to seek out basic counseling classes. It was a win-win for the healers and their clients because with learning communication skills it enhances everyone's life.

While continuing my own study, one evening while I was reading yet another book on counseling techniques, a small flyer fell out of the book. It was advertising Reiki training as a means of expanding ourselves and deepening our healing abilities. I had no idea what Reiki was and tossed the flyer aside because I figured I was already well versed in the healing arts and didn't need someone's classes.

It didn't matter that I tossed that flyer aside, didn't matter that I wasn't seeking to take more healing classes. Something deep-rooted in my core nagged me to find out more about Reiki.

Through some computer searches I soon discovered that Reiki was a Japanese technique to help a person relax and allow their body, mind and spirit to heal. Reading also that Reiki invited the God source to flow through and assist people in restored health; peaked, my interest. The word 'Reiki' translates to mean Universal Life Force Energy. Upon my research I soon realized Reiki and Spiritual healing were both drawing from, the same Loving source. Both channeled Gods healing energy, both healed on physical, mental, emotional and spiritual levels and both methods even used hand placement guided by intuition. The only difference I found was that Reiki had symbols for students to use as a means of increasing their focus on healing and Spiritual healers did not use symbols. Deciding, that as much as I liked what Reiki was and meant, I didn't think added training would make much difference for me.

To my surprise it seemed as if I wasn't going to get off the *Reiki Bus* that easy. Over the course of a week I was bombarded with Reiki information that I hadn't actively sought out. Reiki flooded my world, without me even trying. I had to admit it all began the moment that flyer fell out of my book and onto my lap. The final synchronicity that influenced me to pay attention was when I found out a friend was a Reiki Teacher. I'd known her for a few years and hadn't heard her mention this Reiki stuff before. Enough, I thought, okay already, with feeling this prompted I will study Reiki.

When I completed my first level of Reiki, I then understood why it had been so important for me to become a Reiki practitioner. It actually opened doors for me that otherwise would have remained closed. My study of Reiki deepened my personal growth, which may never have happened if not for the Reiki groups I attended. Practicing Reiki eventually led me to providing Reiki treatments for staff at the Counseling Agency, Hospice, Hospitals and private homes. I went on to further study of Reiki ultimately learning levels two, three and the Master-Teacher level. Becoming a Reiki Teacher took time and dedication, I didn't take it lightly knowing the responsibility incurred with each level. Having achieved the Masters level through one Teacher, I sought out yet another Reiki Teacher and received a second Master-Teacher certificate. Providing the teachings of Reiki helped many people to access that healing energy which is always right there within them. You see, Reiki is not some energy or force that the Teacher gives to the student, more accurately the Teacher holds the space for the student to access that Universal Healing Energy that is free and within each of us. For me, it was gratifying; such an honour to share the energy of love, Reiki, with others.

One of my favorite things about Reiki is that there is a strong community where we gather together to share experiences as well as treatments for each other. It's where there is love, support and a place to BE your-self.

As long as I intentionally opened to Love, it touched lives anywhere I was. Early one morning, while working behind the front desk at the Counseling Agency, I could hear one of the counselors rummaging around the file room, sighing as if frustrated. I asked her if she needed any assistance. She replied there was an important report she had to give at a Government Agency, which could influence more funds being provided to our Agency. She was confident in giving the report, but now her many papers had fallen from her hands and lay scattered all over the floor. Although the pages were numbered, she felt certain there was not enough time for her to get them properly organized and get to that meeting on time. I didn't think twice, as I got up from behind the desk and walked into the file room. I asked her if she had ever heard of Reiki. She had, but didn't know much about it. Asking, if I could gently place my hands on her shoulders and invite Reiki, she said sure, but sounded unimpressed. I touched her shoulders and prayed silently, "*may all the Divine healing energy of God be focused here*". The moment my hands made contact with her shoulders she exclaimed she could feel a soothing energy moving through her entire body. I remained in quiet prayer for about twenty seconds then removed my hands. She had tears in her eyes as she profusely thanked me for sharing Reiki with her. As she gave me a quick hug, she whispered to me that all her tension was gone now. I explained to her that "*I*" had not done anything except focus and invite love in; the serenity she was feeling is a result of her own connection with her inner Divine. It was important for me to always provide the truth about healing; it's not the hands-on-healer who is restoring your health when you go in for a Reiki treatment. The Reiki practitioner is merely the vessel or conduit who maintains a loving space for clients to meet with their own God-Source and restore their own health. The more experienced the Reiki healer, the wider the channel they are for allowing love to flow in, but, ultimately I never forget who the real healer is. The end result to this few seconds of loving intent is that she picked up and sorted the papers quickly and I later heard that her report was well received. Soon thereafter additional funds were donated to our Agency.

That brief interaction of sharing Reiki, led to that counselor telling the Agency Supervisors how I impacted her through channeling Reiki; which led to the Supervisors asking me if I would be willing to offer Reiki treatments to staff & volunteers. Of course this was a dream come true for me. A room was dedicated for use within the Agency to accommodate Reiki sessions and evolved into a sacred space where staff could go to quietly meditate.

With the constant practice of kind thoughts and compassionate action my consciousness radiated peace in all areas of my life. This was now an automatic mindset, I no longer needed to apply effort to *'think'* positive or apply mindfulness exercises because now my mind functioned at this healthier level all on its' own. My intuitive knowing was amplified as a result and my clairvoyant perception more clear and accurate.

An exceptional happening occurred in the wee, early hours one morning. I woke around 1:00 a.m. feeling the need to say a prayer of protection for my daughter. I had no fear around this sensing, in fact, I didn't even wake my husband. I simply said a prayer for my daughter and went right back to sleep. The next morning I received a phone call from my daughter. She was enthusiastically telling me how last night around 1:30 a.m., as she was alone, ending her shift at the pub; a deranged, angry person burst in and attacked her. My daughter told me she had no idea where she got the strength, but suddenly she was able to physically remove the enraged person and get them outside the door. Me, I smiled and proceeded to tell my daughter of the feeling I had woken to at 1:00 a.m.; to pray for her protection.

So there it was, validation right in front of me, when I placed my intention on *how can I help* opportunities showed up all around me, even when in bed sleeping! To this day, I recall the many times prayer has intervened to assist and knowing that we can pray on behalf of others is reassuring.

Life had become a joy being partnered with a higher power and now that I trusted myself and the spirit realm, I was ready to check out more of my latent abilities. Common sense kept my feet firmly planted on the ground as I explored more in depth, around my psychic sense.

Chapter #20

FROM PSYCHOTIC TO PSYCHIC

I'D BECOME A FAMILIAR FACE at the Spiritualist Church, a member in good standing and often was there helping to set up for the Sunday service. It was with eagerness that I accepted the Ministers invitation to join the Church Board of Directors. My College training had been office administration and bookkeeping so I was interested when offered the Treasurer position. Soon enough, the Board let me stretch my creative muscle by allowing me to design posters and create tickets for upcoming events. I always loved playing with design and computer programs. That was relaxation for me. They were a great bunch of people to be meeting with for the purpose of running the Church. All were genuine, compassionate and fun loving. As a registered charitable organization we not only helped our own congregation but also individuals and families in our community. I learned much alongside my friends at the Spiritualist Church. Also, during the time I was mentally ill, the Church members kept me in their prayers. I am certain their generous and loving intentions contributed to my restored health.

Even though, I rarely tapped into spirit contact anymore, I could no longer deny the profound yearning to further explore my clairvoyant aptitude. Fact was, not using all of my natural human senses felt like something was missing.

To describe what it was like for me not applying my now healthy psychic sense, I would compare it to having a broken arm. Imagine having your arm broken, casted for a long time and unable to use your arm until it completely healed. Then one day you realize the arm is like new and usable once again, so the cast comes off. Now consider your arm as being a strong capable arm; but you don't use it? It was like that. I no longer had a broken mind, my spirit was renewed and so was my extrasensory perception.

Recognizing my God given senses, I began attending various workshops for the purpose of developing my Mediumship. For those that may not know what Mediumship is, it is a form of communication between physical and non-physical beings. In Mediumship our goal is to provide factual evidence of who the spirit person is, to prove existence of the eternal soul. Mediums do not predict future events, we do not mind read and truly we are not meant as entertainment. What Mediums do is offer validation that your loved one has survived the death of their physical body. The thing about me, with my background of mental illness, I became cautious about whose classes I went into. Over the years I had seen how many *quack-a-doodles* are out there promoting themselves as experts. I prefer my teachers to be sound of mind. These days, I knew to search out people with credentials that had been around long enough that I could check out their experience and skills. I trusted my Minister's mediumship classes, having seen her skill level at providing accurate proof of spirit contact, consistently. Also, there were many world renowned mediums that came to town, some were Tutors from the England based Stansted College. Under their experienced guidance, I soon became very proficient with my spirit communication skills. Unquestionably, I felt at home and in my element as I opened my senses more fully.

In addition to workshops, I attended years of weekly Mediumship development training within a group of dedicated people. This provided me the opportunity to explore my full potential. I soon learned the importance of discipline, discernment and responsibility. Through providing proof of the continued existence of our spirit, I noticed how profoundly this helped the people who came for readings. Some people connected more deeply with their belief of God. Others were helped to get in touch with their grief and move towards acceptance. Then there were some who felt encouraged to live their own life more fully.

I felt humbled to be a part of helping people this way. It became very apparent as to how healing it is to reunite people with their loved ones who had crossed over to spirit. As in providing counseling sessions for clients I was equally mindful with people coming for clairvoyant readings; encouraging people to not become dependent on coming back too often. My school of thought was to help people live their lives without relying on constant proof of the spirit realm.

Over the years, a few times, people have asked to hire me for their home parties and do readings for their guests. I do have friends, who are very skilled psychics, who provide psychic readings at parties. Most certainly they do good work through this means. For me, it never felt comfortable that I provide readings this way. My preference is to access spirit communication while in a quiet, private atmosphere. In my experience, the people I've been providing mediumship readings for tend to require privacy to express their emotions. Whether a private reading, or a group party, one way is not better than the other. Clairvoyant readers just need to honour their inner knowing and do what feels best for them.

Currently, my calendar was definitely full of everything I loved; counseling sessions with clients, secretarial work, Reiki treatments, Mediumship readings, and helping on the Agency Board and also the Church Board. There was plenty of time for family, friends and fun too. Amazingly, I had more than enough time and energy to do everything I wanted. Most likely it was due to following my passion. As long as you're pursuing your anointed path, you'll have energy and time to spare.

My secret was that I no longer said yes to anything that didn't light up my heart. *"No thanks, I need to be elsewhere"*, was an important statement I said often. I kept all my evenings and weekends free to indulge in what I call self care.

Delicious foods, afternoon naps, a good book, movies, hikes and often I'd take off and spend a night or two on a spiritual retreat. Life was now relaxing, fun and I had several outlets for expressing my creative nature. My journey just kept getting better and better.

During my exploration and development of suppressed talents along with embracing my new found independence, I'd lost sight of Ron. He must have felt shell shocked; here I went from insecure cling-on to outgoing career woman zooming along with happiness.

One day, I had a long hard look at our relationship and it scared me. Ron was not interested in the same pursuits as me. I invited him on retreats, to Church, to the Agency social gatherings, to sweat lodges, walks; none of these activities held his attention. But at the same time he was inviting me on his fishing trips, camping trips, work excursions and I had no interest in his stuff either. Sometimes, even when Ron booked flights or drove back to his home town to visit family, most often I didn't go. Not because I didn't want to see family, but due to me already being enrolled in either classes or retreats. If I canceled those pre-paid commitments, I would not receive a refund of money. Besides that, I just knew I needed to be in those group activities, for my continued well being. Ron and I could have planned the timing better, so we could both vacation, but for whatever reason Ron's work schedule seemed to clear when my calendar was full.

With some sadness, I started feeling like I was missing out on a part of life I could never get back; spending time with my own husband. Oh NO, not good!

Here's what Ron and I did to make it better though; I bought a book called 'The Five Love Languages' written by Dr. Gary Chapman. We learned to speak each other's language and found activities that we could share in common. When you love someone as much as we adore each other, you make it work. Movies and popcorn, drives to visit old friends, walking the dogs and hiking, meals together, oh and Potluck parties at our home; we began playing together in these activities. Our friendship deepened. Not to make it sound all *bliss and no blahs*, I will say, as in any long term relationship; we had our occasional battles. With Ron's patience and my grit we were a good balance for each other regardless of the dips and corners. Before long we were both back in sync, taking the dips and corners of life gently and together. Once again, we had become supportive towards each other.

It's with reverence that I recall the day Ron approached me saying he'd like me to teach him the technique of Reiki healing. I was astonished and overjoyed at the same time. With Ron and six women in my class, it was my privilege to share the healing practice of Reiki. As they allowed their *inner healer* to surface, we all deepened and widened our compassionate nature. In the process, we became more able to project love towards all aspects of our life.

Ron and I practiced mindfulness which helped us remain conscious of one another. Balance within our relationship was enhanced as a result.

Respecting my-self meant staying within my boundaries of integrity. As these years of good health continued it became more and more evident that I was out-of-integrity considering I was keeping a huge secret. When you hide anything from view, eventually it erodes your self esteem. Regardless, I wasn't ready to step out of the closet just yet and talk about my experience with mental illness. Fear stopped me from sharing the knowledge I held. My fright was of being asked to leave the Agency and no longer being accepted as part of their team of helpers and I was also frightful that the people seeking me out for healing sessions would stop coming because they'd assume I was still mentally ill. Coming clean meant taking a big risk and perhaps having to deal with huge, undesired change.

Someone, a long while back, told me it is SELFISH if we have something to tell that could benefit others and we don't pass it on. Still, for the time being, I remained silent.

Chapter #21

THE WISDOM OF CHOCOLATE

W HEN AT THE COUNSELING AGENCY and in session with people, it was a strict policy that we must never accept gifts from appreciative clients. On occasion tokens of gratitude were offered and in these times I would respectfully quote the Agencies policy. There was one exception to this policy that I was ever so grateful of because, to me, turning away someone's gift was an act of disregard. The exclusion was: gifts could be accepted as long as the client was agreeable that all staff would be the recipients of their generosity. In every situation, calling for this to be said, clients were happy to know their present was honored and shared amongst all.

The reason I'm explaining the gift policy and exception to the rule is to better describe a gift giving scenario that took place between a client and my-self. After the eighth counseling session the client was ready to end meeting with me. To my surprise she offered a gift basket as a means to express her gratitude of having a safe place to share her intimate story. Explaining the policy and the exception, this client was happy to know everyone at the Agency would be able to enjoy the treats contained in the basket she had thoughtfully put together. As I said my goodbyes and walked her through the common area, I raised the basket to place it on the front desk. That was when my eye caught sight of a large bar of white chocolate wrapped in cellophane and tied with a beautiful blue ribbon. I could see this white chocolate was of high quality because it was stamped with a crest and wrapped so eloquently. Being a chocoholic, of course I took that white chocolate bar out of the basket before setting it on the front desk. I'm quick when it comes to decadent treats.

It wasn't easy waiting until the end of the day to bite into that bar! Hungry and tired after a good days work, I got into my vehicle, pulling the white chocolate treasure from my purse. With great care and anticipation I began to unwind the cellophane from that innocent looking treat. Thinking of the generosity and thoughtfulness of the person who provided the gift basket, I promptly chomped into the chocolate with a giant bite. Immediately I was wishing I had not done this. The bar was not white chocolate; it was a bar of fancy white soap! If you've never had to pick waxy soap out of your teeth, you won't be able to comprehend the bitter, nasty, lingering taste of soap that remained with me most of the night. Lesson learned, sniff first.

Geez, I thought I'd graduated a long time ago from that class of, *don't cram anything in your mouth before sniffing.* The memory is still far too fresh in my mind from when I attended a classy house party where there was a long table set up with desserts, cheeses, meat dishes, salads and what I thought was decadent homemade chocolates. Of course, looking like chocolate, I popped one over my lips, expecting the smooth chocolate to melt in my mouth. Well, apparently raw fish wrapped in seaweed doesn't melt. There was no napkin in my hand or nearby and there were lots of people standing next to me. I politely chewed. It was a hard lesson, choking down fishy bits.

What is it with me and chocolate I wondered? One thing came to mind. It was the dear memory of sharing chocolate with my Dad when I was a child. He used to take chocolate bars in his lunch kit and as I got old enough to realize this, I began sneaking into his pre-packed lunch and taking the bar, devouring it greedily. Soon Dad put a stop to me taking his whole treat; as he enjoyed that chocolate during his coffee break at work. Being rather creative though, I devised an ingenious way to indulge in Dad's chocolate bars. Taking the bar, carefully unwrapping it, cutting the chocolate in half, eating what I considered my portion and then re-wrapping the remaining chocolate bar, strategically stuffing the empty half with paper filler. Back in the sixties chocolate bars were easy to unfold and put back together without any notice.

Eventually Dad began trying to outsmart me. He would hide his chocolate bar somewhere in the house and take it just as he was walking out the door to work. Ah, but, he'd forgotten I have good radar for finding what I want! All too often Dad would go to his hiding spot only to discover a crumpled up, empty, chocolate wrapper. Sometimes I was generous and left him almost half of the chocolate bar. To me it was open season on Dad's treats!

We never grew tired of this chocolate war, even after I married, Dad kept trying his best to stump me. Such was the time I went over to visit my parents, knowing they had just gotten back from staying with relatives who lived in the United States. As customary, Dad brought back the famed Frango mints from their vacation. They were the best tasting treat I'd ever come across. He said he'd hidden them so well, I'd never find them. Then he added *if* I found them, I could keep the whole bag. I sat across the table from Dad, glancing around the areas I could see. My eyes rested on the bulletin board near their phone. There was a tiny key pinned on that board. I wondered what that key was for. Then my eyes scanned the living room and paused on a decorative unique coin bank, it had a mini chain and lock wrapped across it. Oh ya, that key fit the lock and inside were all his Frango mints. I tossed him one on my way out the door with my loot.

Not to go on and on reminiscing of all the many times Dad's treats were pilfered by me, I'll simply say, fondest memories remain close to my heart and there isn't a time, I bite into chocolate, when I don't think about my Dad.

Ha! Wondering if Dad didn't help strengthen my psychic muscle back then; Chocolate being a great motivator.

Chapter #22

MEDICATION FREE

C HOCOLATE AND ALL THE SILLY fun aside, on October 26th, 2002, a very serious decision was made by me, as I took my first step to lower my psychiatric medication.

There were no more fears of psychotic episodes because I knew with certainty my inner work and applied effort had indeed changed my consciousness from one of illness to one of health. This was not a whimsical *knowing of wellness*, based on a short term phase of feeling well. No, no, this time I had spent the past four years noticing my responses to stressful and challenging occurrences in my life. Upon experiencing consistently that I handled every aspect of my life by staying in the present moment, showed me the new level of conscious awareness I had achieved.

Yes I was still on medication, the dose was 1000 mg of Valproic Acid (Epival) daily, yet at no time did depression, euphoria, paranoia or any form of delusion break into my thinking, anymore. From past situations, I knew the mental illness was regularly pushing past the medication and spiking my brain chemistry into psychosis; this no longer was the case. The difference now was that my thinking, my emotions, even my physical activities and spiritual life were all in balance. No more crazy brain. Just plain living life and being able to easily embrace whatever came up throughout my days was all the proof I needed. I did not require medication in my system any longer.

There was even an image I created in my mind, to strengthen my resolve. Within my mind's eye I'd think about being an elderly woman in my nineties, rocking in a chair on my front porch and saying to myself one of two possible things;

> ONE; *you did it Ann. You ended the cycle of mental illness within your body, got off all the medication and remained well. Good on you!*

> TWO; *even though you didn't break the cycle of mental illness Ann, good on you for trying to heal when you were young and strong enough to endure another psychotic episode. You haven't failed, because at least you tried.*

You might wonder why I would need to strengthen my resolve if I actually believed I was well. The reason being; over the many years of being a mental patient, I'd heard all the professionals tell me if I felt better it was only as a result of the medication working AND if I ended my medicine therapy, they all assured me my psychosis would return. My 'it-se-bit-se' fears lingered because of hearing this repeated to me over the past nine years. It took courage for me to let go and put my own belief of wellness to the ultimate test.

Earlier in the week, approaching my Doctor and asking for his assistance to lower my current dosage of mood stabilizer, was denied. A concerned, *Why Not,* was my plea. Reminding the Doctor that I had already been taken off the antipsychotic and sedative medications, without incident, I was certain He would change his mind and help me lessen the remaining medication. I was currently taking 1000 mg of Epival and my hope was to lower that dose under my Doctors supervision. To my disappointment, the Doctor was not in favour of this and proceeded to tell me all the reasons why it was too risky. He had no doubt I would end up in another psychotic episode and I had no doubt I would remain well on a lesser dosage. Seemed we were at a stalemate. His final comment to me was that I should go back and talk with a psychiatrist and if a specialist agreed to attempt lowering the Epival, then he would support me to do so.

In all fairness to this Doctor, I understood his reasons for not cutting back on my measurement of Epival; after everything he'd seen me go through! Thanking him kindly for his advice, regarding the psychiatrist, I walked away from the appointment knowing the support needed would not be found in a psychiatric office. Past experience taught me that common psychiatric methods, only encouraged remaining on medication. My feeling was that I needed people around me that would believe in my wellness and support my choice to lower medication.

After careful consideration, I decided to attend the next support group for those afflicted with mental illness. It had been several years since I had met with this group, but I recalled it being a place where other patients encouraged each other. Although there was a psychiatrist that facilitated the group, it was an open, casual forum. There were people of various ages, numerous social backgrounds that included both men and women. My hope was to hear optimistic words from others. My outlook was that perhaps some people in this group may have successfully lessened their medication or had gotten completely off their prescription.

When first diagnosed, back in 1993, this monthly group became a safe haven for me to express myself amongst people who could relate to my experience. At this present point in time, I did not feel backed from anyone there. The support group unanimously tried to discourage me from entertaining the thought of lowering my medication. The psychiatrist present remained quiet until near the end of the group's effort to convince me of the many dangers. I finally stopped attempting to share with them of the inner work and transformation I had moved through. It seemed no one could hear me or maybe they just didn't believe me? Everyone was now sitting quieter in their seats and the Doctor took this opportunity to speak. He asked one of the men patients present if he would be willing to share with me his experience of going off his psychiatric medication. This particular man had been quiet throughout the group and now he leaned forward in his chair, eyes sincerely gazing into mine as he said, *"Ann, I too felt I had done all the inner work and that I had succeeded in healing all aspects of my chemical imbalance. After asking my psychiatrist to help me lower medication to the point of getting right off of it, he agreed to walk me step by step and support me to do so. My Doctor is sitting right here with us."* he smiled and gestured towards the psychiatrist facilitating this group, then continued *"He held my hand through the entire process, which took a few months. Then the day came where I was able to stop taking all medication. I remained well for exactly twelve days. Nearing two weeks of no medication in my system, my psychosis returned and I had to be hospitalized. It took a long time to find the right dosage again, to manage my illness. I just want you to know, be aware of the risk involved and ask yourself is it really worth taking that chance?"*

Upon hearing this, I wanted to ask him if he had covered all aspects before reducing medication. Not wanting to upset the apple cart, I didn't ask if he had included developing a strong foundation within his spiritual nature. He may or may not have, I don't know; but the one thing for sure that I did know is that I had.

In appreciation of his candor and the whole group's participation to offer me their perspective on this matter; I went home to digest the possible risks. It didn't take long for me to realize my desire to end medication superseded any concerns other people had raised.

**JUST FOR THE RECORD; I do not suggest anyone
who is taking Doctor prescribed medication to
ever lower their dosage, on their own accord.**

My forty-fourth birthday was only five days away when, as a gift to myself, I lowered my mood stabilizing medication for the first time. This was done in secrecy, not even Ron knew. Medication went from 1000 mg of Epival to 750 mg.

I stayed at this dosage for eleven months. October 28, 2002 had been my start day and it was now September, 2003.

Given that I was remaining well, I wanted to lower the medication a bit more. But first, this time, I confided in two close friends. After stating my intention to decrease psychiatric medication, they agreed to be my support team. The reason I chose them as my confidants was because both had spiritual awareness, were Reiki Practitioners and they were also trained in medical knowledge; one was a paramedic and the other a midwife.

The second lowering of medication took me from 750 mg of Epival down to 500 mg. Ron still did not know of my lesser dose. After what he had gone through, as a result of the severity of my mental illness, I was afraid he would try to intervene and stop me.

Since I couldn't blame him for possibly expecting the worse, I decided to wait and tell him when my medication was no longer therapeutic. That way I believed he would see firsthand that I was sound of mind without medication. Still not telling my Doctor what was going on, for obvious reasons, I continued decreasing the Epival dose. This was done with care and very slowly over a period of years. I most certainly was in no rush.

Staying at 500 mg. of Epival for the next five months was easy. I was diligent about taking that quantity every day. It was important to me. Being gentle on my body, mind and spirit during this process of ending medication, was essential. Frequently I chatted with my support friends and felt grateful to be able to share my success with someone.

February 2004, marked the date I lower the dosage again. Going from 500 mg down to 250 mg felt satisfying to me. Cutting the Epival down in my system this much, clearly, it was no longer of a therapeutic value. This was when I entrusted Ron and brought him into my confidence. Surprisingly he was on board with my choice and proud of the courage it took for me to progress in my health.

Every couple of months I was supposed to go into my Doctor office and get a renewal prescription along with a blood test to keep an eye on my Epival level.

As it so happened, my Doctor was off on holiday a lot and I was mostly seeing his fill in associates. Lucky for me they were not paying close attention and no one asked me why I wasn't coming in for regular medication refills. Thing is, with cutting my medication down so much, I had lots of Epival to spare so I didn't need to get as many refills. I wasn't hiding what I was doing. At any time a Doctor could have noticed in my medical history that I was not coming in for those refills or blood tests. So I went about taking care of myself, knowing if anyone asked I would tell the truth.

April 7, 2004, approximately one and a-half years of lowering my Epival dose had already gone by. I booked an appointment with my regular Doctor, who was actually in the office this time. His greeting was always the same, *"How goes the battle, Ann?"* I used to always reply *"pretty good"*. This time I replied *"I'm great, no more battle"*. He looked surprised as he invited me to tell him more. So I did, I told him everything. Then I waited for his response. He quietly flipped through some papers in my file. I waited. When he was ready he spoke in an even, calm voice and proceeded to remind me of the dangers of lowering my psychiatric medication on my own. He talked to me of the previous psychotic breaks that required hospitalization. Then he implored me to raise my medication level back up to a therapeutic range.

Slipping through the medical cracks, unnoticed for quite some time, I explained to the Doctor that I had absolutely no intention to increase my medication. Pointing out my success, with less medication, and recapping our previous patient/doctor talk, I expressed how obvious it seemed that I would have to do it without his support. My sincere apologies were stated too as I recognized his good intensions towards me. When it sunk in and my Doctor more fully understood the precautions and responsibility I took for myself, he seemed to appreciate what I had done. Sharing with him, the good support team I surrounded myself with and my cautiousness in lowering my dosage ever so slowly, gained the Doctors respect.

Nearing the end of my appointment, we both agreed that 250 mg of Epival was good as long as I remained well. I promised I'd follow through on regular blood tests and have more frequent follow up appointments. The Doctor smiled as I stood up and reached for the door knob to leave, he then asked that I not lower the Epival any further; that I did not promise.

August 2004, it had been a solid four months staying at 250 mg of Epival. I kept my promise to my Doctor, doing follow up appointments and regular blood work more often. But when I felt it was time to lower my dose yet again, I did not ask his permission, I simply made an executive decision. I lowered again and was now at 150 mg.

Remaining well, on my next check-in visit, I told my Doctor of the more recent lowered dose. He was clearly not pleased with my choice, yet, he concurred that I had indeed not suffered a psychotic break. He did tell me he was glad that I had common sense to include Ron and two friends that had some medical knowledge. The Doctor then asked me if he could have my permission to talk with Ron. This request told me that my Doctor sincerely wanted the best for me. I saw his request as taking an active part to ensure my health. Ron's meeting with my Doctor went extremely well, it put my Doctor at ease and I noticed he was much more supportive in my efforts to get off medication after that meeting with my husband.

February 2005, Now that I had stayed at 150 mg of Epival for six months with no problems, I wondered *'what am I waiting for?'* Yet, I didn't feel ready to let go of that imagined safety net. Instead of stopping the medication altogether, I cut the half of a pill in half again to make the dose 75 mg. Silly really, the medication was definitely not making a difference in my system at this tiny dosage. Fear, that's all it was, that voice of doubt lingered.

August 2005, another six months gone by, I chipped the tiny bit of medication and took what I think might have been about 37 mg of Epival. Somewhere in my psyche I was carrying around all the warnings from past Doctors and well meaning family and friends. Their voices were echoing in my head, *"If you get off medication you will end up on the psychiatric ward, ill again."* Their fear was only mirroring my own self doubt, that's why I still hung onto that tiny crumb of Epival.

It was hard to end the last bit of medication. Harder than I ever imagined it would be. The mind is a powerful force and what you tell yourself tends to dictate your actions. My Self talk was all about fearfully not really trusting my own judgment. The nasty *'what If's'* swirled around my brain. *What if* I'm wrong and the mental illness comes back when I end medication all together? *What if* I'm fooling myself into believing my chemical makeup has changed but really it hasn't? *What if* the professionals are right and it's only a matter of time before another cycle of bipolar disorder strikes me? So, with all that bull-crap in my mind, I continued taking 37 mg of Epival, for nine months longer. My close friends all emphatically tried to convince me to let go and trust completely, but I wasn't quite ready yet.

My long time Doctor had retired before I dropped that 37 mg, but at least he knew I had whittled it down that low and remained mentally healthy. It was my new Doctor who read through my medical history, interviewed me and then encouraged me to let go the last bit of Epival. She sympathetically assured me that medication was not in the least, keeping me well. Her gentle reminder that it was only an incorrect, psychological attachment keeping me on Epival 'dust' that finally helped me *put my big girl panties on* and free myself.

May 31, 2006 was the first day in thirteen years that I was medication free. From the start of lowering Epival through to getting completely off this medication, took three years and seven months.

The reason I chose May 31, as my medication free start date, was because that had been my Dad's birthday. This was a significant date which I would never forget.

When I was a child my Dad would sometimes say, *"The nut never falls too far from the tree."* Usually I heard that remark when playfully acting silly. He liked to tease and remind me that I come by my twisted sense of humour honestly.

There was a different reference about nuts and trees I had heard him say once, which deep down remained with me throughout all these years; *"The Mighty Oak grows from the nut that stands its ground."*

I sent my Dad a thought this 31st day in May of 2006, *"Hey Dad, this Nut stood her ground and I'm growing into that Mighty Oak!"*

There's only one thing that can ever really stand in our way and that would be, **our own thoughts.** When I couldn't trust my own at least I could trust in the, Divine Intelligent Consciousness; that was far beyond my own.

Chapter #23

SOARING

ONSIDERING IT TOOK ME NEARLY four years to get off all psychiatric medication, there was much that happened during that time frame. Like a momentous and rapid learning curve, my comfort zone expanded as a result of the new experiences.

It seemed the Counseling Agencies Supervisor saw potential in me, as she encouraged me to take on more responsibilities in the Agency. Enjoying every aspect of my work I soon decided it was time to *kick-it-up-a-notch*, so I studied more advanced counseling skills through additional classes. Before long, I was seeing not only individuals but couples, groups and teaching self esteem workshops through the Agency.

In my past, I had never even entertained the idea of helping others in this capacity. Most importantly, my work and studies were helping me to further know myself. I could now embrace the freedom of expressing myself without fear.

Nothing is impossible! My early years' right up through adulthood had me paralyzed with fear. I saw myself as weak, stupid, ugly and believed myself to be mentally ill. Therefore I was. Wow, so it's true what the Bible says, *'As a man thinks so he is!'* There are many books written that support this very truth. What you THINK about yourself; that is who you are or will soon become.

When I couldn't see anything worthy in myself the only thing left was for me to fall into God's love. Sobbing and trusting. Letting go of trying to impress others or be like them, provided me the peace to simply accept myself as is. Knowing that I am a child of Gods, good enough as I am.

In essence, even though I couldn't see anything good about myself back then, I just *believed* that God accepted me. That started to ball rolling to change my thinking. I saw myself THROUGH DIVINE EYES, which eventually led to greater joy in living.

Along the way, it became evident I was beginning to expand into a whole new skill. Being invited as guest speaker through various organizations such as the Counseling Agency, Heart and Stroke Foundation, Spiritualist Church, College Class and Awareness Center; helped me make the decision to peek in on a group called *Toast Masters*. They are highly regarded for helping people to develop aptitude in public speaking. Although I didn't stay with *Toast Masters* long, the few weeks I participated, my confidence improved tremendously.

Another way my public speaking improved and developed into a level of comfort, beyond what I imagined I could ever attain, was learned through my Church. After the past few years of allowing my natural abilities of spirit communication to flourish, I was soon invited to do inspirational speaking through the Church. This meant I was also required to provide proof, of life after death, through my mediumship. This platform work was pleasant to me. I felt serenity as I tapped into and spoke on matters of uplifting inspiration. The aspect of mediumship helped me to clearly view how healing it is to provide people with accurate evidence of loved ones in spirit world.

Quite often it was not just people that came through to communicate from spirit, animals communicated with me too. One such time, that impacts me to this day, was during a public demonstration of clairvoyance I was part of, alongside three other established Mediums. As soon as I stood up to connect with spirit world and provide evidence, I immediately witnessed a spirit dog running towards a woman in the audience. As customary, I first asked this woman for permission to share the spirit communication that was coming through. Upon her invitation to continue I stated, *"There is a large breed black dog beside you, He is appearing young and vibrant yet I sense he passed as an older dog, yet died unexpectedly. Do you recognize this dog I've described and how he died?"* She did know the dog and became emotional. Asking if she'd like me to continue and hearing a yes, I stated, *"This dog is a combination between black lab and a healer."* The woman burst into tears exclaiming enthusiastically that indeed her dog was a cross between a black lab and a blue healer. I was thankful she had a friend sitting next to her that was consoling her as I continued, *"This vibrant dog of yours is bringing my attention to his brown leather dog collar and wanting you to know that he appreciates that you have kept it, but also conveyed to me that it's time for you to 'let it go'. Does this make any sense to you?"* After she took a couple deep breaths, she bravely shared that indeed she did keep his leather collar and told me she felt the dog died because the collar was too tight. Upon hearing this and realizing the depth of healing this dog was providing, I continued,

"Please understand and let these words settle into your heart, YOU did not keep the collar too tight. This dog passed-on of complications through old age. YOU DID NOT HARM YOUR DOG." Both of us took a moment to wipe tears from our eyes as we gratefully thanked her dog for providing this level of comfort. As her grief shifted, even from the platform I could see relaxed joy in her eyes. Her last comment was, *"I always wore his collar snug and it had never been a problem, but I kept wondering if it played a part in his death. I needed to hear this today. Thank you, I feel so much better now"*.

This natural ability, all of us have, of spirit communication is through the grace of God. I know many people will understand what I mean by the above comment. It's all about having a strong foothold or foundation in knowing LOVE and setting an intention for Gods truth, evidence and uplifting assistance to come through.

This feels like a good place for me to speak directly to an issue I've heard uttered at me from a small group of people. These individuals have condemned me for accessing spirit communication. They have told me I am channeling evil or tied to immoral, wicked ways. I want to acknowledge my respect towards them for standing strong in their belief and their understanding of who God is. I also appreciate that they are being sincere in their efforts to *help* me. It is easy for me to completely accept that they mean well toward me. Within my acceptance of how others choose to believe, I also commend myself for standing strong in knowing God the way I do. Regardless of threats and judgment from people, at the end of the day, I feel at peace between myself and God; and so must we all. No longer do I seek approval from people, especially when it comes to my spirituality. For sure, it didn't used to be that way, though.

When I was confused, intimidated and trying to be 'the good girl' there was a long period of time I tried to ignore my natural abilities and follow other people's beliefs; that professed using our sixth sense as bad. Quite honestly, after a while, it felt like a sin against God for me to ignore my awareness of all levels of life that surround us. How I reconciled my confusion of the big question, *is it okay to speak to spirits?* I referred to my Bible. If you are a person looking to develop your mediumship (spirit communication) the Bible happens to be one of the best guide books ever! It warns of the dangers associated with false prophets and spirit beings that are capable of fooling us. Yet, the Bible also records many time's where spirit contact assisted people.

As a result of my own research and personal experience with mediumship I quickly determined that indeed there are cautions we must use. You have to know the rules of the road in order to drive safely. Rule number one that I follow; absolutely no spirit contact until you've developed a strong relationship with Creator God. My thought on it, is to follow the ABC's of spirit communication;

A= Absolutely (in alignment with),

B= Beloved,

C= Creator.

Aside from learning to be more comfortable in my own beliefs and walking to the beat of my own tambourine, many other new encounters happened along the way. The dearest to my heart is when I learned to be a grandmother!

My grandson was born in October of 2005. I was there for his arrival and as his Dad laid his blanket wrapped, wee body into my arms, I welcomed him with murmurs of love. Another level of gratitude filled me, not just because I was holding my Grandson but because I appreciated, that in my mental wellness, I would be a competent, loving Grandma to this beautiful child.

By the time I met my son-in-law my mental illness was non-existence, so he never witnessed my torrents of psychosis. Oh but, my son and daughter had witnessed a lot of peculiar behaviour from me, when I was in episodes of mental illness. Had I remained unbalanced I would have missed out on being a participating and responsible Mom to them now. My kids watched my transition from weirdness to wellness, thus, their trust of me was now intact and undamaged. Their restored respect was apparent to me when they sought out my opinion on matters in their life. My certainty that I was completely trusted by all my family was when I had been given the privilege of babysitting my Grandson. He and I would have play dates together as I cinched up his car seat belt and took off on day trips. Pushing him in his stroller as we took in the many sights gave me pure delight. His sweet natured baby babble caused my cheeks to hurt from smiling so much. During our overnight sleepovers I made sure it was all about the fun and of course the food!

All through the cycle of the nearly four years, while decreasing and eventually ending my psychiatric medication, many new experiences transpired. Some were challenging to the extreme. When they say *what doesn't kill you strengthens you*, believe it. The extreme trials taught me I actually could do anything I set my mind to.

Thankfully, in my life, there were many people who saw my potential and were eager to push me onward. One such person was the Minister at the Cowichan Spiritualist Church of Healing and Light. She has known me for over twenty years now and seen the devastating effects and severity of my previous mental condition. During my healing process and eventual restored health it was she that recognized my authentic spiritual abilities of inspirational channeling, spiritual healing and mediumship. With her trust in me it strengthened my belief in myself.

Another person was the professional therapist at the Counseling Agency, who was also my Supervisor. She offered me a job as her assistant, which meant I stopped working the front desk of the Agency and began doing follow up calls with clients, typing reports, matching counselors with clients, helped with counseling classes and did intake sessions with new clients.

Even when I doubted my skills, she didn't and that was enough to get me over the hump to see for myself that I was qualified.

Truthfully, sharing sessions with clients and groups taught me a lot about being unpretentious. The people I met in sessions helped me open my eyes wider and perceive life from many different angles. Depth of character comes from exploring our inner thoughts and we need each other for that.

Speaking of exploring, I expanded that to my physical activity too. I discovered a new fun exercise and joined a group of Tai Chi students. This teaching is amazing for developing concentration and building muscle strength while relaxing. Doing Tai Chi, by my-self, was not as satisfying as being in the synchronized flow of an entire class. There's something about being a part of a group, that connectedness with others.

Soaring into new adventures, experiences and challenges took its toll on my time spent with relatives. After carefully considering our busy lives, although we loved our work, Ron and I pampered ourselves to a long holiday. Twenty-one days of driving where ever our hearts took us. Our first destination was to go back to Ron's home town and visit our family. I kept my schedule clear so this time I could go with him and do some catching-up with my relatives. We ended up covering three provinces in Canada then crossed the USA boarder and explored nine States. What an adventure! Yet, nearing three weeks of being gone, I was missing the Counseling Agency, Spiritualist Church, Hospice, friends and family back on the island.

After arriving home, little did I know, my life was about to expand even further; into territory I had not yet experienced.

Soon after I returned to the Counseling Agency, my Supervisor asked me if I'd be interested to create a two hour lecture on stress management and be the presenter. The Heart and Stroke Association had requested a counselor to be a guest speaker in their Life class. My heart thumped in my chest as my old thinking crept in causing me to doubt my capability as a lecturer. Thankfully, I'd learned enough about self talk to quickly snuff out that spark of doubt and quickly accepted the opportunity to do this. Now two hours is a long time, especially for someone green, like me. I asked my Supervisor to proof read my talk and help me tweak it. When the day came for me to present my topic, I felt nervous excitement. I remember feeling my legs shake slightly as I heard the class facilitator introduce me. So what I did was immediately use humour and honesty to ease myself into this new role. The response from the class was elevating. They too could relate to what I was feeling and had a good chuckle along with me. Afterward, I got great feedback from the class and the Instructors invited me back to present in more of their classes. Through being listened to, understood and appreciated these class participants helped me feel even more bonded with people.

In the privacy of my home, the gratitude I felt brought tears to my eyes. Having experienced the earlier part of my life as a misfit and now feeling acceptance, helped me to appreciate the blessing of oneness with other inhabitants of this Earth. Never will I take for granted sharing this world with others. We need each other to motor through life and experience new aspects of ourselves. Every person is a teacher and student simultaneously. I really understand that now.

Another new territory explored was marathon walking. I'd ever done anything like this before and I decided either *'go big or go home'*. So big it was. I did my first marathon walk with 56 kilometers (36 miles) of hilly terrain. The team at the Counseling Agency had done this walk before, so they gave me great tips to prepare myself. We started at 5:00 a.m. and I finished almost twelve hours later. Part way through this lengthy walk I was met with a magnificent surprise. A friend and fellow Spiritualist had taken the time to bring a brightly coloured helium balloon to me. It's a precious memory that remains as I recall her keeping up with my stride as she tied that balloon to my arm and offered words to inspire me to the finish line. The combination of her thoughtfulness and that funky balloon, bound to my arm by a ribbon, bouncing around in the air; helped me plod on when I really wanted to crumple onto the side of the road. Oh my goodness, I was doing the shuffle as I headed towards the finish line. My muscles were painfully asking me to rest, but I pressed on and it was worth every step. There was yet another splendid surprise waiting for me. Just as I reached up and rang the signal bell to indicate I was crossing the finish line, there stood my Mom and two of her friends along with Ron. They had all come to watch me complete and celebrate my first marathon. That in itself was profoundly reinforcing. The loving hug I shared with my Mom will forever stay with me as one of the best moments in my life.

Also over this time frame, of lessening medication, Ron built an addition onto our home. This gorgeous, very large room was specifically built to support me in offering Reiki classes, clairvoyant readings, and to facilitate spiritual groups. He created the most beautiful, bright room with hardwood floors, a library and three walls of huge windows that sported an ocean view. This spoke hugely to me of his trust and respect of me. Ron had seen me at my worse and yet always seemed to bring forth my best.

In silent thought, I reflected on possible future endeavors while sitting in the newly built wellness room. Day dreaming of spiritual groups I could facilitate. For anyone, this is a good practice to plan ahead and set achievable goals; just imagining what you'd like to bring into your life. Through this means of visualizing what I would like to begin, I began spiritually coaching individuals, teaching active listening classes, teaching Reiki and hosting gatherings like the Sharing Soup Circles.

It was tremendous joy for me to facilitate groups and one-on-one sessions alike. To elaborate a little regarding the soup circle I facilitated, each participant would bring a vegetable to add to the soup stalk I had simmering in the crock pot. While the soup brewed we all went into the wellness room, sat in a circle and shared healing stories. Then we indulged in some delicious soup together.

Along the route, of imagining what I could create in my life, I came across some naysayers. They're the ones that grumble, *"It will never work"* or *"You're not authorized to do that"* and my all time favourite *"You're going to burn out and get sick again"*. If I agreed with any of these kinds of statements, then I would never have followed through on my plans. I learned to listen to MY wisdom and disregard what other people thought. Ultimately, it makes little difference on whether anyone encourages you or discourages; your success depends on what you belief about yourself. Therefore, believe the best for yourself and let that unfold.

Remembering when I used to be terrified of social gatherings, I reveled in the realization of how much I enjoy socializing now. Why the difference? Basically because I liked myself and therefore there was no pressure to impress anyone. Even though there were still many times I made some social blunders and *oh yes* there were still those people that used my slip-ups to try to embarrass me; none of it bothered me as I could only see the humour in my bungles.

When out shopping, it was clear that my adding and subtracting had not improved and I continued confusing myself when trying to make change. Yet, through being able to laugh at myself there was no problem for me around feeling embarrassed anymore. If people tried to shame me when they saw my lack of math skills, it was like water running off a good rain coat; nothing negative stuck to me.

Well established with balanced self esteem, I got up to some fun ideas and created opportunities for myself and other people to play. Ron and I formed a block party in our community. The party covered three streets and included a baseball BBQ for families. The beauty of a block party is that it involves all the neighbours, so in truth, I can't take credit for the activities as each person combined made it happen. For a while I became filled with *glee,* whatever I thought might be interesting to experience, I was all over it. As said in the popular footwear ads, "**Just Do It**".

What enabled me to live my life fully was that I always took the time in the morning and at night to center myself in prayer and then listen to my heart. Prayer was me talking with God and meditation was me listening to God. You'll feel the presence of love if you place your attention on it.

To those that say they do not have time for prayer twice a day; stop with the excuses and be honest with your-self. Prayer can happen in the morning upon waking and last for five seconds all the way up to whatever length of time you want. As well as evening prayer, that can be done as you climb into the comfort of bed. There is always time if you want it. The question to ask your-self is 'do I want to access conscious prayer' or 'do I prefer no prayer'. Do what you like and do it without guilt or excuses.

There is a popular story that has been passed around for years. It's about a young aboriginal boy asking his grandfather, *"It feels like two wolves are inside me, constantly fighting, one is good and one is evil. Please Grandfather tell me how to make them stop this fight?"* His grandfather replies, *"It is easy Grandson, simply feed the wolf you want to win, then the other wolf will starve and die."* As did mental illness, I no longer fed into it and therefore it passed away.

Knowing there are several more people that propelled me forward through their belief in me. I thank them all and wished I had enough space in one book to acknowledge each one. You all know who you are and your support and love that you've shown in many different ways has helped me change my life for the best.

Since it's not possible to talk about all of the amazing ways people have helped me, I will resolve to just share this one more. Her clairvoyant reading for me, took place during a time that I was in the thick of depression and saw very little hope for myself. She connected with the spirit world, gave me accurate evidence of people I recognized and then proceeded to tell me the disruption of my mind will be restored to peace and that I will move into doing community work that will assist others. During this time of sadness, I could never have guessed I'd be able to help others in the community and yet her prediction in this came true several years later. She also told me of a book I would write, she saw the cover and contents adding that I would be past my fiftieth year of age, before it was completed. *I was currently still in my late thirties.* She told me sharing my experience within a book would significantly help certain individuals. I can only hope that she was correct in that prediction. This session, with this medium, provided a seed planted that grew and flourished within my mind. Although she never did describe what the book was about, I have a feeling it was this one she saw coming. After all, as I send this book off to the publishers, I'm a few years past my fiftieth year of age.

Much can happen in a short time. A great deal of learning took place between the years 2002 through 2006 and I'm not even touching the tip of the ice-burg in this book. When opportunities for a new experience came along, I jumped on all of them. Fun, that's the only word to describe how it all felt to me. Fun.

For example, drumming circle caught my attention and without knowing exactly what that was, I jumped in with both feet and my hand-made, native drum. So there I am in the presence of a Master

African drummer and me not realizing the entire class are using African Djembe drums. Heck, I didn't even know what a Djembe was? Still not cluing in, as the percussion began, I merrily pounded on my traditional native drum. For those that do not know the difference between drums, like I didn't back then, Djembe drum and my drum were completely different structures. I stood out from the rest and not necessarily in an *easy on the ear* kind of way. At that time I figured it was all about spirituality and expression. So did I stop the *thud-thud-thud* when everyone looked at me kind of strangely? Of course not, I was in my groove. Apparently, I found out soon enough, this was an actual CLASS to learn HOW to play the Djembe drum. Oops. But on the other side of oops, lucky for me the Teacher had a spare Djembe to loan me and hence my first lesson in blending my drum beat in with the rest of the percussionist.

Point of interest: there was no embarrassment for me within this blunder, I and several others had a good belly laugh and carried on. Before the end of this drumming circle not only had I picked up some great tips on playing the Djembe, but I also picked up some sweet African dance moves. Our Teacher got some of the more advanced drummers' tapping out a joyous melody and the rest of us moved in unison with dance!

This from a person, me, who would have never considered dancing in front of anyone let alone perform a lively African dance in front of a class. When I was ready to view life with less seriousness, I enabled myself to play and have fun no matter the circumstances.

My thirst for new adventures inspired me to join an expression singing group. This meant we blended our voices together, without the use of instruments. I had never been comfortable singing by myself let alone in a group of people. I had never sung because I cannot carry a tune. But, when the day came for the weekly singing practice, I showed up even though I felt the fear. Long story shortened; my experience with this group was extraordinary. They helped me open up to express my voice fearlessly. Quite a healing took place, not that I am pitch perfect, yet at least I am no longer ashamed of my own voice.

While with the Counseling Agency I noticed how effective meditation and relaxation techniques were in sessions with clients. As my interest to learn more about using my breath for relaxation formed, I met a very fascinating couple. My new friends were; one, a counselor and the other a well known hypnotherapist. After reading the hypnotherapist's book and listening to several of his fabulous meditation CD's, I decided to take his classes. Through his mentoring, class material and my consistent practice I became a hypnotherapist. Although certified, I did not go on to become a registered hypnotherapist. My training and level attained did not go wasted, it deepened my own meditation practice which influenced me to offer individual and group sessions from my home wellness room. This did not feel like work to me, all of this was pure enjoyment as I developed my awareness.

Soon after hypnotherapy training, there was a distinct urging within my core that it was time for me to start my own mediumship development group. Exceptional people who wanted to explore their natural born abilities joined me weekly as we practiced our spirit communication. We developed our communication skills with both people of the physical world and non-physical. Basic counseling teaches us how to speak respectfully and how to listen compassionately and I brought this aspect into our group as a way to share spirit contact with someone who would come for a clairvoyant reading. On occasion, a reading most certainly can require the medium to access a depth of listening to help someone release past grief and loss issues.

Each person brought with them, to the mediumship group, their own individuality and experience. Some only stayed a short time while others participated weekly with me, for years. Development of spirit communication, in our group, is a sacred time of accessing the Divine Love of God present within. Once that contact and foundation is built, accurate spirit communication from loved ones was easily proven through all participants. This strengthened everyone's faith of God's existence and gave us tangible proof that our souls do progress after the death of our physical body. It was never about messages in our group, more so it was about learning how we can be in service to assist others, through our mediumship.

Words can't describe the gratitude I feel towards the many people I've met on this side of the veil and the other side. Simply put; physical friends and spirit friends.

Along my path, I spent much time participating in workshops where I could learn different perspectives of seeing life. One group that I ended up co-facilitating through the Agency was '*Parenting after divorce or separation*'. It was through a chance meeting with one of the *Child and Family* Therapists, in the Agency file room, that spurred my interest. She was an experienced professional that I'd come to highly regard. When she offered to take me under her wing and bring me into her parenting group, I have to admit I felt intimidated. Here I'd been married for well over twenty years, there was no divorce or separation within any of my close family members and I wondered how I would be able to fit with this group. Upon sharing my thoughts with the Therapist, she smiled knowingly at me and told me it could be helpful for this group to meet someone who is in a long term relationship. She added that perhaps I could bring a whole new aspect to the group, giving hope that relationships can thrive. Setting my doubts aside I attended the group and stayed for two years as a group facilitator. Much growth happened for me during this group that opened my eyes to appreciate the many different ways to face personal challenges. It was saddening that this group ended due to lack of Agency funding, yet no one gave up hope that perhaps through effort, money could be raised to create another group down the road.

Many other types of groups drew my attention; I was like a kid in a candy store, wanting to participate in them all. Of course that wasn't realistic being that there are only limited hours in a day! Following my interests, I chose activities, classes and retreats being mindful of maintaining balance in all areas of my life; emotional, mental, physical and spiritual.

The best way to express what these years felt like to me is, FREEDOM. Giving myself permission to do what I wanted fearlessly.

Chapter #24

ACCEPTANCE OF CHALLENGES

WHAT WOULD LIFE BE WITHOUT challenges? Possibly life would then be Heaven. Remarkably, I've learned that my own personal heaven can be experienced even in the middle of a crisis. For me, it is all relevant to my state of mind. My perception of *Personal Heaven* is a place inside myself where I feel calm, centered and capable; no matter what is going on in my world. I attain this place of serenity through intentional prayer combined with faith.

It was a shock, to all my family and friends, when I got a call from Ron's employee telling me they'd taken Ron to Hospital. He had suffered a heart attack and landed in the intensive care unit. Ron is my closest friend, my Husband and my Rock. If there is such a thing as *Soul Mates,* we are. The thought of losing him, felt unbearable. My focused prayers remained constant and through that stance I was able to maintain my center of peace. I knew Ron's health was completely out of my control, yet I held strong knowing if he still had more to do on this earth, God's love would assist him to be well. In my personal heaven I was able to acknowledge the reality of Ron's physical illness and stay calm in order to be helpful where I could. Remaining at peace also afforded me the ability to feel into my sadness of Ron's condition. Just because I felt at peace did not mean I didn't experience the swelling of emotions that required releasing. Better *out* than *in*, I often say. Suppress anything and it can hurt you whereas allowing the tears to flow provides release and relief.

What a day of celebration when I got word that Ron could come home! Ron told me he recognized his heart event as a wakeup call, a second chance. I too felt that way. We had a look at what areas in our lives needed tweaking. The one area that stood out for both of us was our eating habits. Since we both worked outside of the home, we had become too reliant on restaurant food and when we did eat at home I was indulging our taste buds with fatty sauces and sugary treats. The Universe provides us opportunities when we make up our minds. Ron and I decided to make better nutrition choices and within twenty-four hours of making that choice, someone inadvertently gave us information about a four month nutrition class about to start. We signed up and attended. By the end of those classes we were both leaner and energized. Ron took up bike riding and I continued with my walking.

Challenges aren't always life threatening or tragic, as in the case of planning a wedding. Although this celebration took place a few years prior, I mention it as an example.

For a long time, I've heard people say, *'instead of spending all that money on a fancy wedding, just give the money to the couple so they can have a good start'*. I couldn't disagree more. I absolutely thank my daughter and son-in-law for choosing the traditional tux and white dress wedding. The planning of this event created closeness and happy memories for all involved; worth every penny. One of my favorite moments at the reception was when my daughter took me into the ladies room and was very concerned because one of the waiters had accidentally stepped on her gown as she walked by the food table and the dress's train tore away from the gown. It was quite obvious too. You might be wondering why this horrid tearing of the gown was a favorite moment. The reason being, I then understood why I had tucked several safety pins on the inside fold of my gown. Within minutes I had her dress all pinned and no one could see there had ever been a problem. Ron and I danced the night away. I believe we were the last ones to leave! Stress can be beneficial to influence forward movement, especially when you see the humour in events.

As we age, it's the memories we create along the way that will keep us company. Keeping this upper most in my mind, I do my best to create as many happy memories as possible. My great-aunt Mary lived to be 103 years old, with longevity in my family I plan to have several truck loads of enjoyable memories to reflect on.

It's always a blessing to experience times of celebrating new beginnings and I learned that there are also blessings to be found in the grief of saying goodbye.

A dear friend, who died of bone cancer, taught me how to enjoy life no matter what challenge you're facing. While she was in hospital, bed ridden and on oxygen, she planned her own wedding. She was wheeled down the Hospital chapel isle wearing an heirloom white lace wedding gown. Later her husband drove her to their home where she greeted every guest at their reception and then went back to Hospital. I spent much time at the Hospital with her and always she was creating fun in her life, even though she knew her time was limited. She was usually playing board games, cards, putting together a scrap book for her family or writing her book. This is where I was able to be of assistance, book writing, since I was good at dictation and a fast typist.

Before my friend died, she got to see her book in print. I had followed her instructions carefully for the cover of the book and printed several copies off my printer, then used my office page binder to finish the book. Each of her close family members, pleasantly surprised to receive a copy, let me know through their appreciativeness how much they treasured having her story in their hands. This courageous friend, who left this earth far too young, showed me through her faith and courage, that we must live adventurously no matter what is going on in our life. With her spiritual awareness, she knew beyond any doubt that she was leaving her pain filled body to be in Gods' presence. She experienced Heaven before leaving this physical world because of her attitude.

Even when it came time to pay bills in our household, I never grumbled, I was grateful that the businesses granted us credit to pay later. Looking at everything as blessings, at least trying to look for the silver lining, kept both Ron and I happily moving through life's trials.

Unexpectedly, a difficult time of opposition came as a result of a woman who was close to my family. She abruptly decided I was no longer welcome to be a part of her life. She cut not only me out, but also Ron and our two children. It was a huge shock for me initially because suddenly this person was yelling at me, telling me what an awful person I was. This was not her typical behaviour; she had never uttered an unkind word towards me before. Usually she was caring and easy to get along with. This particular day, she was so incredibly angry at me that I begged her to stop putting me down or she risked damaging our relationship. That got me more of the same rage. I tried everything I could think of to ease her anger. Asking what had I done and how can I make things better? Through her blasts of blame it sounded to me as if she thought I had intentionally tried to upset her in the recent past. With her suddenly perceiving me as her enemy I wondered if maybe she was going through an anxiety attack or rage due to depression. What confused me is that I had consistently been very good to her. Taking her shopping, to appointments and spending time visiting with her. I thought everything was great between us. To my knowledge, I had not said or taken any action, that I was aware of, that would warrant this sudden hatred towards me? My reasoning mind searched for a logical shred of truth that would help me understand her sudden disliked of me and my family. This mental state she was in lasted longer than I believed it could. She would not take our phone calls nor would she allow us into her home to talk this out. Only she knew why she was angry, the rest of us consoled our hurts by accepting she was no longer associated with us and we moved on to focus on living our lives.

To say this woman did not cause hurt to my family and I, through her shutting us out without any explanation or willingness to discuss it, would be dishonest. So, after a solid month and headed into the second month of ignoring us, I found a way to let go of my feelings of persecution and confusion. Through my faith in a Divine intelligence, I enabled myself to reach to a higher love. As per my habit, I merely prayed. This helped me put things into perspective with the realization that I definitely had not done anything to deserve her behaviour towards me. I let go of any personal responsibility because it was her choice to act out this way, not mine.

That is when a phenomenon happened. A book literally fell off a shelf in my home and landed near my feet. I picked it up and looked at the title, *Tao Te Ching* by Stephen Mitchell. The first page I turned to was sixteen and it reads;

Empty your mind of all thoughts. Let your heart be at peace.

Watch the turmoil of beings, but contemplate their return.

Each separate being in the universe returns to the common source.

Returning to the source is serenity.

*If you don't realize the source, you stumble
in confusion and sorrow.*

*When you realize where you come from, you naturally
become tolerant, disinterested, amused, kind hearted
as a grandmother, dignified as a king. Immersed in
the wonder of the Tao, you can deal with whatever life
brings you, and when death comes, you are ready.*

This focused my mind on peace. I practiced page sixteen to the letter and there was no more upset for me. I enabled myself to let go of my concerns of this persons conduct and felt at ease once again.

The timing of this part of my life coincided with my scheduled guest speaking through the Church. My heart filled with gratitude as I realized my inspirational talk would be on the **Tao Te Ching**, page sixteen to be precise. After my talk, many of the congregation members approached me expressing how helpful my topic was and that they intended to put it into practice too.

A few weeks later the woman, that had been angry towards my family and I, phoned. She explained that her *nerves* had gotten the best of her and that she had exploded on several people that were close to her. Her gracious explanation helped me have more understanding as to what happened within her mind and her sincere apology made it easy for us to spend time with her again.

Ultimately after evaluating the whole of what took place, I was left feeling satisfied with myself. Rather than fall into despair of being treated disrespectfully, I fell into prayer to support my hurts.

The book that fell, practically on my feet, helped me get on with my own life while I contemplated her eventual return to peace.

Forgiveness doesn't say it is okay that someone hurt you; it says that you are okay with moving on. I read these words posted on the internet one day and although I have heard them said for many years, finally, I truly understand their meaning now.

Troubles, upsets, worries, discord and even things that cause happy stress in our lives; usually require our sincere effort to motor through and gain from the experience. With honesty I can say that I have not yet mastered remaining within a peaceful heart all the time. Heaven within me, at this point, requires much conscious effort on my part. My triggers kick in occasionally and instead of responding with reverence, I have been known to react emotionally. Being a work in progress I'm okay with this and it's with contentment that I acknowledge I'm much quicker to find my way back to love than I used to be.

My promise to myself; I will continue to seek for higher ground during times of divergence.

Chapter #25

INTENTION CREATES

W HAT YOU THINK ABOUT MOST you become and what you place your attention on grows.

As a child I had both positive reinforcement and negative criticism from family, friends and strangers. Our minds are like sponges at a young age and can be easily influenced one way or the other. It's not surprising then that some children grow into well developed, happy adults and some do not. The complex workings of the human psyche is beyond my comprehension, nevertheless I absolutely understand one simple thing. No matter what messages a child has been stimulated with, when they grow into adulthood, they then have the freedom to agree or disagree with past suggestions.

As far as I can tell, it's much more complicated if a person suffers from a chemical imbalance that causes their brain to misfire. Sure, they still have choice to seek medical assistance and follow through with techniques to help them change their thinking habits, but sometimes mental illness causes loss of ability to even recognize there is a problem in the first place.

May none of us ever judge another, based on the fact we don't know what it's like walking in those shoes that belong to someone else.

Something about myself; having come through mental illness to mental wellness, is that I absolutely had to put away the blame game. This was not an easy task. For far too long, I wasted precious time clinging to my stories of victimhood. In my mind, the 'poor me' stories excused me from taking responsibility for my Self. If I had of held onto my old incorrect beliefs I would never have experienced wellness and contentment. I would not have initiated favorable circumstances into my life.

It was often frustrating for me to deal with body chemistry that often prevented the electrical impulses of my brain to carry forth completed thoughts. Instead messages within my mind were disrupted, which sometimes confused and frightened me. I understand, when you are dealing with a mental illness, it's as unique to each person as finger prints are to humanity. It is my guess that retraining your mind to think differently is perhaps similar between a person who suffers chemical imbalance and one who does not. Both have to repeatedly make effort to replace their negative thoughts with positive and uplifting thoughts. The only difference I've noticed is that possibly a person with mental illness has to take medication to become balanced enough *before* they are able to do the mental exercises to attain a healthy mindset.

Regardless, I know from firsthand experience, changing a mentally ill mind to a mentally healthy mind, medication free and without any therapies; *IT CAN BE DONE*. There is a natural permanent cure for mental illness, in some cases. The first step; is desiring wellness.

Although I was born with a genetic makeup where it was most likely that a chemical imbalance would disrupt my mind, and it did, I was able to eventually transform that physical illness to one of chemical balance. It was through the repetitive practice of positive thought. My diligent effort combined with faith of a loving intelligence beyond my own, ended the cycle of mental illness within me.

To be clear, I did not learn to manage my illness or to cope with my illness nor did I exchange medication for some other form of therapy. What happened is that I cured the chemical imbalance within my body. It no longer exists thereby I no longer require medication or any form of safeguarding. This statement is easy to make because living life has been the test. Through various trials and tribulations I have remained of a balanced mind and dealt with these challenges without any form of psychosis.

When telling others of my experience with mental illness, there have been many theories people have presented to me. It is a wide variety of speculations I've heard. What crops up most frequently, when in discussion about mental illness, is the age old question: *Which came first, the chicken or the egg?* What people have said is, *which came first, negative thinking or chemical imbalance?* At this time, I feel my fear based thoughts triggered the chemical imbalance that was already physically within my body, from birth. I believe my predisposition to have psychosis came first. If you have a hereditary gene that is known to create illness in the body, it may never become activated. On the other hand, as with my hereditary gene, my insecurities and suppressed anger triggered the activation of the inherited illness. Another way a person with hereditary chemical imbalance can be triggered; is by taking drugs.

Admittedly I could be wrong? Yet most likely, in my opinion, mental illness may never have been triggered if my thought process had been less fearful. My theory is based on rationalizing, through looking at different people's responses in times of stressful challenges. Some people handle difficult situations in stride, some have heart attacks, others suffer insomnia, still others will develop various physical side effects and then there are some of us who release brain chemicals that cause psychosis. Some families seem to have a long line of the same conditions passed from generation to generation. Seems to me it depends on your physical DNA configuration as to how your mind and body translates the stressful thoughts. I'm sure some will agree and others will disagree with my point of view and so I confess, no one may know the whole truth of this matter. Alas the grand mystery remains, what came first?

Respectfully, I do not ascertain that anyone with mental illness can become mentally well by applying the same methods that worked for me. I simply reveal it is possible that what worked for me may make a difference in someone else's life too. My main message is; *yes, severe mental illness can be cured, I have done it.*

You bet it can be done. I trust there are others out there, who haven't shared their experience yet, that have healed completely from mental illness too.

I have a friend that tells me he was abused both mentally and physically as a Child. He believes having heard nothing but negative messages all his life has caused his unhappiness in the present. So currently he excuses his addiction to drugs by blaming it on his childhood. I concur that addiction is not easy to let go of, yet by seeking help, it can be done; if a person wants it. Constantly seeing your unhappy circumstances as a fault of someone else strips you of your power. My hope for this friend is that he will come to forgive his past and take responsibility for his present choices. Right now, his thoughts are focused on how to maintain his addiction and having such a strong will he's quite proficient at getting the drugs that make him feel better. If he ever decided to use his strength of will to seek solution to his addiction, he would be equally successful at that too.

You're in the driver seat, no one else. Choose your thoughts wisely. When in psychotic episodes I couldn't choose my thoughts but with accepting professional help through medication I was soon returned to balanced mind where I could then apply mental exercises. Eventually I recognize how to surrender and rely on God when I couldn't trust myself. Slowly, with determination and faith the old thought patterns gave way to a positive, constructive mind set.

As life became more fun, many things I thought about were coming into my world. It got to be quite astonishing. There was the time Ron and I needed a new work truck to provide efficient service to our customers. Ron described to me his hoped for model, year, colour and price range for a truck. We both held faith that we'd find this perfect truck, at the right time for the right price. Within two weeks, we got a phone call from someone who learned there was a private sale on a work truck. Upon viewing the truck, Ron was overjoyed to find out it was the exact colour, year and model he had hoped for. Oh, and the price was within his budget.

For many years I have maintained a prayer alter where I like to kneel in private, to pray and meditate. My legs often tingled and went numb from being in the kneeling position. I began thinking about what might suffice to give me more comfort. Without a doubt I knew what I needed; a prayer stool made of wood, hand painted, that was low to the ground where I could be in a kneeling position yet have my weight supported. I even went so far as to imagine this stool would have been previously used in a sacred way. Within days of thinking about this type of prayer stool, a friend and I decided to go shopping on one of the nearby islands. One of the shops had gorgeous pillows of various sizes stacked all around their store. I thought about buying a giant, colourful pillow to sit on at my Alter; but really I wanted a wooden, hand painted stool. As I lifted some pillows from a stack, I noticed a wooden, low to the ground, hand painted stool underneath the pile of pillows. Quickly and with excitement I tossed the last few pillows aside to discover this stool was almost identical to the one I had hoped for. After asking the sales person what the price was, I found out it was affordable. As I paid for my new prayer stool, the clerk told me it had come from one of the temples in India and had been used to sit in a kneeling position, during prayer. To be sure, I didn't focus very intently on the image of what I hoped for, more so it was a prayerful feeling and a knowing that if it was for my best, it would happen. And it did.

Same holds true of my desire to have a native drum. I had a subtle thought of how wonderful it would feel to meditate as I drummed. Over the course of several weeks I came across a few native drums for sale; some new and some second hand. Deep inside my hope was that I'd find a drum that would have significant meaning and spiritual value to me. None of these drums, so far, spoke to my heart. Trusting Divine timing, proved challenging as I patiently waited for a drum to show up. It was wise for me to wait because a few more weeks went by and as it turned out, I was given a gift of a native drum. This gift was handmade by an acquaintance who had gathered the drum materials himself. With honour and the greatest respect to the animals that provided the material, he caringly built the drum with love. This drum holds many levels of sacredness for me and one level being my appreciation of this man's generosity. It was fascinating how this gift came to me, this friend had no idea I had been praying for a drum to help me in meditation.

There have been times where I prayed for and held a strong vision of something coming my way and it didn't happen. Such as the time I was hired in a company as an entry level, computer data typist. This was during my years before the Counseling Agency. I wanted to be promoted and even saw myself in the position of secretary. I was certain through my intention and skills I would be promoted and given a raise. Lucky for me that did not happen, the company ended up under investigation of fraud. If promoted, I would have inadvertently been involved in the illegal activities going on. Thankfully, as a casual data typist, I was not considered in the loop of thieves.

When we place our focused intention on something it will grow, yet, we must understand the common sense of it all too. For example, no matter how diligently I focus healing prayers at a root rotted, dead plant; it is not going to suddenly come back in full bloom over night as a result of my invoking healthy vibes toward it. Perhaps there are enlightened beings that can do this; I'm not there yet though. In my opinion, what could happen is through my intention to restore the plant to health, I may be inspired to change out the soil, add some nutrients and follow through with appropriate watering. Perhaps then, it's likely the plant would have a second chance to grow, if there's any spark of life left within it.

Another thought, if I desire something and visualize it happening, feel it happening, meditating on it daily as if it has already come into being; does not necessarily mean it will occur. There is something people refer to as the law of attraction and yes I believe there is such a law. It seems to me the only way this magnetic law attracts things to us though, is based on what is truly within our consciousness. You can't fake it nor just think what you want and attract it. The law of attraction works at a depth of honesty and sometimes honest work.

It's important to me that I concentrate on what I want in my life, fully expecting the best in all ways. Yet, I don't become disappointed if I do not receive my desired outcome. I hold no attachment to my wants and desires, I contemplate what I'd like to see in my life, I will even take steps to achieve certain goals and then I allow life to simply unfold as it will. I stay very happy this way, no disappointments and no frustration.

Too often I have heard spiritual friends complaining, as they beat themselves up, thinking that they haven't been diligent enough to summon things through the Law of Attraction. The only things you can summon to you through the law of attraction are those things that are deeply rooted in your subconscious or in the core of who you are. My conclusion based on personal experience is that we can only attract the truth that lies within us.

YOU ATTRACT WHAT YOU ARE, SO BE YOUR BEST.

Considering my Self a truth seeker my realization is that I do not know what makes this universe tick, nor the answers to overcome severe mental illness. Yet, I do know how I became mentally healthy and off medication. To give one piece of advice to someone struggling with depression or any form of mental discord it would be; *'Put your attention on love, replace all thoughts that are fearful with ones that are uplifting. Pray sincerely.'* By the way I believe we don't have to use words for a prayer, crying, is a very strong prayer that will invoke the law of attracting God's assistance in your life.

Besides the occasional release through tears, I had restored my ability to laugh and feel joy. Ron and I had both learned to play and have fun, together. Life was too short not to indulge in silliness now and then. Most often Ron would catch me tap dancing down our hallway to put a load of laundry on or doing ballet leaps across the patio while I played with our dogs. It was really a sight to behold when Ron and I would waltz together, to our own humming, throughout the kitchen, dining room and living room. After the previous years of sorrow and chaos when I was mentally unstable; it was refreshing to feel this content now.

As in most long term relationships, laughter and dancing gave way to disagreements from time to time. Now and then those arguments could escalate to the point where one of us would stomp out of the room in a huff of anger. We could have continued along that unhappy road, but thankfully we brought something new into our relationship and this tool always helped us find common ground. What happened was I got upset with Ron over some misunderstanding, this time it was me stomping toward the front door to go for a long walk. With my hand on the door knob I found the presence of mind to say a silent prayer. *"God will you please guide me to a peaceful outcome"*. Instantly, I had an urge to go get my deck of Angel Cards and instead of throwing the front door open and slamming it behind me, I went and grabbed my deck. No words were spoken between Ron and I while walking back into the kitchen. Simply shuffling my Angel cards and then spreading them across the counter, I chose a card for myself. Right in that moment I asked Ron if he would like to hear about my feelings, while I used the card to inspire my honesty. Promising him what I talked of would be about me not him. He took a seat beside me and gave me his full attention. I flipped over the card titled, *Support*. What surfaced from me was that my upset towards Ron was a result of not feeling supported in a recent choice I had made. My next com ment came from a more vulnerable place as I choked out the words, *"I feel like I'm always looking for your approval"*. At hearing this, Ron reached out and placed his hand on my arm. We then talked about his feelings, then mine, then his again; we must have sat together for over an hour, really caring about the other. As we wrapped up our talking and decided it was time to get on with the day, Ron suggested I pull one more card. I tossed the 'Support' card back into the deck shuffled it up good, Ron cut the deck and I pulled one last card. Low and behold it was the card named

Support again. Our laughter was unanimous; obviously I needed this card to pop up in my face again. This card *support* implored me to go deeper in order to understand a simple truth that was being missed.

The truth was: I HAVE ALL THE SUPPORT I NEED FROM THE DIVINE ESSENCE, WHO IS WITH ME ALL THE TIME. From that point on, I stopped expecting Ron to support my every idea.

Using the cards to get to the bottom of what we really were trying to say to each other helped us enhance our relationship. The Angel Cards helped us get out of the blame game and take responsibility for our own thoughts and actions.

Through our willingness to hear each other and respect our differences we were now looking, very much, in the same direction. Family was most important to us and we both enjoyed our chosen professions; so life became a breeze. We were about to celebrate twenty-seven years of marriage when we decided to have a serious look for our dream home on acreage. With both our children now grown and building lives of their own, most people thought we would be seeking a smaller place, but they couldn't have been more wrong.

It all started when Ron came home excitedly describing an older home his customer lived in. Ron had been awarded the contract to build a new home for this man and that meant his old house would soon be up for sale. After hearing Ron describe huge windows, floor to ceiling rock fireplace twelve feet in length, six bedrooms, three bathrooms, recreation room, living room, large laundry room and on and on he went. I wondered why he was thrilled about this particular place because to me it sounded like a mansion and we definitely were not on the market for something that humungous.

Six bedrooms, did I hear him right, I wondered? What did Ron think I was going to do, quit counseling work and clean house all day!

After he started describing the out buildings then I thought perhaps he is being blinded by his want of his own carpentry shop. Totally not impressed, I did my best to discourage him from pursuing it any further. Never mind the size of the house, I told Ron, but the price is way out of our budget.

Almost a week went by before Ron's eagerness for me to see this gigantic home, wore me down, and I agreed to go meet his customer and have a look at the place. To my surprise I felt a spiritual brightness when we first drove up to this house. Corny as it sounds, I actually did feel like I had come home. It wasn't that the house was ritzy, 'cause it wasn't, more so it was a seventies style, sprawling, two storey house with beautiful trees, shrubs, flowers and two acres of gorgeous lawn with fringes of forest on three sides. The price was a stopper for me though. Now what happened is quite a lengthy story and I'll keep it short. Basically I'm certain, because of the way events unfolded, that we were meant to be living on that particular property. Things fell together effortlessly and it was on Ron's birthday that we signed the papers and bought the house. It was on my birthday that we physically moved into our new home. There are more coincidences though.

After Ron and I moved in, we started talking about how to make the best use of all our space in this home. Right about that time, our daughter, her husband and their baby, found themselves in limbo with their home sold and their new place unavailable until four months. We were thrilled to move the three of them into our home and with the massive space; we hardly ever saw each other. They truly blessed our home with laughter, activity and a sense of family closeness. We were sad to see them go, but their newly purchased home was eventually ready!

Ron and I were not alone for long. Our son and his girlfriend were saving up to travel abroad for a year. We encouraged them to let go of their apartment and stay with us for five months. We appreciated them taking us up on our offer because through them, again our home was blessed with the closeness of family and fun. Miss them we did though, when it came time for them to travel.

It wasn't long until we found our next victim, friend that is, to pull into our home. Ron and I found out we had ourselves a little sanctuary in this place and loved to share our space. It was two friends that were in process of moving when an unexpected hitch in their plans created chaos in their lives. After we approached them about the space we have, they also moved in for a few months until circumstances settled. I was in heaven! Our friends shared much in common regarding family values, spiritual endeavors and the love of pets. Well in our household, you better like pets, they pretty much rule the roost. We missed our friends dearly, when we eventually had to say goodbye as they moved into their new home. To this day we stay in touch as much as possible.

Over the course of time, I continued working at the Counseling Agency and helping out at the Church. Ron created a very large vegetable garden and transformed our shops and house with further renovations. One of the first things Ron built was yet another large wellness studio for me. I had been missing that space from when we moved from our previous home.

As soon as possible I began teaching spiritual classes, facilitating communication groups and providing individual healing sessions. Soon I opened my door for other spiritual facilitators to hold their workshops from our home too. It was an interesting mix of people that graced our home and many new friends were made. I came to understand why we needed such a spacious home.

Ron and I had a deal. One section of the property housed his construction equipment and carpentry shop; another section was reserved for spiritual activity. For starters we had an outside fire pit complete with running water and cook shack to accommodate groups of people for potlucks and other outdoor gatherings. There were pathways that meandered through the forest of trees and shrubs on our property that was perfect for admiring the many varieties of natural flowers. Zen like, on one half of the yard; functional on the other half.

Not to lose sight of further dreams we hoped to create together. Ron and I often sat back and discussed the unfolding of our lives. It was without a doubt a collaboration of our attention on what we wanted and allowing it to happen. When two people who love each other hold similar visions it can be a powerful combination.

Ron and I wanted to design a spiritual walking garden on the property, maybe a labyrinth or maze. We weren't quite sure how it would look or where we should put it though. I left it in prayer and trusted the intelligent consciousness, beyond our own, would inspire us to create something easily doable.

It didn't take long for something unique to transpire. Our spiritual garden came into being as a result of me following my impulse to teach an eight week spiritual development class. This class was based on listening to your intuition and so one of the participants did listen to her inner wisdom and by acting on it, she brought me a book titled, *The Medicine Wheel Garden* written by E. Barrie Kavasch. Now she had no idea we were considering to build a spiritual garden, so I was thoroughly impressed by her ability to trust her instincts. Through her suggested reading, Ron and I were inspired to build a Medicine Wheel Garden on the Zen side of our property.

As they say, there are no coincidences, the location for this garden actually found us. While looking over the forested part of our yard we noticed a lone cedar tree surrounded by a thirty foot perimeter of ferns and twigs. That cedar tree became the center peace pole, representing the three directions of above, below and here. With Ron and my son's help we cleared ferns and moved in topsoil. Then

I began slowly, shovel full by shovel full, carving out the path ways. It was a moving meditation filled with mindfulness, as I envisioned possibilities of world peace, while working. Soon I was ready to spread the carpet of pebble size stones to define the paths. Then, I walked around the property and chose four, ten foot long, fallen branches that were straight enough to be erected as directional poles. My son and Ron placed each pole at one of the four directional gates; north, south, east and west. Over 1000, softball size stones, were patiently gathered by both Ron and I, then placed to outline the medicine wheel paths and four quadrants.

Nearing the middle of June, we were ready to have several friends come and join us in a blessing ceremony over the garden. After the sacred ceremony we all shared potluck and laughter. Actually, truth be known, we had some snickers and chuckles while standing *in* the medicine wheel garden during the blessing. There was about thirty of us standing in a circle within the garden, placing crystals and saying prayers for world peace. Right in that precious moment a car driving down the road pulled over and a man ran from the driver side, into the heavily treed part of our property. He didn't notice us in his state of emergency but we could definitely see him as he relieved himself against one of the maple trees. I'm certain most of us looked away to give him privacy. Oh how hilarious was this, I'm still having a chuckle over that perfect divine timing. Now that's a true blessing, HUMOUR.

That night, after everyone had gone home, I marveled at the gracious love that surrounds us all. Within, above, below and all around; every living thing is love and is loved.

To acknowledge the sadder, more painful events that occur in our world I will say it's not always easy to *feel or see* love all the time; and that remains one of humanities biggest challenges. What helps me to stay focused on love is to act on kindness in all areas of my life. I figure if I am doing my small part by just being nice to others and generous of heart then at least I am not contributing to the chaos. Rather than be part of the problem we all need to find a way to BE a part of the solution.

When I hear of violent deeds perpetrated by individuals or groups, my mind immediately goes to the recognition that all of us have that potential to be harmful or helpful. Instead of judging an act of violence, anywhere in the world, I remind myself that I need to have a look at myself and ask, *"Am I being violent anywhere in my own life?"* If I am scowling at someone, swearing at someone under my breath, gossiping about others or even just thinking unkindly towards someone; those are all acts of violence.

Then of course there are the many other acts of violence; lying, cheating, stealing, manipulating, hitting, killing, yelling, and cruelty in any form. My habit is to do self examination every now and then, a check-in with myself. If need be, I clean up my act when I notice any violent behaviour seeping into my consciousness.

If you want change in the world the best place to start is with yourself.

Chapter #26

SMALL STEADY STEPS

H AVE YOU EVER BIT OFF a huge chunk of food, found out it was too much to chew and it darn near choked you? Well I have. As a kid I believed that the more I could cram in my mouth meant I'd be getting the better of the deal. Greedy-guts learned the hard way not to bite off more than I could chew.

Taking more than I can handle in any area of life, causes me discomfort.

During the years of struggle with manic episodes, it was sometimes my overly excited, emotional bursts that caused me to take on more than I could handle. Whenever I was in euphoric crazy-brain, I thought my skills were greater than my actual level attained.

Such was the time when I figured my abilities to prepare drywall, for painting, surpassed all others. The minute Ron drove away, as he headed off to work, that was my cue to get the hallway wall prepared for painting. My intention was to surprise him when he got home, showing him how capable I was to sand a wall and get it painted. Running outside to our shed, I grabbed drop sheets and the electric sander. Little did I know when Ron talked about sanding a wall to prep for paint; he meant a light hand sand to gently rough the surface. After three minutes of using the electric sander on the wall, I could barely breathe for all the dust. Stepping back to admire my handy work I was a bit stunned to see the huge dip I'd created in the wall, from sanding too long in one spot. Oh no, now what? Firstly, I ran back to the shed and found a paper nose and mouth mask. Secondly, I ran back to the shed yet again to find the carpenters goggles. Next I buzzed that wall from top to bottom with that electric sander. Took me darn near all day! Trying my best to even out the waves of uneven sanding was like trying to smooth out icing on a cake using a serrated edged knife. Smooth couldn't happen while using the wrong tool. By now my house looked like it had been bombed with sacks of flour and I looked like the abominable snowman. The only thing not covered by drywall dust, were my eyes! Desperate to finish off the mess I'd created, before Ron walked through the door, I took a broom to the wall knocking down remaining dust. Around that time my brain cleared and the horror of what I'd done to a perfectly nice wall, glared back at me. As my weary body sat slumped over our kitchen table crying, Ron walked in through the front door. I had succeeded in surprising him.

In comparison to this drywall sanding fiasco, it was similar to my approach of using self help techniques. In the beginning, having learned several exercises to develop positive thinking, I tried implementing them all at once. My thought was to take giant steps, actually leaps, in order to become *well* faster. That only served to overwhelm me, which caused great discomfort and falling flat upon my face.

Again biting off more than I could chew, like the sanding episode; left me in a mess. After a while I soon figured out that slow, small and steady steps kept me on the path of wellness.

Years later, having come to know the joy of mental balance, I often pondered how I had accomplished this. One day, over a cup of tea with a new friend, I was able to share my thoughts of how my affliction with severe bipolar disorder was healed. Describing what I had done to become mentally stable and medication free seemed to be of great interest to him. I concluded my comments by saying, *"life these days are filled with my gratitude of what is possible through God"* In response, He thoughtfully exclaimed, *"Ann, it's nice to meet a fellow member; you're describing page 59 of the big book!"* I had no idea what he meant? Hearing I was not aware of the book he spoke of, he chuckled and said, *"I'll drop over tomorrow with your own copy of the big book and then look up that page, you'll soon understand why I mistook you for a member."*

The next day my friend dropped over with a copy of the Alcoholics Anonymous hand book. He asked me to turn to page 59 and read. There were twelve steps described and to my amazement, they mirrored what I had done in my process to be healthy. Below I have listed the simplistic ways that helped me to create wellness in my life.

1. I admitted I was powerless. (rock bottom)

2. I came to know there is a Power greater than me; that can restore my sanity.

3. I made a decision to surrender my will and life over to God.

4. I took stock and had a look at my own behavior.

5. I had admitted my wrongs out loud to others.

6. I asked God to correct my thoughts and align me to be in Divine truth.

7. I humbly asked God to remove my shortcomings and restore my mental health.

8. I thought of all the people I had wronged and asked God to help me set things right.

9. Whenever possible I went back to people and apologized for any harm I may have caused.

10. I continued to take personal inventory and when I made a mistake I quickly admitted it.

11. I sought God through prayer and meditation to strengthen my foundation in him.

12. Having had a spiritual awakening I do my best to carry a message of hope to others.

Without knowing it I had been following the steps from the A.A. hand book. Upon realizing this, I felt reassured for trusting Gods voice within my heart. Listening to Gods guidance, nudge me forward, is the only way I could possibly have known to climb that particular twelve step ladder.

We often have all the answers right there within us and around us; thing is WE HAVE TO TAKE ACTION. Knowing or memorizing these steps will not make a difference. It's our childlike innocence, to humble ourselves, trusting in a consciousness far beyond our own, where we find out there really is a state of *God's Grace* that restores us. This state of *Grace* provides us the peace, strength and resting time we need to nurture and heal ourselves. It's where we can 'rest easy' and let God carry us for a while.

After your nap though, get up off your butt and do the necessary steps to free yourself completely. If you fall down, pick yourself back up and keep on moving! We're not alone on our individual journey and every time one of us restores our health, we are actually helping the whole world to get another step closer to world peace. Imagine that, world peace and why not? At least let's make the best effort we can to ensure we are doing our part to create harmony. Harmony within you equals harmony all around you.

Let your light shine and we will eventually have so many bright lights blazing that every dark corner of the world will be illuminated.

Chapter #27

ONE PHILOSOPHY; BE KIND

F OR A WHILE, MY MEDICINE wheel garden was where I observed quiet sanctuary and prayed as I placed symbolic stones. The stones solidified my prayerful intentions. They fortified my conviction of peace by merely seeing them there in my garden. The stone cairns reminded me of each and every prayer I had stated as well as fond memories of friends who had placed their own prayer stones in the garden. Every spring the medicine wheel pathways would all be thickly carpeted with green weeds. I thought of it as a moving meditation when I would kneel in solitude while plucking out the greenery to once again reveal the stone paths.

Soon enough my Grandson had reached the age where he was interested to help me clear the garden pathways. I taught him how to enter through the east gate and honour the seven directions of east, south, west, north, above, below and here. When I walked him over to the North directional pole he innocently exclaimed, *"Oh Grandma, the North Pole, this is where Santa Claus lives!"* So cute, I thought, enjoying a heartfelt giggle.

Every now and then my Grandson would come to our home and spend a night or two. It was an adorable sight to watch Grandpa go hand in hand with his Grandson across the property, looking at all the interesting insects along the walk. Now and then Grandpa would let him help out around the carpentry shop, sweeping sawdust or hammering a nail or two. There were many chores that a young boy could help us with and he was eager to pitch in to stack wood or clear the lawn for mowing. After getting the work finished, it was play time. Out came our ATV four wheeler and with me revving up the engine my Grandson would chuckle with anticipation, as he climbed aboard. What a sight we were, helmets gleaming in the sun and on rainy days mud flying from the wheels; as the dogs ran alongside us. After a long day of fun, just before bed, it was our habit to pour a big bowl of grandma's special cereal soaked in magic milk and chow down together. The cereal was actually bland tasting, organic, gluten free, kamute flakes. The magic milk, in truth, was soya milk mixed with protein powder. Go figure, my Grandson loved it. Once tucked securely into bed, he would describe to me some make believe characters and it was my job to create an amazing bedtime story from it. My favorite made up story was when he gave me the characters; a bear, a rabbit, a fox and a jet plane. That took some quick thinking to work out an entertaining story line using this strange combination of characters. I'm sure it's obvious to all that eventually that jet plane was high-jacked by the bunny rabbit, right? Bunny had a good purpose in mind; he was giving his friends a ride to the finish line so that they would all be winners.

One of the many sleepovers with my Grandson, he decided he wanted to help me do laundry in the morning. The help was welcomed! We started by stripping the beds and while tugging on the edges of my bed sheets, trying to pull them off he came upon an image of Jesus on my bedside table. Being a curious little man, he wanted to know who the person in the picture was. Giving the simplest answer I could think of, I said, *"His name is Jesus and he lived hundreds of years ago. Jesus was kind to everyone and taught the world to also be kind. He often helped people get better if they were sick. He is in Heaven now and whenever we want, we can tell him we love him and he will hear us."* Then I added, *"Did you know that Christmas is to remember that Jesus was born, it's his birthday celebration"*. Now I felt like I was on a role and looking forward to telling my Grandson more, but with the innocents of a young boy he said, *"That's good Grandma, can we go play checkers now?"*

One of the funniest moments was when my Grandson noticed I had a painting of Lakshmi, an Eastern Goddess, hanging in my hallway. *"Who is she and why does she have so many arms!"* he wanted to know. Not quite sure how to explain why she had so many arms, I distracted him with a Popsicle, deciding to get my facts straight before I attempted an answer. Later on, being a bright and observant fellow, he noticed my statue of Buddha and rubbed the ceramic big belly. In mid-rub my Grandson spotted the wooden carving of Ganesha, which was an Eastern symbol depicting a boy with an elephant head. Intensely scrutinizing this carving he insisted I explain why this person had a head that looked like an elephant? It was easy for me to tell him the meaning of the image; it represents *families love for each other*. But, oh no, that was not what he wanted to know, it was the elephant head that needed explanation. Feeling that the story behind this was a bit too graphic for young ears, there again, another Popsicle spared me trying to help him understand Gods and Goddesses from another culture.

All the while, when it came to my curious Grandson, I was mindful to have previously asked his parents their beliefs before sharing mine with their son. My Daughter knew and appreciated some of the ways I understood spirituality and her only request was that I keep it simple.

There are many views of God, I can't even count or name the various religions. Eastern, Western, ancient, new age and so many philosophies and doctrines. Who's right, who's wrong and who cares! To get to the nitty-gritty, the way I see it, there are really just two categories of understanding God. You either believe or you don't. I also appreciate that it really doesn't matter if you believe in an intelligent consciousness beyond your own or not, because that Divinity knows you regardless. Fact is you're alive, therefore you are spiritual and when life comes to an end I trust we will all go back to the same source from whence we originated, no matter your belief. The real Church is within your own heart. To me the only philosophy is, Be Kind.

Personally, I do reap a lot of benefit from attending Church and spiritual gatherings. It's the friendship of like minded people and the positive inspiration that recharges my batteries. I find Church also helps me release negative views created by some of the chaos in this world. Another thing I adore about Church, it's a place where I can reach out to others and not only receive assistance but also offer words of encouragement and compassion.

Bottom line is kindness. I like to hang out with people that accept and reciprocate kindness.

Being kind isn't always easy, especially when someone has flipped your switch and sparked your trigger. Kindness is a choice. With practice the decision to be nice comes more naturally. Some of the ways I have trained myself to have kindness as my first response, is by filling my home with images of saints, ascended masters, angels and beautiful crystals. Let me tell you, if you wake up grumpy, roll over and are immediately staring into the eyes of an image of Jesus; it quickly helps you snap your thoughts back onto love. Some other ways I have found to maintain a happy mind is through gardening, whipping around my yard on the ATV, raking leaves and stacking wood even. My home is kept clutter free so my space feels open and inviting. Even house cleaning can be uplifting and gratifying, of course, over the years I've learned not to be obsessive. Moderation in all things!

There are several rituals and spiritual tools that have helped me stay focused on a healthy, balanced life. When I'm happy, I'm most likely to respond kindly, even if someone has triggered me. So my goal is to maintain a balanced level of happiness, which entails doing things I enjoy. Self care is essential. Respecting my personality trait and honouring that I like variety in my life, I tend to change my rituals every now and then. Certain practices seem to be enjoyable for a while and then I move on to try others; occasionally going back to old rituals that still light up my heart.

A while back, I came across a yard sale and purchased a long string of deep red rubies, at a very affordable price. The previous owner told me she had gone to India, handpicked these rubies and had a local woman string them. She was pleased when I told her that I was going to use them for a sacred purpose. My intention was to create a set of prayer beads. Research was needed so I found out every detail required, off the internet, to make my own. Upon understanding the process, I restrung 108 of these rubies following specific directions. Next, I began chanting *Om Ma Ni Pad Me Hum*, as I pulled one bead at a time, across the string. I repeated the chant 108 times for each bead I pulled. These six syllables chanted have many meanings. One is; Generosity, ethics, patience, diligence, renunciation and wisdom. There is a precise hand position used with prayer beads and I followed it to the letter. I received much value from this ritual and practiced it daily for months. When it no longer felt uplifting I stopped using the prayer beads and moved into a different practice.

With my Reiki teachings, I often followed the practice of chanting the five Reiki principles to myself.

1. I release all anger

2. I let go all worry

3. I do my work honestly

4. I am kind to all living things

5. I am grateful and humble.

Along with the five principles, I often used particular Reiki symbols to focus my intention on sending myself healing as well as out to individuals and the world. It's all intention.

Other times I used Tibetan brass bowls and occasionally crystal singing bowls. Often my African Djembe drumming served as meditation and on different days Native drumming. Allowing my intuition to inspire me, there were many techniques used to facilitate relaxation; singing, dance, drawing, writing and many other meditation techniques. One at a time of course, it surely would not be relaxing to attempt doing all the above during the same sitting. By the way, when I chose a tool and performed my ritual, it did not take long. Usually I gave myself fifteen to thirty minutes first thing in the morning before my day began. This would establish mindfulness, gratitude and relaxation for the whole day.

Although some spiritual practices have come and gone, there is one practice that has remained a constant in my life. It is saying the Lord's Prayer. I remember as a child, we always said the Lord's Prayer at school and it has always and still does hold devout meaning for me. That prayer covers everything. It addresses God, acknowledges the sacredness of the Spirit, requests that we receive only what we truly need, reminds us to forgive others and that we are also forgiven, grants us loving guidance and protection. As far as I'm concerned it is the perfect prayer when stated with sincerity. Even though I was sad when the Lord's Prayer was taken out of schools, I comprehended not everyone valued this prayer being taught to their children.

The Lord's Prayer, when I said it to myself, helped me feel closer to life. Depth and meaning was felt every time. To my surprise the Church I attended, yanked the Lord's Prayer out of their service after having prayed it every Sunday for years. At first I couldn't understand the decision to do this; but I had to accept the loss I felt because the majority ruled.

What happened for me, over losing the Lord's Prayer from the Church, is that I learned a precious lesson. Just because I gained a lot of value from something didn't mean it was important to others and that was simply Okay. Truth is, it really didn't mean I was *losing* the Lord's Prayer, I continued saying it as I always had. No big deal.

What I am about to share, regarding the Lord's Prayer, happened immediately after *I let go of* my upset of having my favorite prayer taken out of the Church.

As I headed up those familiar stairs of the Counseling Agency, a staff member told me there was a kitchen supply store having a going out of business sale. Thanking her for the information but deciding I had no reason to go there because there was nothing needed for my kitchen, I went about my day as usual. Ironically, a few days later while helping a friend, I had to drive past that precise kitchen store. The urge to go in was so strong that I parked the car and out of curiosity entered the store. Searching that store for an hour and finding nothing needed, I headed for the exit door. Just as I was about to leave there was one item spotted, that Ron might want, a wine bottle cork. With the massive sale prices the cost was under a dollar, so I stood in line waiting my turn to pay. And I waited and I stood in line longer and I waited. Inching my way closer to the cashier, I saw the lineup was not moving because some customers were distracting the clerk with questions. The long line had me waiting so far back I was smack-dab in the middle of an Isle, between shelves of items for sale. Feeling impatient, thinking how silly of me to wait for *this* long to pay for a bottle cork? Just as I was going to step out of the stalled line up; I heard a voice, well, more accurately I heard a thought, pass through my mind that said, *Look to your left!* I did look to my left and there on the shelf, eye level to me, I saw several ceramic angels. They were delicate and painted in various pastel colours with tasteful sparkles on their skirts. That inner voice guided me to move the ceramic angels that were in the front and reach into the back of the shelf. Following this urge, I pulled out one angel that was hidden behind all the rest. This angel stood about eight inches tall and on the skirt was written the Lord's Prayer. A tingle of warmth ran through my body with the realization that I was being gifted by Universal love. My budget for ornaments was limited so when I flipped the beautiful decoration over and saw the price was out of my range I sighed and put the Angel down. Amazingly, a woman behind me whispered *"it's 75% off that sticker price."* I almost did a happy dance right there in the crowded store. The Angel with the Lord's Prayer, delicately written on her skirt, is now placed in my wellness studio. She is a reminder that what we truly love, comes to us when the time is right and if it is what we need.

No matter what phase of life I'm in, all activities aside, I hold to only one philosophy; just be kind.

Chapter #28

ENLIGHTENED VISITS

My Dad, Stan Clarke, died before he ever got to see me reverse the effects of mental illness and become healthy. For a long time I felt let down that my Dad never had a chance to see me at my best.

Dad had always been comfortable speaking in front of groups and especially enjoyed himself when socializing. I just know he would have beamed to see his daughter living life with exuberance and participating in community activities.

Such is life, I figured, you never know what direction it will go. Through Dad's early departure, I learned there are no guarantees that you'll be able to see your loved ones or sit down and have a cup of tea with them when you want. Whether it be with family or friends; phone calls, computer chatting, letter writing or the face to face time is deeply appreciated in my life now. When it comes to people in my life, nothing is ever taken for granted and I do my best to leave everyone feeling uplifted, as I walk away from any visit.

Having to admit I didn't always appreciate my Dad's authoritarian role when he was alive, truthfully, it would lift my heart to hear his opinions once again. He may have come across gruff the rare time, but that was just his way of dealing with pressures of life; his generosity equaled his gigantic kind heart. My Dad would do most anything to help someone. One of my favourite memories of Dad is when he would dress up as Santa Claus and surprise the neighbourhood kids with treats.

But nothing surpassed the contentment I felt when watching Dad enjoying a plate of Mom's homemade apple pie as he sipped his tea. No matter what worries or concerns that sat on his shoulders from time to time, that pie put him right in the center of his own personal heaven. Holding onto my memories of those sweet moments, I decided I better put away my sadness of Dads absence and accept the change.

After Dads death, I knew his spirit lived on, yet still missed his physical presence. My perception of death is that a shedding of our body takes place and then our spirit returns from the origins of where we first came, to be in the presence of our Maker. Hopefully that's not the end though. I like to believe, when we pass into spirit, our own conscious awareness will determine what level of existence we experience. This would provide each of us with the comfort of being with like-minded souls in the spirit world. Then my hope would be if we choose, we could expand our awareness and move into new areas of existence, eventually reaching enlightenment. That would be awesome if we still have room for growth and development on the other side.

Many people talk about the possibility that we might end up watching our individual life review alongside Angelic counsel. This seems like a fabulous thing, if it's true. Being in the presence of pure love, I imagine it would be much easier to grasp an accurate view of who we had been and why we made the choices in life we did. Well, I guess I'll have to wait to find out the truth of it all, I won't know what happens after physical death, until I get to that part of my journey.

Thing is, I learned a long time ago not to dwell on how the Universe works. Its' okay to wonder and ponder, but too much of trying to put your puny logic to it, can be disastrous. It has actually played a part in me going bonkers and landing in the Hospital psychiatric ward. Some things, we just don't know yet.

What really tickles my funny bone is when I hear spiritual leaders think they know all the answers. On the other side of my giggle is the sadness of realizing, these proclaimed leaders, teach what they think they know and in their process do much damage to their listeners as a result. There are certain individuals who consider themselves experts on spiritual matters, when I come across ones that profess this, I run, not walk, away from them. We must not be spoon fed spiritual beliefs. The one sure way to know you're God guided path is to seek earnestly and have a look at what the Word says. Oh yes I am, I'm so totally going there! Read your Bible people, read it with sincere intention to guide you truthfully. The Bible is not a religious book, well in some cases I stand corrected, yes it is for some religious sects. But, if we open our minds and hearts, we can get past the manipulations people have used the Bible for. The Book has a wealth of common sense, guidance and truth. It also has some distortions, historic and otherwise, yet we don't need to get caught up in that if we choose to seek the simple loving message contained within it. Just saying; it's got some good information in it. There have been times I've gone on a mining expedition within those pages and have come up with Gold.

Way back, when I used to be confused about whether accessing my psychic nature was in alignment with God, there were some well intentioned religious people that condemned me for even talking about my psychic abilities. For a long time I took on their judgments and thought there was something wrong with me having a sixth sense. One night while brooding over this dilemma, my Grandmother popped to mind. When I was a child, she had given me a Bible with embossed gold lettering on the front cover that spelled out my name. What the heck, I thought, I'm going to pull out that old Bible Grandma gave me and see what the Word says about psychic impressions. Upon finding parts in the Bible where it describes psychic communication as part of our natural human existence, comforted me. Ghosts, Angels and departed loved ones are acknowledged in the Bible as returning from the spirit realm and at most times, helping people. There are also many warnings and teachings in the Bible of the dangers in communicating with the spirit world. Sound advice, as it's not a game nor is psychic communication a feather in our cap. Most assuredly, at least for me, the psychic is an ability we all have and it's there as a *guidance beacon* to help us see the light of God; or for those of you who have trouble with the word God: To help us see the light of love. In my experience seeing the light of love has been quickened as a result of communicating with the spirit world. Intention, common sense, responsibility and discernment; especially discernment, are necessary for receiving Divine guidance.

Being an avid reader it soon came to my attention that many books have great information on the human psychic ability. With interest I noted several books coincide with much of the biblical guidance. Just to name a few; *A Course In Miracles, Silver Birch, Tao Ti Ching,* and *White Feather.* Then there is *Sermon On The Mount,* by Emmet Fox, which is one of my favourite books. Any of Joyce Meyer's books are uplifting and informative too, I adore her. Her manner of inspiration fuels me to get up and get on with life. Here's the thing, just read or watch what interests you and ignore others if they disapprove your choice of material. We're all so different and our interests will naturally vary.

My Parents believed in a greater good, a higher intelligence that was acknowledged as God. They followed the golden rule as best they could and provided my brother and myself with a basic foundation in Christianity. Fortunately in my Parents' home there were no strict formalities or harsh religious beliefs. We were not forced to attend Church and as I got older I felt freedom to choose my own way of expressing spirituality.

As sad as I had been, that Dad never got to witness my success of a peaceful heart and sound mind, I received proof eventually that he indeed was aware of what I'd been up to while he was gone. The first time I knew for certain that Dad had popped in to see me, from the other side, was during a Church service. Sure, I did have the rare occurrence of 'happenings' around the house that reminded me of him, but nothing I could prove.

As I sat in the Church congregation listening to the inspirational talk, I thought I felt the presence of my Dad. Later on in the service the speaker attuned to her clairvoyant senses and told the parishioners she was seeing a spirit man who was wearing a woman's wig, high heels and seemed to be acting clownish. She thought this was a pretty funny sight! As she carried on with more details, she went on to describe my Dad's physical appearance accurately then proceeded to correctly explain his personality. I was positive this was my Dad, yet didn't put my hand up, I wanted more proof. Next she said he liked to play a card game called 'solitaire' and he had worked within the forest industry. Hearing these details, my hand shot up like a rocket as I admitted to the medium that indeed this was my Dad. She smiled and asked *"what's this about him being dressed up as a woman and clowning around?"* I explained that he used to sometimes be in skits with his friends and at least once I remembered him dressed up just like she described. As soon as I acknowledged she was in communication with my Dad, the details of what I'd been up to lately, poured through the medium. She said my Dad was feeling very emotional and happy that I had placed a red rose on the Christmas table this year and then said a prayer for him. *"Oh yes"* I exclaimed *"I did do this!"* She added that my Dad also wants to talk about the watch that had been his. She told me my Dad says I keep it in a safe place. She even described the engraved letters on the watch, but that she couldn't read what they spelled out. I responded cheerfully that there was an inscription on the watch and that not only was this watch kept in a safe place, but that it was kept in a locked safe. She smiled knowingly then told me, *"Your Dad would like you to sit somewhere quiet while holding his watch as you think about him, because he wants to show you something."* Then she added, *"Your Dad is very proud of you and loves you."* Hearing from Dad, I cried tears of joy.

At home later, grabbing the security safe dial, I spun the combination wheel and opened the thick metal door. Taking out Dad's watch, I held it between my hands thinking of him. Over many past years, I had taken this same watch, where no one could see what I was doing and prayed over it that it would work again.

During my childhood a man called *The Amazing Kreskin* used his mind over matter ability and apparently got broken watches working again. What a disappointment finding out I didn't have that ability and how silly I felt that I had believed it might work. The difference now was that the Clairvoyant at Church had given such profound accuracy, describing my Dad; I completely trusted his message that he would like me to spend some time with that watch. Actually believing, once again, in the possibility *energy* might get the watch working? Being a person who enjoys formalities and ritual, I found an old photograph of Dad and placed it on a table as I lit a white candle. While sitting cross legged on the floor, holding the old broken watch in my hands, I thought of all the cherished times spent between Dad and I. Chocolate bars, fishing for trout, holidays with my parents and his silly antics of joking around. My thoughts were only of Dad and how much I loved him when suddenly I noticed that his watch was ticking! His watch kept perfect time for the next ten years. My Mom was surprised to hear this because in her own description, that watch never did work properly! Mom went on to tell me the story behind this watch, saying it was an expensive one back in the 1950's, she had to work and save up her money to buy it. My Dad obviously appreciated Mom's gift because just before he died, he made certain there was a note stuck to this watch, with a request that it be kept and eventually passed to my son. It now resides with the intended owner, my dad's grandson. Mom's gift watch to Dad is the source of many good memories shared with the family, to this day.

Then, another day, a different psychic, Dad came through one more time. This medium not only gave accurate evidence of my Dad but also described in detail what I had been doing lately. Dad then relayed his message through the clairvoyant. He came to tell me that he has been watching me all these years and is so very proud of my courageous effort to follow through and become well. He said that I had managed to break the cycle of mental illness and that through me others will be inspired that they too can heal through anything. My tears rolled down my cheeks as I smiled and thanked him for letting me know he was indeed aware of what I'd been up to.

There was yet another spiritual event that took place, where I know it was my Dad who came to help. It was a few weeks before Christmas and I was decorating our tree. Ron suggested that I not use the ancient, practically antique, string of lights because they were on their last legs. I knew he was right, but they held sediment for me. Those particular lights used to adorn my Parents tree when I was kid. I plugged them in to check that they all lit up and they did, so onto the tree they went. The next day that string was burnt out. Rats, I figured I could squeeze just one more season from them. Nobody was looking, I double checked, then I said a prayer out loud, *"Come on Dad, if you can hear me, turn the lights on for one more Christmas will ya? Please and thank you."* Not really believing the lights were suddenly going to come on, I left the room to grab a tea. When I came back to the tree to remove the string of burnt out lights, I was astounded to see the lights were working. They remained lit up throughout the whole Christmas celebration. Thanks Dad, was all I could say.

Many friends have relayed similar accounts of loved ones coming to visit from the spirit world. It's very uplifting to know this is possible. Something that seems mutually agreed upon by most, is that spirit people do not pop in all the time. I believe this is probably so that they do not distract us from paying attention to our lives on earth. It would be adversity to our well being if we paid too much attention to the spirit world. I know this from firsthand experience. Remembering all too well when I imagined spirit friends with me 24/7. Certainly I was not living in the present moment when that was going on. My head was in the clouds, my thoughts were diverted onto fantasy and I missed out on living life.

Bona fide spirits of love are never going to be 'playing' with us all day long nor 'talking' with us all night through. We're either being fooled by spirit tricksters or fooling ourselves with our vivid imagination. Either way, genuine spirit contact is easily recognizable through the brevity, accuracy and uplifted feelings that remain with you.

Currently, I choose to experience my life with both feet firmly planted on the ground. Over these many years I've developed my mediumistic capacity in a responsible way. No longer do I seek spirit communication willy-nilly and without thoughtful intention. Readings are done only through attunement with God. The Lord's

Prayer is a great way to start any spiritual sessions. My clairvoyant readings for people are done during specific appointment times or pre-booked public demonstrations. With this discipline in place, I can relax to enjoy my life, without being bombarded with random, psychic noise.

Someone asked me once if I was afraid I'd miss hearing an important spirit communication by being too structured in my discipline. Good question and my answer is that anytime there is authentic spirit communication needed immediately, my team of angelic helpers know how to get my attention. And yes, they have done so from time to time.

Many experiences come to mind where my divine spirit helpers have knocked on my psychic door, unexpectedly, to have me give an impromptu reading. One such, unexpected spirit visit, happened as I was diligently loading clothes into my laundry machines. It just so happened that an acquaintance was standing beside me as we discussed our current plans for the day. Suddenly I got a *heads up alert* from one of the long time spirit helpers I knew and trusted. This communication was most comfortable, subtle and profound all at the same time. The woman standing beside me hadn't known me long so I used discretion with how I broached this subject. To be respectful I started out by saying, *"I realize this might sound odd, but not knowing your feelings on spiritual matters, I'm curious to know if you'd be comfortable with me talking about life after death and spirit loved ones?"* If she had said no thanks, that's all garbage or I think it's against God, I would have ended the spirit contact and carried on talking about my day-to-day routine. On the contrary, I saw a huge smile spread across her face as she acknowledged her belief that spirit people, especially loved ones, often do come back to give us proof of their continued existence. Very happy to hear this, I asked and received her permission to share this spirit communication with her. This spirit person was a capable and skilled communicator;

he made it easy for me to hear him. I was able to give my friend his name, accurate physical description, what job he did in life and as an added bonus this spirit man sang me a humorous song I'd never heard, which I immediately repeated word for word. She recognized everything I said and upon hearing me repeat the song words, tears poured down her face. Regaining composure, she explained how some friends and her had made up a little ditty and would sing it to him when he came to visit, I had relayed it precisely. Next I repeated his reason for coming to chat with her, she was grateful for the encouragement he brought with regard to a specific challenge she was facing. My heart humbled at the realization I was witnessing a rare and sacred moment. Certainly I could not take credit for this magnitude of spirit communication; only through Gods graces could such a thing take place.

Not that these spectacular spirit enhanced moments happened to me every day, but for reasons I don't understand, when they did happen it was truly helpful for all present.

A different time and different person, we decided to go for a coffee at a funky local cafeteria to get to know each other. Her depth and sincerity was a joy to be around, I had a feeling we'd become good friends. As she chatted with me, a spirit man showed up beside our table. Using my intention I dismissed him and demanded he leave me alone! This type of thing wasn't commonly happening to me, yet at times it did occur. To maintain my peace of mind, I only accepted contact from spirit people when either in specified appointment or through my recognized spirit team giving me the A-Okay. Today, this spirit man was being very insistent to be seen and heard. With me being just as insistent, I ignored his antics because I couldn't sense my spirit helpers giving me the *thumbs up*. Boldly this spirit man leaned on the table, between my new friend and me, smiling a gorgeous smile directly at me. That was it. I finally caved in and asked if my new acquaintance would feel comfortable if I talked about a spirit being communicating from the other side? Not only was she comfortable with it but she had experienced psychic activity many times and held no doubt around the validity of it. I proceeded to describe the handsome young man with dark hair and then added he said he was her brother. At first I thought I must be wrong because my new friend was rather quietly staring at me without acknowledging if I was correct or not? I continued by describing how he passed away. It was then I saw the emotion in her eyes and heard her disclose that, yes, her brother was in spirit and my description accurate. He just wanted her to know he was there. He then winked at me and said he didn't require my help anymore because he could communicate directly with her now. Well, his sister and I became friends for a period of time before life had us going in different directions. During that short time of knowing each other, it was fascinating to see how helpful contact with her brother had been. Although he never told her what to do, he always offered his encouragement and support to live life joyfully.

Along with being accurate in my clairvoyant knack, there were also times I was unable to provide evidence that made sense to a person. Soon I learned not to let it trouble me if I couldn't make the connection. The thing with mediumship and communication with spirit is: some days it's clear and easy viewing and other times it's like plowing through a thick fog with zero visibility. There are also those times where I felt and plainly saw spirit people, but the person didn't recognize them. When this happened I simply *cut myself some slack* knowing that even the most experienced clairvoyants occasionally misinterpret evidence. Then too, I recalled times where a person phoned up a week or so later to confirm that, having checked with family records, indeed the spirit person I described was recognized. Many variables determine spirit contact, including the intentions of the person who claims to want a reading.

Over the years I've talked with people, who are highly developed in their psychic awareness, who want to help locate missing people in the area or offer their assistance to the police on more serious cases. From time to time, I have to admit, the thought has crossed my mind too. Knowing that we absolutely can give accurate proof of evidence from time to time; reason tells me why wouldn't those of us with developed abilities help the community this way? My excuse was: authorities would never take me seriously, considering my past *certified mental illness* history. One friend, being rather clever, pointed out to me that *if* I gave accurate details to locate someone who had been missing, that I wouldn't have to worry about my credibility. So I had to concede that my friend is correct and with that my honesty got to the core of the matter. My deeper fear was actually the thought, *what if I can't do it and I end up looking like a schmuck.*

Around this time of considering these options and admitting my own doubts, someone I regard as more family than friend, popped over and told me there was a man missing and presumed swept away on one of the local rivers. My friend asked me if I would be willing to attune my senses to the matter and see what I come up with. Why not I figured, there was nothing to lose, it would just be between her and I. Upon lifting my thoughts above the mundane, daily routine, I started to describe a part on the river that was coming into my minds' eye. Grabbing a piece of paper and pen I began drawing a line representing the river, then added particular twists and bends on this line. I told her I saw a pool of water, where it was very deep and had a strong undertow. It felt to me that this missing person was now crossed over to spirit but that his body would be found near that pool of deep water, snagged below by a water logged stump. Immediately she pulled a map of the river out of her pocket, she belonged to a department within the emergency services and had come prepared to mark down what I might come up with. To my amazement, as she traced her finger along the actual map river route, the section I had drawn on my paper was a perfect match to a particular area of river on her map. She then told me she knows the river like the back of her own hand because it has also been her 'playground' for years. She said in this section of river there truly was a deep pool, with quite a dangerous undertow.

To get to the outcome; her team searched that very section of river by the deep pool and although the man's body was not found snagged in that pool, he was found just a short ways further down from that area. My confidence was boosted when she told me they had already combed this whole part of the river previously and had not seen him anywhere. She believed it was most likely his body *had been* snagged in that deep pool, out of view, yet could have become dislodged and would have then been swept further downstream. I know it's a stretch; this may or may not have happened. One thing for sure though, my hand drawn replica of the river precisely matched her map and he was located just down from that area I'd sensed. Sad as it was that this man had died tragically, I was learning that perhaps I could develop this ability further.

My confidence waned as I opened my psychic senses on other occasions, with no verifiable proof or information leading to find missing people.

There were times I'd take notice of what was going on locally, with serious crimes, finding that my ability to *know* who did it or where they were hiding; was completely inaccurate. How I knew this is by paying attention to those particular news issues and checking my psychic answers compared to the true outcome of police investigations. Wrong, wrong and wrong, so after that I decided to let go of pursuing my investigative *clairvoyant ventures.*

A certain seed of assurance remains with me though. It is possible, sometimes, to *remote view* whether a missing person has survived and where they will be located. My dear friend, who I consider my soul sister, has been a strong encourager for me to further believe in myself.

Although I've not pursued developing my psychic eye to find lost people and pets; this is definitely something I'd like to aim for in the future. My thought is if you're wrong, wrong and wrong then pull your socks up and practice, practice and practice; until you get it right.

Enlightened visitations from loved ones in spirit do happen, yet when sitting with a medium for a reading it is wise for us all to remember that interpretation still has to get through the belief system and personality of the clairvoyant. An open mind helps us allow and a discerning mind keeps us from being gullible.

When it comes to visits from the spirit world, a photo is worth a thousand words. During an Easter dinner party at our home I had taken several photos. Later as I looked over the snap shots I'd taken of family and friends. Incredibly one photo shows four people with beautiful bright orbs resting on different parts of their bodies. One man had several orbs floating upon his knee, calve and foot. I happen to know he wears a leg brace on that part of his leg! One woman had a large orb hovering over her arm that happens to have tendinitis. Another person who suffers from a form of mental discord had one orb by her forehead. The fourth person had orbs around their tummy, but I don't know if they actually had stomach troubles or not? I assume those orbs were assisting people in their healing, why else would they show up in photos hovering over the injured areas. Seeing this photo reignites my passion to be sending more healing prayers out to the world.

Speaking of orbs, another photograph I snapped of my oldest dog clearly shows her head tilted downward, looking directly at a giant size floating orb. Good Ole Molly seemed to be keenly interested in that mysterious bubble. She was close to seventeen years old when she died, shortly after the photo of her and the orb was taken. I'm certain her spirit helper was keeping her company near the end and comforts her in her passing.

Chapter #29

OUT OF THE CLOSET

I T HAD BEEN CLOSE TO eight years that I had been working at the Counseling Agency. Time does fly by fast, especially when I'm having fun. It was through challenges, play, family, friends and just simply living life that I learned more about myself than ever could have been imagined. Thing is, in order to learn more about myself I had to place my attention there; on me.

Through being mindful and paying attention to my thoughts, it became easy to notice what was working great in my life and where I would like to make changes. Ultimately learned, was that I could experience anything I put my mind to. The only thing that ever got in the way of living fully was me.

One of my most profound *AHA* moments was realized while self pondering. During my meditation on self evaluation, my concern was focused on a couple of people in my life who were obvious about their lack of respect for me. These folks spoke harshly and sarcastically towards me, at times pointing out the faults they saw in me. My initial feeling was hurt and upset of not being accepted or appreciated by them. The *AHA* popped into my mind suddenly and literally whisked the discontent away. Here is my self realization: *"Aha! They are not seeing me. They are seeing reflections of what they harbor within their consciousness. All the criticism they direct at me, gives them a sense of comfort. I must not take this personally as it has nothing to do with me."* Yup, felt great realizing this. But, it was also imperative that I see my part in this. Asking myself, why was I continuing to keep my company with them? My sense was that I felt deserving of this criticism, as if part of me still held the incorrect belief that I was less than everyone else. This felt like a fit to me and I was thankful to have grasped it at this point in time. Amazing how my own subtle poor thinking had hid itself deep into my subconscious. Now aware of my bit of lingering low esteem, I could release it and move forward into better self image. Strangely enough, I felt appreciation for those two people. It was through their harsh behaviour that I was able to recognize an area in my own consciousness that needed tweaking. Still I was faced with the reality that I didn't want to be associating with people that needed to comfort themselves by being critical towards others. Making effort to set boundaries hadn't worked in past so now I felt confident to stop chatting with them altogether. This didn't mean that I ignored them, it was easy to smile and say hello in passing because they are good people at the core. My decision to stop visiting with them was based on not wanting to be around their critical habit. Another bit I learned about myself was that I could still love the person, appreciate the core essence of goodness within and at the same time give myself permission to walk away from unpleasant behaviour.

There was tremendous satisfaction felt through experiencing what I had co-created in my life. I say co-created because without God as my partner, my mind would have continued to reside in the muck and thereby remained stuck. Through trusting in that Divine Holy presence of pure love, I found my true Self, well at least a healthy portion of my Self. I expect for the rest of my life I'll be exploring and identifying deeper levels of Me. Sure hope so!

That song, Amazing Grace says it all, *I once was blind but now I see, was lost but now I'm found.*

In 2008, while continuing my work at the Agency, I came across a flyer advertising an upcoming workshop with the very well known Dr. David Burns. I was familiar with his best seller, *The Feel Good Handbook.* As I signed up for his classes, I had no idea of the significant impact Dr. Burns would have on me. It happened on the second day of his workshop when my shift from holding a long time secret moved into being authentic with my Self. For far too long I'd felt as if I was keeping a part of *Me* hidden away in a closet by not sharing my first hand experience of recovering from severe bipolar disorder. To explain further how this class impacted me to push open that closet door and come out, I'll need to describe my first encounter in his workshop.

My counseling Supervisor and I attended Dr. Burns' two day workshop together. Both of us fervently taking notes and thoroughly enjoying his topics of discussion. Anxiety, mental illness, strength based strategies and his personal case studies were disclosed. Dr. Burns appeared knowledgeable, personable, humorous and unpretentious. I was glued to his every word.

On the second day of his class, I became personally drawn into his topic on mental illness. Dr. Burns was sharing with us, one of his client success stories. As he described coaching this client through severe mental illness to mental wellness, he went into a poignant description of how he supported the client through psychotic episodes. What I heard him reveal reminded me of my personal challenge through past episodes and I couldn't control my sobbing. Forgetting the Agency Supervisor was sitting next to me, I allowed myself time to surface feelings I'd forgotten about. With my Supervisor not understanding why I was reacting emotionally to this part of the class, she merely reached out to me by asking if I was okay and did I need to talk. Managing to calm myself, I briefly explained my personal ties to mental illness through my Mom; still not disclosing my diagnosis though. Trying to quietly tell her how Dr. Burn's words impacted me, felt rushed and was impossible during class. So, I asked her if she had time to meet with me for tea after the training. A nod indicating yes and with that, we both once again turned our attention back to Dr. Burns. Thankfully he hadn't noticed my emotional reaction, as he continued describing how he helped clients to challenge paranoid thoughts. He supported his client with use of many positive techniques. Nearing the end of his lecture he was adamant that these methods he used to assist patients, were only successful based on the determination and effort applied by the client. True, I thought, so true! I knew exactly how much effort and dedication it took to become mentally well.

For me, there was one missing part of the puzzle that Dr. Burns did not talk about during his classes. That was the area of our natural, intuitive and psychic abilities. Perhaps the link between psychic activity and mental illness has yet to be acknowledged and adjoined through the medical profession? I don't really know because I've not had contact with all that many professionals in the field of psychiatry or the science of the mind. Most assuredly, I had not directly talked to Dr. Burns so I have no idea what his actual views on the matter are.

My view is that the sixth sense is a fact both in humans and all life forms alike. As we evolve, I'm hopeful it will become more and more common place for our Doctors to acknowledge this natural capacity we all have.

While still sitting in the class, I was digesting all the reasons I had been sobbing. One, I was filled with joy to hear a Doctor of his stature acknowledge that mental illness can be healed. Two, I heard how he coached his client and I recognized how I'd basically done similar steps on my own. Three, I felt some grief, realizing that none of the professionals working with me, supported my hope of getting off medication. It was joy, gratitude and grief; all strong emotions that surfaced in an unexpected place and time. It was much food for thought, no wonder the tears.

An overwhelming urge to tell my Supervisor of my personal journey through mental illness, pulsed in my throat as we headed to the restaurant. I knew if I didn't act on that desire right now, I probably would never tell her. As we got seated at the table I felt thankful the waitress had given us a private, quiet space. Feeling anxious knowing I was about to finally divulge my past, I thought it best to relax with some pleasantries first. After discussing our views of Dr. Burn's workshop, without any further wavering, I asked if I could explain why I was triggered during the topic regarding mental illness.

Not being able to recall the exact words I said, to my recollection it went closely to this;

"What I am going to tell you will probably put you in a position where you might need to end my job as assistant to you. Also, I'm guessing the Agency policy will dictate that I am no longer going to be able to counsel clients or facilitate groups. As much as I'd miss working for the Counseling Agency, I feel it's long overdue that I tell my experience. In 1993, I was diagnosed with a hereditary mental illness and placed on psychiatric medication. My mom has the same diagnosis; bipolar disorder. I was hospitalized repeatedly between

1993 through 1998. Over the many years I did my best to develop a healthier attitude through classes at mental health, individual therapy sessions and spiritual beliefs. In the year 2000, I knew I was well yet the Doctors did not agree with me lowering medication, so I remained on them. As you know it was this same year I took the counselors training and from there you know better than anyone how my behavior is and what my counseling skills are. You're also aware of my inspirational speaking at my Church and speaking publicly on stress management through The Heart and Stroke Foundation. What you may not know about me is that I also have developed my psychic muscle, over the years and now do public demonstrations of mediumship alongside other experienced mediums in the community. So, to get to my point, over a period of four years I weaned myself off medication and have now been medication free and completely healthy for several years. I want you to understand that I have never lied about my history of mental illness; it's just that no one ever asked so I didn't elaborate. I'm telling you now because my emotions were triggered today and I realized that I'm feeling out of integrity keeping my experience quiet. I fully understand if you are annoyed with me for not coming forward sooner. I know the Agencies policy and that anyone with a diagnosis of mental illness certainly are not permitted to go into session with clients. I hope I haven't put you on the spot, if you need time to think this through before talking to me about it, we can meet again to discuss it. What do you think?"

My Supervisors' response was one of respect, graciousness and support. Of the many things she said to me this day, I clearly remember hearing her say that I was a person she would never be concerned about in session with a client. She told me, as far as she's concerned, I was welcome to stay on as her assistant and continue as a lay counselor too. It was a relief to be accepted and trusted to remain with the Agency.

We talked further and discussed some details of how I recovered from such a devastating illness. In one of my comments, I affirmed that one day I'd like to write a book on how I went from hereditary, severe mental illness to stability of mind and emotional wellness. My desire, I told her, is to instill hope to those who feel defeated. It was heartwarming to hear her encouragement and support of my intended book.

Up until the year 2009 I stayed working with the Counseling Agency, but in order to dedicate my efforts to writing this book, I ended my work with them. Enjoying the Agency as much as I did, it wasn't easy for me to completely let go. Hence, I continued keeping an eye out for the occasional Agency workshop and participated from time to time.

This Counseling Agency certainly provides a much needed service in our community. Knowing how funding can be such a challenge for them to stay up and running, my hat goes off to all the staff and current volunteers for their dedicated service.

Even though I'm only in my mid-fifties, seems to me that it's been a long expedition; yet worth every step. There is not one moment from my past that I would wish to change, knowing how important every painful and joyful experience was. All of it was necessary for me to realize the truth;

OUR OWN THOUGHTS, PLACE US IN
MADNESS OR PARADISE.

Chapter #30

OH YES YOU CAN!

W<small>E WERE NOT INTERESTED IN</small> planning a vacation, Ron and I loved being at our home. There was always plenty to keep us active. Besides our work we had over two acres of property to maintain along with caring for pets, garden that would need harvesting soon and of course more potlucks to host.

This particular year, 2009, a random email showed up on my computer. While looking over the email flyer I realized it had been sent from a Hay House Publishing website, which I must have subscribed to but forgotten. Through pouring over the contents I was captivated by the announcement of their upcoming cruise to Alaska. Several of my favourite Authors were going to provide inspirational lectures aboard and there was also a 'Writer's Workshop' for the duration of this cruise. One place I always wanted to see was Alaska and knowing I would be surrounded by spiritually uplifting people as well as an opportunity for more writers training, influenced Ron and I to sign up for this Cruise!

During my walk towards and into wellness, several Authors had been dear to my heart. For the past many years I thought of all of them fondly and with appreciation. What a thrill knowing I was headed to my favourite destination along with many favourite authors and the love of my life, Ron.

Over the years, Ron and I had endured our battles and come through immense challenges together. I am ever so grateful it was him by my side the whole way; Ron has the tolerance of a Saint and a deep compassionate heart.

Packed with enough clothes to last a week and then some, I grabbed Ron's coat lapel and yanked him hurriedly toward the gang plank of our ship. OH, I mean guided him gently toward the gang plank. With a wink and a nod we were on board and headed to Alaska!

Now well into the cruise, there were book signings scheduled with each Author. While standing in a lineup to meet Louise Hay I could see how incredibly long the line was behind me and decided it would be best to move myself along quickly when it came my turn to speak with her. My intention was to say a simple *"thank you"* as she signed my book and then be on my way. Well, I had good intention but my enthusiasm gave way to what actually happened. With sincere emotional gratitude caught in my throat, I could barely speak to Louise Hay. Through tears I attempted sharing the depth of my feelings towards her, but my emotions got in the way. Realizing my sentiment was slowing the lineup I got a grip on myself, smiled at Louise Hay thanked her for signing my book and started to walk away. Right then she stopped me for a moment offering more time to talk with her. A surge of warmth filled my heart. Her generosity immediately put me at ease and it was in that moment I was enabled to look into her eyes, saying *"Thank you so very much. Your work and dedication has helped me heal through a devastating mental illness. I'm happy now."* So with that, I headed back to my cabin feeling a personal satisfaction of having thanked Miss Hay. What a fabulous woman Louise Hay is, even upon meeting a total stranger, her kindness shone through her sparkling eyes.

There was another book signing on board that was important to me. This time Ilyanla Vanzant would be offering her time to meet with as many people as the schedule would allow for. When I had been in episodes of depression and lost hope, her books inspired me to trust my process. Often times I would copy her prayers onto recipe cards and carry them in my pocket; to remind myself how to connect with God. To be expected, when I met Ilyanla Vanzant, my emotions showed up front and center. Her gracious words, upon meeting me, clearly let me know her intention was to give me her undivided attention. She did so by looking into my eyes as she spoke with me. I felt a heart to heart connection had been made as I thanked Iyanla and we shared a lovely hug.

The following day, I took my place near the end of the long line up for another book signing opportunity, this time with Sonia Choquette. Her books and on-line courses had been beneficial and interesting. I held her in high esteem. Funny enough, what I thought was the very end of the line soon became the front of the line. To explain what I mean; suddenly ALL the people of the lineup in front of me began walking away. I stopped one of them asking if they were leaving because Sonia was not signing books right now. The woman told me all of them left the lineup because the Author had to stop signing books in order to get to her lecture. Assuming the Author had been Sonia Choquette, feelings of disappointment swept through me but I realized sometimes that's just how it goes and we have to deal with feeling let down. Just as I was going to walk away, a professional looking woman began placing pens on a table near me. She smiled at me and said, *"oh lucky you, you're first in line to see Sonia."* I was delighted. Sonia Choquette is a quality inspirational speaker and spiritual teacher. Surprisingly I didn't cry this time, but my smile must have been from ear to ear as I approached her and was able to thank her in person.

There is nothing more satisfying to me than taking the opportunity to thank someone for the assistance they've brought into my life. Whether it has been through; books, lectures, or a good listening ear of a friend. Also, I believe that this was another puzzle piece to my own healing journey. Expressing the joy I felt within and directing it outwards in gratitude.

Now there was yet another author I had hoped to thank and that was Wayne Dyer. I had been reading and listening to his inspirations for many years. I admired him and his philosophies of living life. He seems to be all about accessing your fullest potential and what an excellent role model he is. Dr. Dyer lives his words. So although there had been opportunity for me to thank him, on board ship, it was not through a planned book signing. Twice, I walked passed Wayne Dyer and both times could see he was with his family. Knowing that he was either relaxing or having a meal, I felt it would be inappropriate to interrupt his leisure time. It was enough satisfaction for me to simply smile at him from a distance, as I thought to myself, *thank you so very much for sharing your knowledge with the world, it has truly helped me!*

Not only was it an honour to meet spiritually awakened authors, but equally a blessing to have met people from all walks of life and from several different countries. All of them had influenced further inspiration within me; in numerous and varied ways. Most all of the people on board this ship were highly aware of the effects of our thoughts upon our own lives; personal responsibility. This being the case it was a common daily occurrence to have several uplifting chats with a variety of people, throughout the cruise. A little piece of heaven on earth; a floating community of kind, thoughtful people all focused on love. I felt profoundly peaceful and at home amongst all these people.

With Ron attending the inspirational lectures that were offered during the cruise and me participating in the week long writer's course, we actually didn't see a lot of each other until evening. At that time, we enjoyed each others' company while walking the deck of the ship, taking in movies, even hanging out pool side and of course eating fabulous foods. When in ports of call we had all day and evening together to enjoy visiting beautiful sites and meeting friendly locals.

Something that was quite significant during this cruise is that I met not one or two people who had reverence for the Bible, but several. This was refreshing because over my past years, I hadn't met many people who held interest of the Bible. What I'm meaning to say is that I enjoyed having some like minded folks around me who could relate to my respect of the Bible, without all the religious mumbo-jumbo.

Bumping into a mixture of passengers on different days and times I noticed none of them talked religion nor professed to be of a certain belief. Yet all seemed to have something in common and that was their deep knowing of a universal consciousness they referred to as God. One woman, of strong faith, ended up sharing dinner with me while Ron was attending a lecture and as we chatted I learned more about her background. Now in her late seventies she explained how she had built up her own company from basically nothing and became a millionaire at a young age. Instead of falling into the trap of materialistic greed, she had created programs to help young people succeed at finding their motivation and life passion. Her vibrant zest for life had me revved up too! As our time together was wrapping up she had some words of encouragement for me, most interesting is that she recommended I read psalm 91. She had not been the only person to suggest I read that particular psalm so now my curiosity was up and I was determined that I'd have a look in my Bible when I got home. For those that may be curious as to what Psalm 91 says, I've written it word for word below. This is taken directly from *The Holy Bible; New Century Edition, Max Lucado/Editor*

Psalm 91

Those who go to God Most High for safety
Will be protected by the Almighty.
I will say to the Lord, "You are my place of safety and protection.
You are my God and I trust you."
God will save you from hidden traps
And from deadly diseases.
He will cover you with his feathers,
And under his wings you can hide.
His truth will be your shield and protection.
You will not fear any danger by night
Or an arrow during the day.
You will not be afraid of diseases that come in the dark
Or sickness that strikes at noon.
At your side one thousand people may die,
Or even ten thousand right beside you,
But you will not be hurt.
You will only watch
And see the wicked punished.
The Lord is your protection;
you have made God Most High your place of safety.
Nothing bad will happen to you;
no disaster will come to your home.

He has put his angels in charge of you
To watch over you wherever you go.
They will catch you in their hands
So that you will not hit your foot on a rock.
You will walk on lions and cobras;
You will step on strong lions and snakes.
The Lord says, "Whoever loves me, I will save.
I will protect those who know me.
They will call to me, and I will answer them.
I will be with them in trouble;
I will rescue them and honor them.
I will give them a long, full life,
and they will see how I can save."
Thanksgiving for God's Goodness.

Admittedly, as I read psalm 91 some parts in the verse I do not understand. What I take away with me, as a result of reading this psalm, is the comfort of knowing we are all protected by universal love, when we tap into it. It's us, it is humanity, which creates chaos and can act out violently. God doesn't make nasty things happen. When I've suffered loss, grief, physical pain; EVERY time I attune my thoughts to divine love through intentional prayer, I find solutions and feel capable to handle whatever situation I'm in. Now that is protection. Not saying I won't get squished like a bug if an elephant steps on me, but I am saying while I'm lying there under that enormous foot my body might feel pain but my consciousness remains at peace for having faith that God will either inspire me to find a way out from under that elephant foot or welcome me to spirit world.

Simplicity is always best. Words escape me in trying to explain what I mean by faith. Pretty much, innocent trust that there is something beyond the four walls is enough. Be kind, be forgiving and be careful around elephants and its all good.

The beauty of Alaska was magnificent. As we were nearing the Hubbard Glacier, 122 kilometers (76 mi) at its widest point, it was a very misty day. No one could see beyond the bow of the boat. From the loud speaker, the announcer said *"Folks, this happens now and then, we never know what the weather will bring us."* A long pause then, *"But, this ship is filled with positive, spiritual people who understand the power of loving intention. Let's all of us focus our intention for the mist to clear and allow us to witness the grandeur of Hubbard Glacier."*

Holey-Moley, as I watched, within minutes of that announcer's request, the clouds and mist receded back. We could all now clearly see the ships approach to Hubbard Glacier – SPECTACULAR, breath taking, truly.

The name of this Hay House Cruise was the *I CAN DO IT AT SEA*. What a strong statement. I can do it. The only limitations are what we ourselves put on it. So when I tell myself *I can do it,* my reply back to myself is always *Oh, yes you can*!

The entire experience was mystical; filled with extraordinary scenery, compassionate people, support and encouragement. I am not only referring to the Alaska cruise, I mean this about my entire life.

A friend recently told me to 'tell my truth'. Glad I finally did.

CONCLUSION

For many years I have been saying to family and friends, live by FROG.

When they ask what I mean by that, I say:

"Fully Rely On God"

THIS BOOK IS MY FIRST attempt to tell people what it was like for me, having suffered psychotic episodes and then finding my way to mental wellness.

If you are someone who suffers mental anguish or if you have a loved one who endures psychological pain; my hope is that my experience will provide encouragement to you that wellness is possible.

One thing for sure, it has occurred to me that some people prefer reading self help books without the authors life experience being shared. Since this book is my in depth account, I am currently writing a companion book to soon follow. The companion book will be a concise guide to offer the simplistic gems, exercises, positive affirmations and coping skills that helped me become healthy and medication free.

As I wrap up my first book, February 2013, my thoughts return to the day at hand. Currently I am teaching Reiki classes from my '*Karuna*' studio as I deepen my own commitment to health. Helping in my community through inspirational speaking and providing Reiki treatments is on-going and gratifying. My secretarial skills are well oiled as I continue working part-time for Ron in his contracting company and occasionally I fill in behind the front desk of a retirement home. Much enjoyment also comes through hosting potlucks and gatherings that include family, friends and new acquaintances. It is our fur family, two dogs, who walk Ron and me often which keeps us agile. They remind us of the importance of play, fun and enjoying nature.

My priority in life is maintaining peaceful living so that I am allowing myself to remain integral and kind. Do no harm and be part of the solution, echoes in my thoughts. People matter, animals matter, plants matter, everything in our world matters. You may have regrets in your life but one thing I can guarantee, you will never regret being kind.

In ending I would like to add, perhaps my road map *Out Of Crazy Town* might not be the direction you or your loved one want or even need; if that's the case, persevere and create your own map and please share it when you're ready. The more diverse experiences circulated, the sooner mental illness will be a thing of the past.

AUTHOR BIOGRAPHY

Grace Ann Carlson (nee Clarke), born November 1st, 1958 in Duncan, BC; grew up in a small town named Honeymoon Bay on Vancouver Island, BC, in Canada.

In the summer of 1975, Ann was one of two girls to be the first hired alongside what had previously been an all men cleanup crew at the Western Forest Industries Saw Mill in Honeymoon Bay. Persistence paid off, after hounding the office staff for weeks, they were finally hired. The two girls had set a new precedence in that area of the mill!

Ann graduated Grade Twelve from Lake Cowichan Senior Secondary School in May 1976.

In September 1976 Ann moved to Victoria, BC to attend Sprott Shaw Business College for one year. To help pay her expenses of renting an apartment in Victoria and attending school, Ann came back to Honeymoon Bay each weekend in order to continue working at the Saw Mill.

After leaving Business College, she ended her weekend job at the Saw Mill and took part time work in a secretarial pool located in Victoria, BC. She also worked as a dining room waitress for Rose Manor, a Victoria senior citizens home.

In 1977 Ann met Ron Carlson in Victoria, BC and they married on June 23, 1979. She ended her work in Victoria in 1980 and eventually took the position of bookkeeper and secretary for her husband's Contracting company.

Throughout her teenage years and on into her adult life Ann suffered bouts of depression that went undiagnosed. Most people, who were close to her, assumed she was introverted and incredibly shy.

Ron and Ann's first born arrived April 1st, 1980, a son, Derrick Carlson. Their second child arrived May 3, 1982, a daughter, Sherrie Carlson.

Over the next few years Ann's mental and emotional state declined further and it was in 1993 that her first diagnosed psychotic episode landed her on the psychiatric ward of a hospital. She was diagnosed with severe, hereditary bipolar disorder and placed on a barrage of medications which included: antipsychotic, sedative and a mood stabilizer.

Her personal experience of moving through mental illness into mental wellness will tug at your heart strings and provoke thought. Ann provides intimate glimpses into her psychotic episodes and helps you understand the logic behind the insanity.

Leaving Crazy Town teaches coping skills, provides guidance and gives hope that mental illness can be healed. Through courage, determination and prayer Ann learned how to master her mind and become medication free.

Her message gives hope and encouragement that freedom from mental illness is possible; in fact it is more easily attainable than some people realize.

2013, currently Ann is writing her second self help book and on June 23 of this same year, she and Ron, celebrate thirty-four years of friendship and marriage.

"Nothing is impossible when we realize the potential that awaits us, deep within.

It's as easy as changing your mind and allowing love to grow you."

G. Ann Carlson

CPSIA information can be obtained at www.ICGtesting.com
Printed in the USA
LVOW081324140413

328972LV00002B/11/P